CHRISTIAN AMERICA
COME BACK TO ME
4th REVISED EDITION

DR. LANCE HURLEY

The Watchman on the Wall

³ and he sees the sword coming against the land and blows the trumpet to warn the people.

⁴ then if anyone hears the trumpet but does not heed the warning and the sword comes and takes their life, their blood will be on their own head.

⁵ Since they heard the sound of the trumpet but did not heed the warning, their blood will be on their own head. If they had heeded the warning, they would have saved themselves.

⁶ But if the watchman sees the sword coming and does not blow the trumpet to warn the people and the sword comes and takes someone's life, that person's life will be taken because of their sin, but I will hold the watchman accountable for their blood.'

Ezekiel 33:6

CHRISTAIN AMERICA
COME BACK TO ME
4th REVISED EDITION

1st Edition, 1stPrinting, June 2011

2nd Edition, 1st Printing, Sept 2012

Revised Edition, 1st Printing, Jan 2017

2nd Revised Edition, 1st Printing, Nov.2018

3rd Revised Edition, 1st Printing, May 2019

4th Revised Edition, 1st Printing, August 2019

Additional materials available from:

Founding Fathers Ministry, Inc.
www.hurleypatriot.org
Lhurley55@gmail.com

Cover design by Dr. Lance Hurley

"Crying Jesus" portrait by Grace McBride

Graphics by Todd Hebertson

ISBN: 978-1-073-61953-5

ACKNOWLEDGEMENTS

There have been many people over the years who have had a great influence on my spiritual journey, and whose support for Founding Fathers Ministry, Inc. has always been appreciated.

I gratefully acknowledge:
The late Evangelist Joyce Still, who prophetically foresaw my ministry, Pastor J.R. Polhemus of Church on the Rock, Castle Rock, Colorado, where my ministry was birthed, and Lee and Jan Melby of United Community Fund who supported my ministry from the very beginning.

I am grateful to the late Dr. Richard Drake of Phoenix University of Theology International, (NOW PRIMUS) for his encouragement to become ordained and to earn my Doctorate degree.

Others who have had a significant impact on my life would be:
James Fitts, Ralph Palmen, Jack Gabler, Rolph Fletcher,(who are all with the Lord) Oralena Valero, Tim Young, Doug Fitzpatrick, Jim Zender, Ken Kempner, Larry Kerychuck, Mike Daves, Todd Boddy, Don Beebe, Frank Abbatte, Don McAlvany and Les White.

I also thank my former Board Members, Mark and Devon Lee Haugebak, who spiritually and financially supported my ministry.

A very special thank you to Bill Runyan, current Board Member, ministry financial supporter, and very good friend.

To my children, Merritt and Elizabeth, to my grand-children Jake, Josh, and Rachel, for whom I pray will grow up in an America where they can still worship Jesus Christ.

Thanks to my former students who so long encouraged me to write this book. I was greatly blessed to have been their teacher.

Thanks to Todd Hebertson for capturing my vision and bringing this cover to life.

I continue to acknowledge the strong encouragement and support that my deceased former wife Sharon gave me in the original writing of this book.

DEDICATION

I dedicate this revised edition to the memory of Mary Ann Gustafson. Mary Ann did graphics on several previous book covers including her last one shown below. She passed away August 2017 at the age of 53 and is now at home with the Lord.

Mary Ann Gustafson

Dr Lance Hurley

EXPLANATION OF FRONT COVER

United States Supreme Court removed prayer from the school in 1962 and the Bible in 1963. The majority members of the Court were Masons, and two of them including Chief Justice Earl Warren were 33rd Degree Masons.

They lifted this phrase deliberately out of context from a letter by President Thomas Jefferson written in 1802: **"...thus building a wall of separation between Church & State"** to justify their decision. **The wall shows the separation.** This topic is the subject of Chapter 18.

Lighting symbolizes the destructive impact of their actions upon the Christian values of our nation and upon our education system.

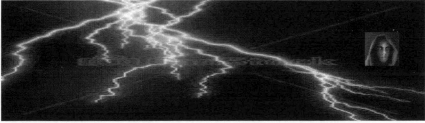

There are two "evil spirits" hidden on the cover. The Reader may wish to search for them!

DR. LANCE HURLEY STATEMENT OF FAITH

I BELIEVE the Holy Bible to be the complete, inerrant, authoritative Word   of God.

I BELIEVE there is only one God, eternally existent in 3 persons: Father, Son, and Holy Spirit.

I BELIEVE in the deity of our Lord Jesus Christ, in His virgin birth, in His sinless life, in His miracles, in His vicarious and atoning death through His shed blood, in His bodily resurrection, in His ascension to the right hand of the Father, and in His personal return to earth in power and glory.

I BELIEVE that for the salvation of lost and sinful man, regeneration by the Holy Spirit is essential.

I BELIEVE that the only way eternal life is received is by faith alone in Jesus Christ and His atoning death for our sins and in a personal salvation given as a gift of God, received by faith.

I BELIEVE in the resurrection of both the saved and the lost – they that are saved unto the resurrection of life and they that are lost unto the resurrection of spiritual death.

I BELIEVE that every believer is commissioned to go into the world and make disciples, baptizing them in the name of the Father, the Son, and the Holy Spirit, and to teach them to obey the commands of Jesus Christ.

TABLE OF CONTENTS

APPENDIX

PREFACE

THE READER SHOULD KNOW THAT THE AUTHOR IS AN ULTRA RIGHT-WING CONSERVATIVE, SOLD OUT FOR JESUS, CHRISTIAN.

The reader may question the accuracy of the first line of my book title, "CHRISTIAN AMERICA," which assumes that America either was, is, or has been a Christian nation.

Many people, including Pastors and graduates of Seminary and Christian colleges would sadly raise the same question:

Does America have a Christian heritage? Our most recent past President at the time of this revised edition has even raised that issue. How sad!

Four main challenges are faced in writing this book.

The groundwork must be laid to prove irrefutably that America was founded as a Christian Nation.

To give credence to the rest of the title, the plea from Jesus: "COME BACK TO ME," I must prove that America as a nation has moved away from God.

Then, I must show the serious consequences that America has endured, due to turning its back on God.

Lastly, I must prove that we must return to God, if we would save our nation from an absolute disaster.

Like many others of the faithful remnant who are sounding the alarm, the verse on the title page of this book has been my motivation for this book. I feel the Lord has placed me in the role of a watchman.

Prayerfully, the Reader will feel that the challenges have been met. It's a tragedy that this book needs to be written.

For six years, I was blessed to have the privilege to teach high school students at a Christian Co-Op. I developed courses on the American Revolution and the Civil War from a Christian perspective.

I used textbooks from well-known Christian universities that contained "watered down" versions of the Christian aspects of America's history.

That led me, with the support of my students, to write my own text.

(I recently had the honor of officiating at the wedding of one of my former students. He had just become a 2nd Lt. in the United States Marine Corps due to my "mentoring" (his words.) Can't put a price tag on that!)

Nothing in this book is being taught in any government school, except for perhaps a few exceptions in the Bible Belt. Our Christian heritage is rarely taught in Seminary and it is not taught in most Christian colleges.

It is no wonder that Pastors believe that "separation of church and state" is in our Constitution, and the Founding Fathers were not Christians.

I once had the opportunity to address an audience of twenty-five Pastors from various denominations.

In a twenty-minute presentation, I explained where the phrase "separation of church and state" originated, that it was not in the Constitution, but a deliberate misrepresentation of a private letter from then President Jefferson to the Danbury Baptist Convention.

At the end, I asked for a show of hands on who had never heard what I discussed. Eighteen hands went up.

I majored in History at college and have always had a love for it. I have read several fine books about America's Christian Heritage. David Barton's" Original Intent" is a great research book.

Bill Federer's "America's God and Country" is full of great quotes on the Founding Fathers. (In 2007, we were both awarded the George Washington Honor Medal by Freedoms Foundation at Valley Forge.)

Mark Beliles & Stephen K. Mc Dowell's "America's Providential History" is another excellent resource.

My overall focus in this book is completely different from those authors. I am applying "then" to "now."

What I have done in this book is to condense all my research to the founding of our country to a much shorter version, and to include information on areas that are virtually overlooked in other texts.

Under revisionist history, the Politically Correct Crowd, Americans United for Separation of Church and State, the ACLU, the One Worlders, ad nauseum, are doing their best to keep Jesus Christ , Prayer, and the Bible out of the public eye.

I discuss the evils of the United Nations, Illuminati, and the Council on Foreign Relations.

This book will prove beyond the shadow of a doubt that America was founded on Christian principles, and that the Founding Fathers envisioned it would always be a Christian nation.

As you read this book, you will be awed by the Founding Fathers strong faith in God, how He directed our nations path in the beginning, and that how many of their statements said then apply most strongly to today's events.

I do believe they were speaking prophetically about this current time.

I was privileged to serve my country as a Captain in the United States Marine Corps

I am deeply saddened as I see my beloved country being destroyed before my very eyes. We live in very perilous times.

Christian America is under attack. We are in all-out war and if we as a nation do not wake up and get involved, America as we have known it in the past will cease to exist.

America has been robbed of its true heritage.

We have been sold a lie by six men(and later 8) in black robes, who deliberately misinterpreted Thomas Jefferson and made up a new law to advance their agenda of removing God and Christianity from America.

I am approaching my 30th year of educating the "church" as to the true Christian heritage of America, and the increasing persecution and attack against the Christian religion. Sadly, the "church" is asleep.

I travel the United States portraying both Patrick Henry and George Washington. I did not seek out this ministry; the Lord orchestrated it completely.

My ministry began by portraying Patrick Henry. (If curious as to how this came about, please visit my website: **hurleypatriot.org** for details.)

Henry failed badly in his first three business ventures.

He decided to become an Attorney. He checked out all the law books he could find and for six months did self- study to set down for the exam.

He got on his horse, rode to Williamsburg, and sat before three Attorneys who quizzed him at great length and "signed off" that he could practice law.

The "Voice of the American Revolution," he has also been called "America's Forgotten Patriot." For a short time, he was Commander in Chief of the Virginia Militia.

He was a delegate to the 1st and 2nd Continental Congress and served six terms as Governor of Virginia.

He turned down the opportunity to be Secretary of State which would have put him on the road to be a future President.

He also turned down the position of Chief Justice of the United States Supreme Court, as well as Ambassador to Spain and France.

Washington encouraged him to run for(and he was elected) to a Senate seat in Virginia. He died before he could take office at the age of 63.

His tombstone simply has his name, date of birth, and date of death.
Years later a relative added this phrase:" **His fame his best epitath**."

Several years ago, the Lord laid it upon my heart to add George
Washington to my ministry.

My direct ancestor served with him at Valley Forge and Yorktown.

In the role of either "Father", what I say is based upon their own words
or those who were present when they said them.

The church is asleep! Rather than be at the forefront of the solution,
they are content to remain the biggest part of the problem.

Most Pastors do not want to learn the truth about our heritage.

"It's not important." "Is it political?" "It's too controversial." "We don't
do drama." "It would not be something our church would be interested
in." "My board would never approve this type of presentation." "We just
want to follow Jesus." (Don't we all?)

The church is now focused on its very survival. It is running scared.
The church is focused on "name it and claim it" and "seeker sensitive."
I.E. "don't rock the boat"(as it sinks!)

As the attack against Christians "heats up," the church is becoming increasingly silent, retreating from the tenants of their sect for fear of being "politically incorrect." They fear losing their 501 (c) (3)status.

"...a time to be silent and a time to speak." Ecclesiastes: 3:7

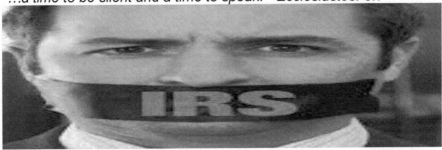

Churches have told the author where he has ministered that "we have decided to go a new direction." Pray tell, where?

The church where my ministry was birthed will not have me back.

" ye shall know the truth and the truth shall set you free." John 8: 32

"The church" should heed the words of President Ronald Reagan when he spoke at a Dallas, Texas Ecumenical Prayer Breakfast August 23rd, 1984:

"WITHOUT GOD THERE IS A COARSENING OF THE SOCIETY. AND WITHOUT GOD DEMOCRACY CANNOT AND WILL NOT SURVIVE. AMERICA NEEDS GOD MORE THAN GOD NEEDS AMERICA. IF WE EVER FORGET WE ARE ONE NATION UNDER GOD, THEN WE WILL BE A NATION GONE UNDER."

The Founding Fathers were strong Christians! They would be appalled to learn that the Bible and prayer have been removed from our public-school system.

The most common comments I get after speaking are:

"I didn't know anything you talked about." "Why aren't our schools teaching this?" "You should be speaking in Congress."

A few years ago, my daughter Elizabeth visited a predominantly "Senior Citizen" church where I ministered.

When it was over, she asked me this question: "Daddy, who will carry on the mantel when this generation passes?" It was a sobering question. If not you dear Reader, then who?

It is my sincere prayer that this book will provide "ammunition" for the reader to get involved (or perhaps more involved) in returning America to the greatness she once had.

There will appear to be several misspellings in several of the quotes, however, that is how those words were spelled at the time.

The **Appendix** includes documents that most Americans do not know ever existed, much less the importance they have in our history.

As the reader begins this study, keep the following quote uppermost in the recesses of your mind. This was from a letter to an autograph hunter and published in several periodicals:

"The highest, the transcendent glory of the American Revolution was this—it connected, in one indissoluble bond, the principles of civil government with the precepts of Christianity." John Quincy Adams, 27 April 1837

CHAPTER 1: CHRISTOPHER COLUMBUS

"your journey has the Lord's approval."   Judges 18:6

Christopher Columbus had a vision since he was a very small boy that he would take the Bible to an "un-chartered land." What guided him was a prophecy about the destiny of the land that he would discover.

A "New World" was to arise in the West to fight a final Crusade against the Arab powers of the Middle East. He claimed this prophecy was given to him by God. (Remember this prophecy when you read the Chapter on Washington's Christian Faith.)

That is why King Ferdinand and Queen Isabella financed the voyage. They agreed to support his quest since they knew it was a Holy Venture.

Quoting directly from Columbus's memoirs "Las Prophecies":

"It was the Lord who put into my mind (I could feel His hand upon me) the fact that it would be possible to sail from here to the Indies. All who heard of my project rejected it with laughter, ridiculing me.

"There is no question that the inspiration was from the Holy Spirit, because he comforted me with rays of marvelous illumination from the Holy Scriptures, a strong and clear testimony from the forty-four books of the Old Testament, from the four Gospels, and from the twenty-three Epistles of the bible press forward ,and without ceasing for a moment they now me to make haste.

"Our Lord Jesus desired to perform an obvious miracle in the voyage to the Indies, to comfort me and the whole people of God.

"I spent seven years in the royal court, discussing the matter with many persons of great reputation and wisdom in all the arts; and in the end, they concluded that it was all foolishness, so they gave it up.

"But since things generally came to pass that were predicted by our Savior Jesus Christ, we should also believe that this prophecy will come to pass.   In support of this, I offer the gospel text, Matt. 24:25, in which Jesus said " *that all things would pass away, but not his marvelous Word."*

"He affirmed that it was necessary that all things be fulfilled that were prophesied by himself and by the prophets. I said that I would state my reasons: I hold alone to the sacred and Holy Scriptures, and to the interpretations of prophecy given by certain devout persons.

"It is possible that those who see this book will accuse me of being unlearned in literature, of being a layman and a sailor. I reply with the words of Matt. 11:25*: "…I praise you Father, Lord, of Heaven and earth, because you have hid these things from the wise and learned and revealed them to little children."*

"I am a most unworthy sinner, but I have cried out to the Lord for grace and mercy, and they have covered me completely. I have found the sweetest consolations since I made it my whole purpose to enjoy His marvelous presence. **For the execution of the journey to the Indies, I did not make use of intelligence, mathematics, or maps.**

(Re read this last statement carefully. Columbus sailed blindly, trusting God to take him to the correct destination.)

'It is simply the fulfillment of what Isaiah had prophesied. All this is what I desire to write down for you in this book. No one should fear to undertake any task in the name of our Savior, if it is just and if the intention is purely for His holy service.

'The working out of all things has been assigned to each person by our Lord, but it all happens according to His sovereign will even though He gives advice. He lacks nothing that it is in the power of men to give Him.

"Oh, what a gracious Lord, who desires that people should perform for Him those things for which He holds Himself responsible! Day and night moment by moment, everyone should express to Him their most devoted grace."   1

Towards the end of his voyage, his crew threatened mutiny as they were becoming fearful and wanted to return home. He finally convinced them to give him three more days to find land. Columbus prayed fervently to the Lord that this venture would succeed.

The ships seemed supernaturally to pick up speed, particularly during the evening hours. Literally on the last day, hours before the agreed upon time to turn back, land was sighted. The date was October 12, 1492.

Columbus made eight landings along the coastline, and at each location he and his men erected a large wooden cross.

Columbus's lifetime vision came to a reality as God's word had now been delivered to this "unchartered land."

The name Christopher means "Christ Bearer!"

Several years later he wrote about America in one of his famous letters:

"God made me the messenger of the new heaven and the new earth of which he spoke in the Apocalypse of St John after having spoken of it through the mouth of Isaiah; and he showed me the spot where to find it."
                                                                2

CHAPTER 2: PILGRIMS LAND AT PLYMOUTH ROCK

"Consider it pure joy, my brothers and sisters, whenever you face trials of many kinds."   *James I:2*

Under the reign of Queen Elizabeth, thousands of Christians fled England to move to Holland where they were free to worship Jesus Christ freely and without any interference.

The Church of England persecuted them because they were basically outcasts. They would not conform to the one and only "state" church.

The Pilgrims had three major concerns about their experience in Holland and why they decided to come to America:

They found it a hard place to raise their children as they were considered "outsiders." Living conditions were very cramped and, they believed the Dutch culture was too permissive. Humanism was being taught in the schools.

When offered an opportunity to begin a new life in America, they jumped at the chance. Forced to finance the ventures themselves, they eagerly signed up to plant a Christian colony in America. There had been several earlier misadventures.

In 1585, Queen Elizabeth I had commissioned Sir Walter Raleigh to settle in the Roanoke area.

This attempt met with misfortune for a variety of reasons.

They made no attempt at farming, so their supplies quickly vanished.

When a new venture later arrived, they found the colony completely deserted.

In 1609, the first colonization attempt at Jamestown began.

This failed miserably due to many factors, not the least of which was the fact the driving force was to find gold and not Christianity.

This was also a poor choice due to the humidity and dampness of the region. Several years later, a new colonization attempt with different motives were more successful.

On August 5, 1620 one hundred and two men, women and children set sail for America on the Mayflower.

They spent sixty-six days in the bottom hull of a ship the size of a Volleyball court.

Besides the confinement and seasickness, they had to endure the taunts of the sailors. They held daily prayer of thanksgiving and the Lord saw them through this most difficult time.

The weather and the heavy currents kept diverting the ship from its original destination which was Virginia. (Note: Virginia is mentioned in the Mayflower Compact.)

After much prayer, they concluded that God had a new site for them, and they landed where the Mayflower had literally been guided.

After landing at Plymouth Rock, they drafted and signed one of the most famous historical documents of all time.

Please read this compact carefully. It is very clearly stated that there were two main reasons why they had undertaken this voyage.

They did not come to America for religious freedom. They already had it.

THE MAYFLOWER COMPACT

"And let us consider how we may spur one another on toward love and good deeds...."   *Hebrews 10:24*

"We whose names are underwritten, the loyal subjects of our dread Sovereign Lord King James, by the Grace of God Great Brita France and Ireland, King, Defender of the Faith, etc.

"Having undertaken**, for the Glory God and the advancement of the Christian Faith** and Honour of our King and Country, a Voyage to plant the First Colony in the Northern Parts of Virginia, do by these presents solemnly and mutually in the presence of God and one of another, Covenant and Combine ourselves together into a Civil Body Politic, for our better ordering and preservation and furtherance of the ends aforesaid; and by virtue hereof to enact, constitute and frame such just and equal Laws, Ordinances, Acts, Constitutions and Offices, from time to time, as shall be thought most meet and convenient for the general good of the Colony, unto which we promise all due submission and obedience.

"In witness, whereof we have hereunder subscribed our names at Cape Cod, the 11th of November, in the year of the reign of our Sovereign Lord King James, of England, France, and Ireland the eighteenth, and of Scotland the fifty-fourth.   Anno Domini 1620."   3

As noted above the two main reasons they undertook this voyage was for "the glory of God" and "the advancement of the Christian faith."

Initially, the Pilgrims aboard the Mayflower thanked God for delivering them from misery and suffering. They went from one hardship to a new one.

They were forced to stay in the hull of the ship and had to endure many taunts from the sailors. They lost one man on the voyage as he was swept overboard.

They had arrived in the dead of winter.

It was doubtful this new colony would survive as they were ill prepared in just about every area of beginning a new life.

They learned nothing from what happened at Jamestown in 1609.They had no houses, no stored goods, no knowledge of the country they faced, nor any knowledge of its inhabitants besides fantastic myths of cannibals and their concerns about the Indians.

In establishing their colony at Plymouth, the Pilgrims faced enormous odds, as Bradford recounted:

" . . they had now no friends to welcome them nor inns to entertain or refresh their weather-beaten bodies; no houses or much less towns to repair to, to seek for succor ... what could they see but a hideous and desolate wilderness, full of wild beasts and wild men--and what multitudes there might be of them they knew not".   4

Governor Bradford had his own personal tragedy.

While the *Mayflower* was anchored off Provincetown Harbor at the tip of Cape Cod, and while many of the Pilgrim men were out exploring and looking for a place to settle, Dorothy Bradford accidentally fell overboard and drowned.

Within six months, forty-seven people including thirteen of the eighteen wives had died. It is difficult to conceive what the mindset of the Pilgrims must have been.

Their strong faith in God was of course immense help in getting through the winter. Then a miracle occurred.

"Behold, I am going to send an angel before you to guard you along the way, and to bring you into the place which I have prepared."
Exodus 3:20

An English-speaking Indian named Squanto showed up one day and befriended them. It was a divine intervention that had guided his life to this place relations between the Pilgrims and the local Indians.

The story of how Squanto came to even be there is an incredible story and would make a book of its own.

He played a key role in the early meetings between the Indians and the colonists. He lived with the Pilgrims for 20 months, acting as a translator, guide, and advisor.

He introduced the settlers to the fur trade and taught them how to sow and fertilize native crops, which proved vital since the seeds which the Pilgrims brought were ineffective.

He showed them how to plant corn and basically saved them from complete annihilation. Squanto was the angel that God had sent, just as He had promised.

When the Mayflower set sail for England, not one single person left the colony. The rise of Christian America had now truly begun.

"The sum of your word is truth...."   *Psalm 119:160*

Patrick Henry denouncing the Stamp Act.

For over a hundred years, the colonies had been very loyal subjects of Great Britain. This relationship was sorely tested when King George III ascended to the throne in 1765.

The French Indian Wars had taken a financial toll on the British. The result was that France lost all her land holdings west of the colonies and the British empire had indeed been expanded.

However, England was still engaged in armed conflict with France. To raise monies for this continuing war, King George III began an era of excess taxation of the colonies.

The first "tipping point" of the American Revolution was the first such tax act approved by Parliament: "The Stamp Act."

The new tax was imposed on all American colonists and required them to pay a tax on every piece of printed paper they used. Ship's papers, legal documents, licenses, newspapers, other publications, and even playing cards were taxed.

Patrick Henry was 29 years old and had just been elected to the House of Burgesses, the governing body of Virginia.

When he arrived at his first meeting, they were discussing the Stamp Act.

He introduced seven Resolves against the Act during his tirade. At one point he said: "Caesar had his Brutus, Charles I had his Cromwell, and King George III may profit from their example."

In response to cries of "Treason, Treason," he said: "if this be treason, make the most of it."

His Resolves were printed in newspapers all over the colonies and his actions lead to that Act being repealed.

See **Appendix IV** for a list of the **Resolves.**

Henry's own written words about the Resolves from his memoirs are far more eloquent than the author can make:

"The within resolutions passed the House of Burgesses in May 1765. They formed the first opposition to the Stamp Act and the scheme of taxing America by the British Parliament. All the colonies, either through fear, or want of opportunity to form an opposition, or from influence of some kind or other, had remained silent.

"I had been for the first time elected a Burgess a few days before, was young, inexperienced, unacquainted with the forms of the House, and the members that composed it.

"Finding the men of weight averse to opposition, and the commencement of the tax at hand, that no person was likely to step forth, I determined to venture, and alone, unadvised, and unassisted, on a blank leaf of an old law-book, wrote the within. Upon offering them to the House violent debates ensued.

"Many threats were uttered, and much abuse cast on me by the party for submission. After a long and warm contest, the resolutions passed by a very small majority, perhaps of one or two only.

"The alarm spread throughout America with astonishing quickness, and the Ministerial party were overwhelmed.

"The great point of resistance to British taxation was universally established in the colonies.This brought on the war which finally separated the two countries and gave independence to ours.

"Whether this will prove a blessing or a curse, will depend upon the use our people make of the blessings which a gracious God hath bestowed on us. If they are wise, they will be great and happy.

"If they are of a contrary character, they will be miserable. Righteousness alone can exalt them as a nation.

'Reader! whoever thou art, remember this; and in thy sphere practise virtue thyself, and encourage it in others."

This was indeed the "watershed moment" in America's history.

King George III did not stop after the set back of the Stamp Act.

He embarked on a series of taxes referred to as "The Intolerable Acts." "The Townsend Act," The Quartering Act," and others, all led to the cry of "no taxation without representation."

King George III said to Prime Minister Lord North :"The die is now cast, the colonies must either submit or triumph."

"Woe to those who make unjust laws..." Isaiah 10: 12

CHAPTER 4: FIRST AND SECOND CONTINENTAL CONGRESS

"Whoever speaks, is to do so as one who is speaking the utterances of God; whoever serves is to do so as one who is serving by the strength which God supplies; so that in all things God may be glorified through Jesus Christ."   *1 Peter 4:10-11*

The colonies petitions to the Crown met with the firmest rebukes. The time for more decisive action had arrived.

Samuel Adams, "The Father of the American Revolution", called for the meeting of the First Continental Congress. All the colonies sent delegates except Georgia.

The "Boston Massacre" and the "Boston Tea Party" had already occurred when the first Continental Congress convened at Carpenter's Hall on September 4, 1774.

This plaque can be seen above in the far-left foreground of Carpenters Hall.

In the plaque, Henry is talking to other delegates and the article quotes his now famous line: "...the distinctions between Pennsylvanians, New Yorkers, and New Englanders are no more. I am no longer a Virginian; **I am an American**."

Patrick Henry was the first Founding Father to use the word "American" in Congress. See **Appendix III.**

Henry also said:
"I know, sir, how well it becomes a liberal man and a Christian to forget and forgive. As individuals professing a holy religion, it is our bounden duty to forgive injuries done to us as individuals.

"Our mild and holy system of religion inculcates an admirable maxim of forbearance. If your enemy smite one cheek, turn the other to him. But you must stop there.

"You cannot apply this to your country. As members of a social community, the maxim does not apply to you.

"When you consider injuries done to your country, your political duty tells you of vengeance. Forgive as a private man, but never forgive public injuries. Observations of this nature are exceedingly unpleasant."   5

At this first gathering Elias Boudinot said:

"Let us enter on this important business that we are Christians on whom the eyes of the world are now turned... Let us earnestly call and beseech Him, for Christ's sake, to preside in our councils. We can only depend on the all-powerful influence of the Spirit of God, Whose Divine aid and assistance it becomes us as a Christian people most devoutly to implore.

"Therefore, I move that some minister of the Gospel be requested to attend this Congress every morning . . . to open the meeting with prayer."   6

The motion carried, the session began with prayer and the first act of the session was to pass a motion that on September 7th, the Rev. Jacob Duche would open the meeting with prayer.

Rev Duche read the 35th Psalm:

"Plead my cause, O LORD, with them that strive with me: fight against them that fight against me.

2 Take hold of shield and buckler and stand up for mine help.

3 Draw out also the spear, and stop the way against them that persecute
me: say unto my soul, I am thy salvation.

4 Let them be confounded and put to shame that seek after my soul: let them be turned back and brought to confusion that devise my hurt.

5 Let them be as chaff before the wind: and let the angel of the LORD chase them.

6 Let their way be dark and slippery: and let the angel of the LORD persecute them.

7 For without cause have they hid for me their net in a pit, which without cause they have digged for my soul.

8 Let destruction come upon him at unawares; and let his net that he hath hid catch himself: into that very destruction let him fall.

9 And my soul shall be joyful in the LORD: it shall rejoice in his salvation.

10 All my bones shall say, LORD, who is like unto   thee, which delivers   the poor from him that is too strong for him, yea, the poo r and the needy from him that spoileth him?

11 False witnesses did rise up; they laid to my charge things that I knew not.

12They rewarded me evil for good to the spoiling of my soul.

13 But as for me, when they were sick, my clothing was sackcloth   :
I humbled my soul with fasting; and my prayer returned into mine own bosom.

14 I behaved myself as though he had been my friend or brother, I bowed down heavily, as one that mourneth for his mother.

15 But in mine adversity, they rejoiced, and gathered themselves together: yea, the abjects gathered themselves together against me, and I knew it   not; they did tear me, and ceased not:

16 With hypocritical mockers in feasts, they gnashed upon me with their teeth.

17 Lord, how long wilt thou look on? rescue my soul from their destructions, my darling from the lions.

18 I will give thee thanks in the great congregation: I will praise thee among much people.

19 Let not them that are mine enemies wrongfully rejoice over me: neither let them wink with the eye that hate me without a cause.

20 For they speak not peace: but they devise deceitful matters against them that are quiet in the land.

21 Yea, they opened their mouth wide against me, and said, Aha, aha, our eye hath seen it.

22 This thou hast seen, O LORD: keep not silence: O Lord, be not far from me.

23 Stir up thyself, and awake to my judgment, even unto my cause, my God and my Lord.

24 Judge me, O Lord, let them not rejoice over me.

25 Let them not say in their hearts, Ah, so would we have it: let them not say, we have swallowed him up .that rejoice at mine hurt: let them be clothed with shame and dishonor that magnify themselves against me

26 Let them shout for joy, and be glad, that favor my righteous cause: yea, let them say continually, Let the LORD be magnified, which hath pleasure in the prosperity of his servant. And tongue shall speak of thy righteousness and of thy praise all the day long."

Reverend Duche closed with this prayer:

"O Lord our Heavenly Father, high and mighty King of Kings, and Lord of lords, who dost from thy throne behold all the dwellers on earth and reignest with power supreme and uncontrolled over all the Kingdoms.

"Empires and Governments; look down in mercy, we beseech Thee, on these our American States, who have fled to Thee from the rod of the oppressor and thrown themselves on Thy gracious protection, desiring to be henceforth dependent only on Thee.

"Thee do they now look up for that countenance and support, which Thou alone canst give.

"Take them, therefore, Heavenly Father, under Thy nurturing care; give them wisdom in Council and valor in the field; defeat the malicious designs of our cruel adversaries; convince them of the unrighteousness of their Cause and if they persist in their sanguinary purposes, of own unerring justice, sounding in their hearts, constrain them to drop the weapons of war from their unnerved hands in the day of battle!

"Be Thou present, O God of wisdom, and direct the councils of this honorable assembly; enable them to settle things on the best and surest foundation.

"That the scene of blood may be speedily closed; that order, harmony and peace may be effectually restored, and truth   and justice, religion, and piety, prevail and flourish amongst the people.

"Preserve the health of their bodies and vigor of their minds; shower down on them and the millions they here represent, such temporal blessings as Thou seest expedient for them in this world and crown them with everlasting glory in the world to come.

"All this we ask in the name and through the merits of Jesus Christ, Thy Son and our Savior Amen."

Jacob Duche Rector of Christ Church of Philadelphia, Pennsylvania
September 7, 1774, 9 o'clock a.m.   7

John Adams wrote of this historical event to his wife Abigail in part saying:

"Rev, Duche read the 35th Psalm. It seemed Heaven had ordained that Psalm to be read on that morning. Washington was kneeling there with Henry, Randolph, Rutledge, and Jay.

"Who can imagine all the emotions with which they turned imploring to Heaven for Divine interposition? It was enough to melt a heart of stone. I saw the tears gush into their eyes."   8

Each day began with prayer. There is a beautiful glass mural of the first prayer in Congress that until recent years hung at Carpenters Hall.

"**Don't want to offend anyone**" was the reason given to the author for the removal of this beautiful mural when he visited Carpenters Hall. The author has included a "black and white" for clarity.

".But seek first his kingdom and righteousness."   *Mathew. 6:33*

The accomplishment of this first meeting of all the colonies was to show a unity of strength, and at the same time hold out hope for harmony with the King. They all approached this convention with great reverence and solemnness.

They knew this was not going to sit well with the King, but they were trying hard to work for reconciliation without having to declare their independence.

Most of the delegates at this venture were still very loyal to the Crown and were very sincere in their approach to him. They prayed that their grievance would open the King's eyes.

The first document drafted in the American Revolution was a petition to the King entitled" **Declaration of Rights."**

The entire document **is Appendix** I. These are excerpts:

"And whereas, assemblies have been frequently dissolved, contrary to the rights of the people, when they attempted to deliberate on grievances; and their dutiful, humble, loyal, and reasonable petitions to the crown for redress have been repeatedly treated with contempt by His Majesty's ministers of state:

"The good people of the several colonies of ......justly alarmed at these arbitrary proceedings of Parliament and administration, have severally elected, constituted, and appointed deputies to meet and sit in General Congress, in the city of Philadelphia, to obtain such establishment, as that their religion, laws, and liberties may not be subverted:

"That the inhabitants of the English Colonies in North America, by the immutable laws of nature, the principles of the English constitution, and the several charters or compacts, have the following rights:

"That they are entitled to life, liberty, and property, and they have never ceded to any sovereign power whatever, a right to dispose of either without their consent.

"Our ancestors, who first settled these colonies, were, at the time of their emigration from the mother-country, entitled to all the rights, liberties, and immunities of free and natural-born subjects, within the realm of England.

"That by such emigration they by no means forfeited, surrendered, or lost any of those rights, but that they were, and their descendants now are, entitled to the exercise and enjoyment of all such of them, as their local and other circumstances enable them to exercise and enjoy.

"That they have a right peaceably to assemble, consider of their grievances, and petition the king; and that all prosecutions, prohibitory proclamations, and commitments for the same are illegal.

"That the keeping a standing army in these colonies, in times of peace, without the consent of the legislature of that colony, in which such army is kept, is against law.

"During our inquiry, we find many infringements and violations of the foregoing rights, which, from an ardent desire, that harmony and mutual intercourse of affection and interest acts and measures as have been adopted since the last war, which demonstrate a system formed to enslave America.

"The several acts of which impose duties for the purpose of raising a revenue in America, extend the powers of the admiralty courts beyond their ancient limits, deprive the American subject of trial by jury, authorize the judges' certificate to indemnify the prosecutor from damages, that he might otherwise be liable to, requiring oppressive security from a claimant of ships and goods seized, before he shall be allowed to defend his property, and are subversive to American rights."   9

This was a respectful petition sent to the King. It was meant to be an "olive branch." King George III ignored it and made no response.

Stung by this rebuke of the King, it acted as a "wake up call" that they were in effect being treated that they were in rebellion.

Talks began regarding what may happen in the future and what steps should be taken now. The issue of declaring independence would certainly lead to war and the colonists from a practical standpoint were ill prepared for an armed conflict.

All eyes were on Virginia. They were the largest colony and had the most influential leaders. (More Presidents are from Virginia than any other state.)

The Virginia Provincial Council, House of Burgesses, Commonwealth of Virginia, met the fourth week of March 1775 to take up the issue of declaring independence from Great Britain.

They had been forced from their meeting place by Lord Dunsmore, the reigning British official. The meeting took place at St John's Episcopal church in Richmond, Virginia. The mood was very serious and somber.

Fate fell to Patrick Henry to champion the cause. He made a motion for the immediate armament of a militia. **(There were two British soldiers at the back of the church listening to this speech.)**

Several cries of "treason, treason" were heard when he made this motion. There was absolute bedlam until two well-known fellow delegates moved to second his motion: George Washington and Thomas Jefferson.

"Sanctify them in the truth; your word is truth." John 17:1

The following are excerpts from the summation speech he gave on behalf of his motion: "...it is natural for men to engage in fond illusions of hope...there is no longer any room for hope.

"A call to arms and an appeal to the God of Hosts is all that we have left. Many say we are weak, unable to fight such a formidable opponent.

"When shall we be stronger, next week, next year?

'Will it be when we are totally disarmed, and a British soldier is stationed in every house? Armed in the glorious cause of liberty and freedom, we are invincible against any force which our enemies can send against us.

"What is it gentlemen wish? What would they have? Is life so dear or peace so sweet as to be purchased at the price of chains and slavery? Forbid it, almighty God.

"I know not what course others may take, but **as for** me, **give me liberty give or give me death**."   10

Henry's motion carried 65 to 60.Entire speech is in **Appendix V.**

Colonel Edward Carrington, **watching through a church window**, was so moved that he said: "Let me be buried at this spot!" He was!

NOTE; Under Revisionist History, it has been claimed that Henry never said: "Give Me Liberty or Give Me Death." This is ridiculous.

Henry was briefly a Colonel in the Virginia Militia and this flag was carried into battle by the Culpeper Militia. Please **read Appendix XIX** for a detailed account on the flag which carries Henry's words.

When the Virginia assembly officially convened three months later in June 1775, every member dressed in homespun rather than imported clothing and had "Liberty or Death" sewed or painted on the breast of his coat.

Henry's words became a rallying cry and helped ensure that his fiery dramatic speech would be remembered as one of the finest in history.

Less than 30 days later, Paul Revere's response to "one if by land , two if by sea," rode through the New England countryside warning of the approach of the British: "The British are coming; the British are coming!"

On April 19, 1775, the infamous "**shot heard round the world**": the Battle of Lexington and Concord occurred.

"...Praise the LORD, who is my rock. He trains my hands for war and gives my fingers skill for battle."   *Psalms 41:4*

Lexington Green

Pastor Jonas Clark was drilling members of his congregation in close order drill. A British regiment passed by and the Commander demanded the colonists lay down their arms.

The colonists refused the command, shots were fired, and five colonists fell. The British suffered only a few minor injuries. The British moved on to Concord where they were routed.

The first official shot of the Revolutionary War was due to attempted gun control!!

The British objective was to seize the weapons arsenal in Concord. In response to this engagement, the colonists became even bolder in their approach.

The Second Continental Congress convened in June of 1775.

The document "**Declaration of the Causes and Necessities for Taking Up Arms**" was adopted on July 6, 1775.

Thomas Jefferson was the principle writer of this document and is the precursor of the ultimate Declaration of Independence.

 This was a wonderfully crafted epistle, clearly outlining the colonists concerns and yet continuing to hope for reconciliation. Complete Document is in **Appendix I**.

Ponder all the references to God throughout this document. The Founding Fathers were strong men of faith.

"If it was possible for men, who exercise their reason to believe, that the divine Author of our existence intended a part of the human race to hold an absolute property in, and an unbounded power over others, marked out by his infinite goodness and wisdom, as the objects of a legal domination never rightfully resistible, however severe and oppressive, the inhabitants of these colonies might at least require from the parliament of Great-Britain some evidence, that this dreadful authority over them, has been granted to that body.

" But a reverence for our Creator, principles of humanity, and the dictates of common sense, must convince all those who reflect upon the subject, that government was instituted to promote the welfare of mankind, and ought to be administered for the attainment of that end.

"The legislature of Great-Britain, however, stimulated by an inordinate passion for a power not only unjustifiable, but which they know to be peculiarly reprobated by the very constitution of that kingdom, and desperate of success in any mode of contest, where regard should be had to truth, law, or right, have at length, deserting those, attempted to effect their cruel and impolitic purpose of enslaving these colonies by violence, and have thereby rendered it necessary for us to close with their last appeal from reason to arms.

"Yet, however blinded that assembly may be, by their intemperate rage for unlimited domination, so to sight justice and the opinion of mankind, we esteem ourselves bound by obligations of respect to the rest of the world, to make known the justice of our cause.

"Our cause is just. Our union is perfect. Our internal resources **are great, and, if necessary, foreign assistance is undoubtedly** attainable.

"-- We gratefully acknowledge, as signal instances of the Divine favour towards us, that his Providence would not permit us to be called into this severe controversy, until we were grown up to our present strength, had been previously exercised in warlike operation, and possessed of the means of defending ourselves.

"With hearts fortified with these animating reflections, we most solemnly, before God and the world, declare, that, exerting the utmost energy of those powers, which our beneficent Creator hath graciously upon us, the arms we have been compelled by our enemies to assume, we will , in defiance of every hazard, preservation of our liberties; being with one mind resolved to die freemen rather than to live slaves.

"Lest this declaration should disquiet the minds of our friends and fellow subjects in any part of the empire, we assure them that we mean not to dissolve that union which has so long and so happily subsisted between us, and which we sincerely wish to see restored.

"Necessity has not yet driven us into that desperate measure or induced us to excite any other nation to war against them. -- We have not raised armies with ambitious designs of   separating from Great-Britain and establishing independent states. We fight not for glory or for conquest.

 "We exhibit to mankind the remarkable spectacle of a people attacked by unprovoked enemies, without any imputation or even suspicion of offence. They boast of their privileges and civilization, and yet proffer no milder conditions than servitude or death.

"In our own native land, in defence of the freedom that is our birthright, and which we ever enjoyed till the late violation of it -- for the   of our property, acquired solely by the honest industry of our fore-fathers and ourselves, against violence offered, we have taken up arms.
We shall lay them down when hostilities shall cease on the part of the aggressors, and all danger of there being renewed shall be removed, and not before.

"With a humble confidence in the mercies of the supreme and impartial Judge and Ruler of the Universe, we most devoutly implore his divine goodness to protect us happily through this great conflict, to dispose our adversaries to reconciliation on reasonable terms, and thereby to relieve the empire from the calamities of civil war."   11

The Colonists were still holding out the olive branch to England.

"Pride goes before destruction, a haughty spirit before a fall."
Proverbs 16:18

King George III does not even read this document he was so incensed.

Based upon his comment after reading the "Declaration" from the first Continental Congress, his "bluff" had been called.

He addressed Parliament with a "Proclamation of Rebellion" and urged them to move quickly to end the revolt and bring order to the colonies.

Removing his protective hand from them, he authorized his troops to use force if that need should arise.

CHAPTER 5: DECLARATION OF INDEPENDENCE CONVENTION

"For lack of guidance a nation falls, but victory is won through many advisers."   *Proverbs 11: 14*

The committee charged with writing the Declarations of Independence

In late June 1776. the delegates met once more in Philadelphia.

Several things were happening simultaneously: a committee was appointed to draft the Declaration of Independence; the Convention itself which was assumed to vote for independence; a committee drafting the Articles of Confederation; another committee formed to draft a peace treaty with France; and George Washington was readying his army.

Thomas Jefferson, Benjamin Franklin, John Adams, Robert R Livingston, and Roger Sherman were the committee appointed to draft the Declaration of Independence.

Adams did a great deal of this work, but he felt Jefferson should be the one to write it for several reasons. Per many sources, the discussion went something like this:

"Reason first, you are a Virginian, and a Virginian ought to appear at the head of this business. Reason second, I am obnoxious, suspected, and unpopular. You are very much otherwise. Reason third, you can write ten times better than I can."

(A bit of trivia: one reason Jefferson was such a prolific writer was that he did not like to speak publicly, due to a speech defect. He is the only President never to address Congress in person.)

The list of grievances included twenty-seven violations of Biblical principles.

(Much of the final version of the Declaration was based upon **Virginia's "Declaration of Rights,"** adopted June 12, 1776. The authors were George Mason and Patrick Henry. These **Right**s may be read **in Appendix VI.)**

John Dickinson headed the committee to draft our first "Constitution": **The Articles of Confederation**. See **Appendix VIII** for the entire document.

The Articles of Confederation referred to the "Great Governor of the World" and (at the risk of starting a major controversy) elected the first President of the United States: John Hanson.

This was the governing document of America from 1776 to 1787 when our current Constitution came into effect.

 It had been decided that all the colonies had to vote for independence, i.e., it had to be unanimous or it would not occur. Not all the delegates in each colony had to agree but the majority would have to agree.

New York was a colony who was there but "wasn't there." They kept waiting for instructions that never came, so they never voted but abstained.

The colony of Delaware ends up being the "key" to the convention. Delaware had three delegates, one loyal to Great Britain and two in favor of independence.

For some unknown reason, one of the latter delegates, Caesar Rodney, leaves early. When it became obvious the tie vote could not be broken, two men set off on horseback to find Rodney.

They catch up with him 75 miles later and convince him to return. This is a 150-mile trip on horseback with no rest. He endures a terrible rainstorm on his way back to the Convention.

He must cross three swollen rivers where the bridges have been washed out.

"I can do all things through Him who strengthens me." Phil: 4:13

He was carried into the convention just in time to cast the tie breaking vote. Never underestimate the power of one vote.

(But there is more to this story. Rodney had cancer. It covered part of his face and he wore a mask to cover it. He had been told his best chance of survival was to go to a specialist in England. When he cast that vote, he signed his own death warrant, because he did die from cancer several years later at the age of 56.)

One of the most salient points of the Declaration was this paragraph: "...We hold these truths to be self-evident, that all Men are created equal, they are endowed by their Creator with certain inalienable rights, that among these rights are life, liberty and the pursuit of happiness..."

The Fathers clearly affirmed that our rights come from God, not from Government.   12

After John Hancock signed, he said: "His majesty can now read my signature. He will not need his glasses. Gentlemen, we must all pull together. There can be no going back. We will assuredly all hang together."   13

Whereupon, Benjamin Franklin said with a touch of "gallows humor": "Yes, we must indeed all hang together, or most assuredly, we shall all hang separately."   14

The delegates went to their knees, many wept, several prayed. They placed the Bible on top of the document.   There was a moment of silence.

Samuel Adams said: "We have this day restored the Sovereign to Whom alone men ought to be obedient…He reigns in Heaven from the rising to the setting sun, may His Kingdom come."   15

"For kingship belongs to the Lord, and he rules over the nations."
                                                    Psalms 22: 28

Fifty-two of the fifty-six signors were Evangelical Christians. Roughly half had Seminary degrees. Five had sons who were Pastors.

(When the British officer at Lexington Green demanded that arms be laid down "in the name of the Sovereign King," Rev Jonas Clarke said: "We recognize no sovereign but God and **no King but King Jesus**.")

 Abraham Clark prophetically said: "Let us prepare for the worst. We can die here but once."   16

What price did the signors pay for the courage of their convictions?

Eighteen months after the signing, twelve were dead.

Two had their wives imprisoned; five were captured and tortured; twelve had all their property seized and burned to the ground; five of them lost sons in the service of the cause.

One was murdered; one was killed in a duel; and one was lost at sea. Many of them died as paupers.

Thus, the Reader can see what a small remnant, relying on God and in the face of overwhelming odds can achieve, if they are vigilant, active, and brave.

The only two signors who became President were Jefferson and Adams.

Adams was so upset when Jefferson became President (and thus lost his bid for reelection) that he did not even attend the" swearing in" ceremonies.

However, later in life, they reconciled and became very good friends.

They wrote to each other on numerous occasions, and on Adams death bed his last words were: "Jefferson survives."

He was wrong. Jefferson had died hours before on the same day, fifty years after the signing, on July 4th, 1826.

John Adams

Prior to his death, Adams said: "…I am aware of the toil and blood and treasure that it will cost to maintain this Declaration, and support and defend these States.

"I can see that the end is worth more than all the means; that posterity will triumph in that day's transaction…"   17

CHAPTER 6: CHRISTIAN AMERICAN REVOLUTION

"For you have been called to live in freedom, my brothers and sisters... use your freedom to serve one another in love."
Gal. 5:13

In the beginning, it was estimated that less than four percent of the Colonists supported the war! (Remember, Henry's motion had only carried 65 to 60.)

At the height of the war only twenty-five percent of the colonists supported the war, about thirty percent gave substantial aid to the enemy, and the rest didn't care. Hmmmm. Sounds like modern day America.

Ponder this dear reader. There is no army or navy, you are short on military leadership, two thirds of the populace are either against you or do not wish to get involved and the mightiest army in the world is already on your shore!

But the colonists were blessed with bold, God fearing men, who much like Gideon,(who will be discussed later) rose to the occasion when called upon to do so.

Talk about courage and a strong faith of conviction!

There is only one logical reason as to why the colonists won the war.

The revolution was a Christian Revolution because it was based on dictates laid down by Jesus Christ.

Jesus says the first thing you do is protest.(The word "Protestant" comes from protesting civil and religious authorities.) Jesus protested by being silent when questioned by Pontius Pilate.

The colonists had protested for over eleven years!

If protesting fails, then Jesus says you must flee. He told his disciples they must flee to the next city if they are being persecuted. (Matthew 10:23).

The enemy was all around them. There was no place to go. Then Jesus says it is all right to fight.

These were among his last words to his disciples before being arrested:

"...When I sent you without purse, bag, or sandals Did you lack for anything? No Lord, nothing. ...But now, if you have a purse, take it , and a bag, and let he who has no sword, let him sell his cloak and buy one.". Luke 22: 35-37

God's chosen man to lead America at this critical venture in her history was George Washington. Washington had been an officer in the British Army during the French Indian Wars.

During one battle, Washington was trapped in a ravine. One of the Indian Chiefs directed fifteen of his warriors to fire only at him. This is depicted in the following painting.

"no weapons formed against me shall stand." Isaiah 54:1

The Chief met Washington years later when he was President and related the following:

"I am a chief, and ruler over my tribes. My influence extends to the waters of the great lakes, and to the far blue mountains.

" I have traveled a long and weary path, that I might see the young warrior (George Washington, from the day he had horses shot out from underneath him) of the Great Battle.

"It was on the day when the white man's blood mixed with the streams of our forest, that I first beheld this chief. I called to my young men and said, mark yon tall and daring warrior?

"He is not of the red-coat tribe (interesting comment since he was in full red uniform)— he hath an Indian's wisdom, and his warriors fight as we do — himself is alone exposed.

"Quick, let your aim be certain, and he dies.

"Our rifles were leveled, rifles which, but for him, knew not   to miss - 'twas all in vain, a power mightier far than we, shielded him from harm.

"He cannot die in battle. I am old, and soon shall be gathered to the great council fire of my fathers in the land of shades, but ere I go, there is something bids me speak in the voice of prophecy.

"Listen! The Great Spirit protects that man and guides his destinies. He will become the chief of nations, and **a people yet unborn will hail him as the founder of a mighty empire."**   18

Referencing this event, Washington wrote the following letter to his brother on July 18, 1755:

"But by the All-Powerful Dispensations of Providence, I have been protected beyond all human probability or expectation; for **I had four bullets through coat, and two horses shot under me, yet escaped unhurt**, although death was leveling my companions on every side of me!" (His hat had also been shot off his head.)

On July 5th, 1776 this was General George Washington's First General Order to his troops:

"The time is now near at hand which must probably determine, whether Americans are to be, Freemen or Slaves; whether they are to have any property they can call their own; whether their Houses, and Farms, are to be pillaged and destroyed, and they consigned to a State of Wretchedness from which no human efforts will probably deliver them.

'The fate of unborn Millions will now depend, under God, on the Courage and Conduct of this army—Our cruel and unrelenting Enemy leaves us no choice but a brave resistance, or the most abject submission; this is all we can expect—

"We have therefore to resolve to conquer or die: Our own Country's Honor, all call upon us for a vigorous and manly exertion, and if we shamefully fail, we shall become infamous to the whole world.

"Let us therefore rely upon the goodness of the Cause, and the aid of the Supreme Being, in whose hands Victory is, to animate and encourage us to great and noble Actions.

"The Eyes of all our Countrymen are now upon us, and we shall have their blessings, and praises, if happily we are the instruments of saving them from the Tyranny meditated against them.

"Let us therefore animate and encourage each other, and shew the whole world, that a Freeman contending for Liberty on his own ground is superior to any slavish mercenary on earth."   19

Thomas Paine wrote an epistle entitled "Common Sense."

It was so powerful that Washington had Paine accompany him throughout some of his campaign and had him read from it to his troops.

This was the most popular section:

"'THESE are the times that try men's souls. The summer soldier and the sunshine patriot will, in this crisis, shrink from the service of their country, but he that stands by it now, deserves the love and thanks of man and woman.

"Tyranny, like hell, is not easily conquered; yet we have this consolation with us, that the harder the conflict, the more glorious the triumph.

"What we obtain too cheap, we esteem too lightly: it is dearness only that gives everything its value.

"Heaven knows how to put a proper price upon its goods; and it would be strange indeed if so celestial an article as freedom should not be highly rated.

"Britain, with an army to enforce her tyranny, has declared that she has a right (not only to tax but "to bind us in all cases whatsoever") and if being bound in that manner, is not slavery, then is there not such a thing as slavery upon earth.

"Should the government of America return into the hands of Britain, the tottering situation of things will be a temptation for some desperate adventurer to try his fortune; and in such a case, what relief can Britain give?

"Ere she could hear the news, the fatal business might be done; and ourselves suffering like the wretched Britons under the oppression of the Conqueror. Ye that oppose independence now, ye know not what ye do; ye are opening a door to eternal tyranny, by keeping vacant the seat of government.

"Even the expression is impious; for so unlimited a power can belong only   to God."   20

Washington endured many hardships during that terrible winter at Valley Forge. He lost over two thousand five hundred men to freezing and starvation.

When many enlistments "were up", he paid them out of his own monies to keep them there.

During this time, Washington was blessed with the arrival of Baron von Steuben. He was a Prussian General and was very skilled in military tactics. He trained the soldiers in close order drill and taught them discipline.

"With upright heart he shepherded them and guided them with his skillful hand." Psalms 78: 75

Baron von Steuben at Valley Forge

They never lost hope in the face of seemingly insurmountable odds. Time after time when Washington and his men were about to lose a significant battle, God changed the weather to confuse the enemy.

This allowed Washington and his men to escape.

One such example was during the fighting on Long Island. General Howe had 32,000 troops massed against Washington's 8000 men and had them surrounded in a semicircle with the colonists back against a mile-wide East River.

Washington could not retreat across the river due to adverse weather. Suddenly a full moon came out, and Washington and his men were able to escape and the British never once saw or heard them!

It was through divine intervention that a disastrous plot was discovered that could have changed the course of the war completely.

General Benedict Arnold, the hero of Fort Ticonderoga, was Commander of West Point. While an outstanding General, he had been passed over for promotion and became increasingly bitter.

His wife was also a strong loyalist which did not help the situation at all. He conspired with the British to turn West Point over to them in return for an appointment in the British Army.

The plot was uncovered at the last moment when a British spy, Major Andre, was caught with the plans in his pocket. He was executed. Arnold escaped and was appointed an officer for the enemy as promised.

Washington proclaimed a day of Thanksgiving for his troops as had this plot not been uncovered, it would have been disastrous for the colonist's cause. The Continental Congress declared a day of thanksgiving as well.

The other key to the war were the Militia: The "Minute Men."

With few exceptions, each militia unit was commanded by a church Pastor, and the members were from his congregation.

Reverend Peter Muhlenberg was one such Pastor.

His congregation was not prepared for what was about to happen at church this one Sunday morning. Muhlenberg's text for the day was *Eccl 3:1: "To everything there is a season, a time for every purpose under heaven a time to be born, and a time to die; a time to plant, and a time to pluck what   is planted...".*

In the language of the day in the mode of things, a time to preach and a time to pray, but those times have passed away.

As those assembled looked on, Pastor Muhlenberg declared, "There is a time to fight, and that time has now come!"

Muhlenberg then proceeded to remove his robes revealing, to the shock of his congregation, a military uniform as a Virginia Colonel.

Nearly three hundred men enlisted under his command that day. 21

"for the Lord your God is going with you."   Deut. 31: 8

So many Pastors fought in the war they were referred to as the "Black Regiment." It was a Christian revolution in every sense of the word.

THE PATRIOT

The author found this movie very historically accurate in many respects.

The main character is a member of the South Carolina assembly and votes against a levy to provide funds for Washington. (Congress had no power to raise money.)

His pacifism changes when one of his sons is murdered by a British officer. This motivates him to form a militia unit.

The movie is very Christian oriented: there are several scenes with prayer, a Christian marriage ceremony, and there are several references to God.

The final battle scene in the movie was recreation of the Battle of Cowpens.(Author toured the battlefield several years ago.)

This was a major victory for the colonists over British regulars. The militia played a major role in the victory.

."...the victory belongs to the Lord."   *Proverbs 21:31*

A church Pastor (armed with a flintlock in the below picture) and a French officer are part of his militia unit, which lends even more authenticity to the movie.

The author highly recommends this movie for the entire family.

An interesting comment about the war came from The House Judiciary Committee in 1854:

"Had the people, during the Revolution, had a suspicion of Any attempt to stifle Christianity or had there been any War against Christianity, that Revolution would have been strangled in its cradle.

"At the time of the adoption of the Constitution and the amendments ,the universal sentiment was that Christianity should be encouraged. There can be no substitute for Christianity."   22

THE FRENCH CONNECTION

France did contribute monetarily to the Colonist cause. This was due to the efforts of Ben Franklin as well as the Marquis de Lafayette. Lafayette was a very wealthy Frenchman.

He believed in America's cause so much that he purchased his own ship and came to America in 1777 at the age of 19! He became a Major General in the Continental army.

"bear one another's burdens, and so fulfill the law of Christ." Gal. 6:2

Marquis de Lafayette

He went back to France in 1779 and won military support for the American colonists. Many French officers served with the Americans.

His tactical cunning was a great assistance. They were played to their greatest advantage at the 1781 Battle of Yorktown. He laid a triangular trap comprised of French reinforcements to the north, American troops to the east, and the York River to the south.

The French fleet blockaded the coast so no British supply ships could get in. After a siege of several days, Cornwallis surrendered on October 19, 1781.

Cornwallis had a subordinate deliver his sword to Washington. However, Washington had a subordinate receive it. Touché!

Lafayette continued his ties with America so much that his grave is buried under soil taken from Bunker Hill. He was posthumously made an honorary American citizen in 2002.

CHAPTER 7: GEORGE WASHINGTON'S CHRISTIAN FAITH

"This is my command-be strong and encouraged. Do not be Frightened, do not be dismayed, for the Lord your God is with you."
Joshua 1: 9.

First a little bit of levity. Let's explore some popular myths.

Did he throw a silver dollar across the Potomac? No. It is over a mile wide and a silver dollar was not even in existence at that time.

Did he chop down the Cherry Tree? The author cannot tell a lie. This was a story invented and later recanted by Parson Weems.   Did he have wooden teeth? No. He had a metal contraption in his mouth full of ivory and other human teeth.

The "anti-Christian" crowd has tried very hard to prove that he was a Deist and not a true Christian at all. This is a ridiculous statement as all evidence points to the contrary.

This was his prayer of salvation: "Almighty God, and most merciful Father . . . since Thou are a God of pure eyes, and wilt be sanctified in all who draw near unto Thee, who dost not regard the sacrifice of fools, nor hear sinners who tread in Thy courts, pardon, I beseech Thee, my sins; remove them from Thy presence, as far   as the east is from the west, and accept me for the merits of Thy Son, Jesus Christ; that when I come into Thy temple and compass Thine altar, my prayer may come before Thee as incense; and as Thou wouldst hear   me calling upon Thee in my prayers and give me grace to hear Thee calling on me in Thy Word, that it may be wisdom, righteousness, reconciliation, and peace to the saving of my soul in the day of the Lord Jesus Christ."   23

(The Masons have done their best to promote Washington in their propaganda, but it is well documented that in thirty years he only attended four lodge meetings.}

His Granddaughter wrote in a letter:

"I should have thought it the greatest heresy to doubt his firm belief in Christianity. Is it necessary that any one should certify, "General Washington avowed himself to me a believer in Christianity?

"As well may we question his patriotism, his heroic, disinterested devotion to his country. His mottos were "Deeds, not Words" and "For God and my Country." 24

"Look to the Lord and seek His strength always."   *I Chron.16:11*

Washington kept a daily prayer journal, paid for a pew in his church and on Sunday nights read to his wife from the Bible.

Remember the Indian Chief who had tried to kill Washington during the French Indian War? After Washington became President, he and other chiefs visited him for guidance on educating their children.

Washington said in part:

"You do well to wish to learn our arts and ways of life, and above all, the religion of Jesus Christ. These will make you a greater and happier people than you are. Congress will do all they can to assist you in this wise intention." 25

(A good book clearly proving the Christianity of George Washington, is "George Washington's Sacred Fire" by Peter A. Lillback.)

The portrait of his prayer at Valley Forge is not a myth. It is an eyewitness account of Issac Potts, a Quaker who lived nearby. He recounted the story many times in his life, both by letter and in talks.

Potts was riding through the woods and heard a plaintive cry. He tethered his horse and crept into the woods and came upon Washington kneeling and praying in the snow.

"Therefore, I tell you, whatever you ask for in prayer, that you have received it, and it will be yours."   Mark 11:24

He crept close, so he could hear what Washington was saying.

Potts would later write:

"If there is anyone on this earth whom the Lord will listen to, it is George Washington; and I feel a presentiment that under such a commander there can be no doubt of our eventually establishing our independence, and that God in his providence has willed it so.

'Such a prayer I have never heard from a man. I did not know that a Soldier could also be a Christian. I am convinced that if God answers that man's prayer, the Colonists will prevail."   26

Potts changed his allegiance from Great Britain to the Colonists.

Rev Henry Muhlenberg noted how "he rode among his army...and admonished each one to fear God, to put away the wickedness that has set in and become so general, and to practice the Christian virtues.

"He sits outside his tent every morning and evening and seems fervent in his prayers."   27

"...the fervent prayer of a righteous man availeth much." James 5: 16

This excerpt is from Washington's' daily prayer journal:

"...Let me live according to those holy rules which thou hast this day prescribed in thy holy word; make me to know what is acceptable in thy holy word; make me to know what is acceptable in thy sight, and therein to delight, open the eyes of my understanding, and help me thoroughly to examine myself concerning my knowledge, faith and repentance, increase my faith, and direct me to the true object Jesus Christ the way, the truth and the life.."

On August 3, 1776, General Washington issued this general order:

"The General is sorry to be informed that the foolish, and wicked practice of profane cursing and swearing (a vice heretofore little known in an American Army) is growing into fashion; he hopes the officers will, by example, as well as influence, endeavor to check it and that both they, and the men will reflect, that we can have little hopes of the blessing of Heaven on our Arms, if we insult it by our impiety, and folly; added to this, it is a vice so mean and low, without any temptation, that every man of sense, and character, detests and despises it."

Washington was instrumental in getting Chaplains for his army.

On May 2, 1778, General George Washington issued these orders to his troops at Valley Forge:

"The Commander-in-Chief directs that Divine service be performed every Sunday at 11 o'clock, in each Brigade which has a Chaplain.

"Those Brigades which have none will attend the places of worship nearest to them. It is expected that officers of all ranks will, by their attendance, set an example for their men.

"While we are zealously performing the duties of good citizens and soldiers, we certainly ought not to be inattentive to the higher duties of religion.

"To the distinguished character off Patriot, it should be our highest Glory to laud the more distinguished Character of Christian.

'The signal instances of Providential goodness which we have experienced, and which have now almost crowned our labors with complete success demand from us in a peculiar manner the warmest returns of gratitude and piety to the Supreme Author of all good." 28

CHAPTER 8: THE CONSTITUTION CONVENTION

"Trust in the Lord with all of your heart and do not lean on your own understanding. In all your ways acknowledge Him, and He will make your paths straight."   *Proverbs 3: 5-6*

The original reason given for this special convention was to address grievances of the Veterans over benefits. They were being paid in "worthless Continentals."

In fact, there had been two military uprisings with blood shed over that issue. Washington met with the leaders and promised help.(Hmm. Are our Veterans being treated any better today?)

Then Madison and Hamilton began to say that we need to address some of the shortcomings of our governing document. There were problems with the current form of government.

Its major defects were that Congress had no power to raise money, had no real power to enforce what actions they would take, and while having a series of Presidents, they were severely limited in the actions they could take.

This was keenly felt during the war, when the army lacked supplies and often went without pay.

Henry believed the defects could be corrected without a special convention. He said: "I smell a rat", because he knew Madison wanted a strong central government and Hamilton wanted a national bank.

Chosen as a delegate, he did not attend. This was a decision he regretted the rest of his life.

After four weeks, the convention was in disarray. Hardly anything had been decided. Twelve delegates, including George Mason, left in disgust.

On June 28, 1787, eighty-one-year-old Ben Franklin asked to be recognized. Franklin was in poor health, and until now, he had just scribbled notes out and had other delegates read his remarks.

Ben Franklin

A loud hush fell over the delegates when Franklin asked to speak:

"The small progress we have made after four or five weeks…with each other is a melancholy proof of the imperfection of the human understanding.

"In this situation of this Assembly, groping as it were in the dark to find political truth, and scarce able to distinguish it when presented to us, how has it happened sir, that we have not thought of humbly applying to the Father to illuminate our understanding?

"In the beginning of the contest with Great Britain when we were sensible of danger…we had daily prayer in this room for Divine protection. Those prayers sir were heard and they were graciously answered…

"All of us who were engaged in the struggle must have observed frequent instances of a superintending providence in our favor.

"And now have we forgotten that powerful Friend? Or do we imagine we no longer need his assistance?

"I have lived a long time, and the longer I live the more convincing proofs of this truth: that God governs in the affairs of man…If a sparrow cannot fall to the ground without his notice is it probable that an empire can rise without his aid?

"We have been assured by the sacred writings that 'except the Lord build the house, they labor in vain that build it.'

" I firmly believe this; and I also believe that without his concurring aid we shall succeed in this political building no better than the Builders of Babel…

"We shall be divided by our little partial local interests; our projects will be confounded and we ourselves shall become a reproach and bye word down to future ages.

"I therefore beg leave to move that henceforth prayers imploring the assistance of Heaven, and its blessings on our deliberations, be held in this Assembly every morning before we proceed to business, and that one or more of the clergy of this city be requested to officiate in that service."   29

Jonathan Dayton said: "The words of the venerable Franklin fell upon our ears with a weight and authority even greater than we may an oracle to have had in the Roman Senate."   30

This speech changed the tenor and atmosphere of the Convention. Franklin's motion was seconded and passed. Each day thereafter began in prayer.

 (The irony is that God used the one true Deist to save the Convention. Who says our Lord does not have a sense of humor?)

From that moment forward, the Convention would complete its task and submit the Constitution for ratification.

The delegates had viewed and researched all forms of government from ancient history as well as those currently in existence.

They summarily dismissed all of them as they felt they were not suitable to the needs of America.

We often hear the argument today that **"If the Founding Fathers believed in God, why isn't God mentioned in the Constitution?"**

The Fathers structured and adopted a form of government that had never existed in the annals of history. Where did the idea of the three branches originate?

Since they were all strong Christians and sought the Bible daily for guidance, is it just possible that they found the answer in God's word?

This author believe that it may have been based upon this verse from *Isaiah 33:22: "For the Lord is our King, the Lord is our Judge, the Lord is our Lawgiver. He alone will save us."*

During his opening remarks of the Convention, Washington said: "This event is in the Hands of God."   31

In a letter to his good friend, Governor Trumbull of Connecticut he wrote that the "adoption of the Proposed General Government' disposed him to the opinion 'that miracles have Not ceased."   32

Washington would later write: "One could "trace the finger of Providence through those dark and mysterious events, which first induced the State to appoint an adoption of the system recommended by that general Convention."   33

Alexander Hamilton said: "For my part, I sincerely esteem the Constitution a system which without the finger of God, never could have been suggested and agreed upon by such a diversity of interests."
                                      34

In a letter to Thomas Jefferson, James Madison said: "It is impossible for the man of pious reflection not to perceive in it, a finger of that almighty God."   35

John Adams said: "Our Constitution was made only for a moral and religious people. It is wholly inadequate for the government of any other." 36

Consider the following phrases from the **Preamble**.

The author has placed a corresponding Bible verse next to the phrases.

"We the people of the United States, to form a more perfect union,

establish justice:	**I Peter 2: 14**
insure domestic tranquility:	**1 Timothy 2: 1,2**
provide for the common defense:	**Luke 22: 36**
promote the general welfare:	**Romans 13: 4**
and to secure the blessings of liberty:	**2nd Cor. 3: 17**
to posterity:	**Genesis 45: 7**
and ourselves	
do ordain	**Exodus 28:14**
and establish	**2nd Cor. 1: 21**

this Constitution for the United States of America."

"Ordain" means to "confer Holy orders upon." Sounds like Christian aspirations from men who had a strong faith in God to the author!

Our Constitution is deeply rooted in Christianity.

WASHINGTON'S INAUGERAL ADDRESS

"Furthermore, you shall select out of all the people able men who fear God, men of truth, those who hate dishonest gain; and you shall place these over them as leaders of thousands, of hundreds, of fifties and of tens."   *Exodus 18: 21.*

On April 3, 1789 Washington placed his hand on the Bible and said:

"I do solemnly swear (or affirm) that I will faithfully execute the Office of President of the United States, and will to the best of my ability, preserve, protect and defend the Constitution of the United States."

Washington himself added the words "so help me God' to the oath of office. Washington struggled with accepting the nomination, even though it was a unanimous vote to elect him as President.

In fact, he was unanimously reelected four years later, and no doubt would have been as well for a third term, if Martha had not put her foot down and said no.

Washington's Inaugural Address clearly shows that he is a Christian. The following are but a few excerpts.

"It would be peculiarly improper to omit, in this first official act, **my fervent supplications to that Almighty Being who rules over the universe, who presides in the councils of nations and whose providential aide can supply every human defect, that His benediction may consecrate to the liberties and happiness of the people of the United States** a Government instituted by themselves for these essential purposes; and may enable every instrument employed in its administration to execute with success, the functions allotted to his charge.

"Every step they have taken to become an independent nation seems   to have been distinguished by some token of providential agency; and in the important Revolution just accomplished in the system of their United government the tranquil deliberations and voluntary consent of so many distinct communities, from which the event has resulted cannot be compare with the means by which most governments have been established, without some return of pious gratitude, along with an humble anticipation of the future blessings which them past seem to presage. These reflections, arising out of the present crisis, have themselves too strongly on my mind to be suppressed.

" Having thus imported to you my sentiments, as they have been awakened by the occasion which brings us together, **I shall take my present leave; but not without resorting once more to the benign parent of the human race, in humble supplication that since he has been pleased to favour the American people, with opportunities for deliberating in perfect tranquility, and dispositions for deciding with unparalleled unanimity on a form of Government, for the security of their Union, and the   of their happiness; so his divine blessing may be equally conspicuous in the enlarged views, the temperate consultations, and the wise measures on which the success of this Government must depend."**

37

WASHINGTON'S THANKSGIVING DAY PROCLAMATION

His **Thanksgiving Day Proclamation** clearly shows the strong Christian faith that our First President had.

"By the President of the United States of America a Proclamation.

"Whereas it is the duty of all Nations to acknowledge the providence of Almighty God, to obey his will, to be grateful for his benefits, and humbly to implore his protection and favor-- ... Now therefore ...That we may then all unite in rendering unto him our sincere and humble thanks--for his kind care and protection of the People of this Country previous to their becoming a Nation--for the signal and manifold mercies, and the favorable interpositions of his Providence which we experienced in the course and conclusion of the late war--for the great degree of tranquility, union, and plenty, which we have since enjoyed--for the peaceable and rational manner, in which we have been enabled to establish constitutions of government for our safety and happiness, and particularly the national One now lately instituted--for the civil and religious liberty with which we are blessed; and the means we have of acquiring and diffusing useful knowledge; and in general for all the great and various favors which he hath been pleased to confer upon us.

" And also that we may then unite in most humbly offering our prayers and supplications to the great Lord and Ruler of Nations and beseech him to pardon our national and other transgressions--to enable us all, whether in public or private stations, to perform our several and relative duties properly and punctually--to render our national government a blessing to all the people, by constantly being a Government of wise, just, and constitutional laws, discreetly and faithfully executed and obeyed--to protect and guide all Sovereigns and Nations (especially such as have shewn kindness unto us) and to bless them with good government, peace...

"Given under my hand at the City of New York the third day of October in the year of our Lord 1789."   38

CHAPTER 9: BILL OF RIGHTS

" Thy testimonies that thou hast commanded are righteous and very faithful."   *Psalms 119: 138*

It is the Bill of Rights that protects us from all the many defects of the Constitution, and considering all the assaults against prayer in the school room, where would we be today without the First Amendment?

These amendments were added by godly men who foresaw how this Constitution could be twisted and turned by evil men in the future.

When the Constitution was presented to the states, America almost went through a second revolution.

The country became divided into two groups; the Federalists who supported the Constitution versus the Anti-Federalists who viewed it with horror, and either wanted it rejected in whole or at least with amendments.

George Washington, James Madison, and Alexander Hamilton led the Federalists. George Mason, Richard Henry Lee, James Monroe, and Patrick Henry led the Anti- Federalists.

Thomas Jefferson was serving as Ambassador to France, but his correspondence clearly stated that he was an Anti-Federalist.

Those drafting the Constitution knew it was a foregone conclusion that George Washington would be the first President. The phrase "first in the hearts of his countrymen" was 100% accurate.

They knew he would not abuse his office. (He did not.) Thus, they saw no reason for fear by giving him broad powers.

The Federalists wanted no amendments to the Constitution at all. Since they were the ones who had drafted the document, they foresaw no problem in getting it ratified.

The Anti-Federalists were absolutely abhorred. They were looking at the future, instead of the present, and praise be to the Lord that they were.

Patrick Henry spoke over five hours at one time against ratifying this document. The author has condensed some of his argument into **Appendix XII** at the end of the book.

See **Appendix XIII** for the Bill of Rights.

The author is adding one of Henry's statements to each of the main concerns, as he believes it adds "you were there" to the discussion.

Considering current events in America dear reader, you decide if Henry's and the other anti-federalist's concerns were justified!!

Their main objections to the Constitution were:

They felt a future President could become a monarchy because he could assume dictatorial powers on his own.
*"If he be a man of ambition, he may seize the first opportunity
to accomplish his hidden design…so away with your President, you shall
have a King."*

There was rule by the minority rather than the majority, due to 1/3 vote in the Senate being necessary to prohibit legislation.
*"Since when does the rule of the minority overrule the rule of the
majority?"*

The Senate could make treaties not in the best interest of America and they did not have to answer to anyone.
*"But then we are told that those who represent us would never do
anything not in our best interest."*

There was no check on the Supreme Court.
*"If you do not put a check on the judiciary, you will one day live under
judicial tyranny."*

There would now be two sets of tax gatherers.
"If under our watchful eyes, at the state legislatures our Sheriffs are sucking out our money with commissions and fees, how will we keep our eyes on another set of tax gatherers in Philadelphia?

Excisemen may come in multitudes...They may, unless the general government be restrained by a bill of rights, go into your cellars and rooms, and search, ransack, and measure, everything you eat, drink and wear."

There was no right to bear arms.
"You read of a riot act in a country that is said to be free, where it's citizens fear to gather in large numbers for being shot by a hired soldiery. I fear we may one day see that act in America."

James Madison basically said the Constitution should be adopted and worry about adding amendments later.
"That government has always been a choice between two evils has been a long-standing maxim. Evils admitted to be removed subsequently, and tyranny submitted to in order to be excluded by a subsequent alteration, are things totally new to me.

I ask, does experience warrant such a thing from the beginning of the world to this day? Since when do you enter into a compact first, and afterwards settle the terms of the government?"

Read Appendix XIX on Virginia's Constitution Amendments and specifically read the wording on proposed Amendment 17 dealing with the right to bear arms.

Madison is often called the "Father of the Bill of Rights." This is a case of perception having nothing to do with reality.

Madison, a member of the Virginia legislature, voted NO to adopting the Constitution with any amendments and thus helped defeat that motion.

Madison then voted YES to adopting the Constitution without any amendments. This latter vote which ensured Virginia's adoption was 89 to 78. It was that close in all the colonies.

(In fact, two colonies, North Carolina, and Rhode Island, originally voted not to adopt the Constitution, but later changed their vote after nine colonies voted in favor. Rhode Island never signed the document.)

Madison wanted to run for Congress. Mason, Henry, and others blocked his nomination. He then went to them and asked what he had to do to gain their support. They said they would support him if he took their twenty amendments to Congress and do his best to get them adopted.

When Madison got to Congress, there were dozens of amendments proposed to the Constitution by all the Colonies.

In perhaps the first political promise ever made and kept, Madison promised to do his best to get them adopted, and to his credit he did.

Madison wrote in one of his Federalist papers: "the accumulation of all powers, legislative, executive, and judiciary, in the same hands whether on one, a few, or many may justly be pronounced the very definition of tyranny." 39

The author finds the last quote somewhat ironical because Madison wanted no amendments, yet there was no check on the Judiciary as there had been in the Articles of Confederation!

Seventeen got through committee, twelve were submitted to ratification and ten were ratified. Praise God for the anointing on those who foresaw what no one else could: what a government could do without any restraints. **SEVEN OF VIRGINIA'S 20 WERE INCLUDED!!**

The Bill of Rights closely follows "Virginia's Declaration of Rights" which has previously been mentioned.

The author has serious concerns about the survival of our "Bill of Rights" due to all the draconian measures contained in the Homeland Security and Patriot Act, and the relentless attack on the 2nd Amendment.

CHAPTER 10: THE SECOND AMENDMENT

"When a strong man, fully armed, guards his own homestead,
his possessions are undisturbed..."   *Luke 11: 21*

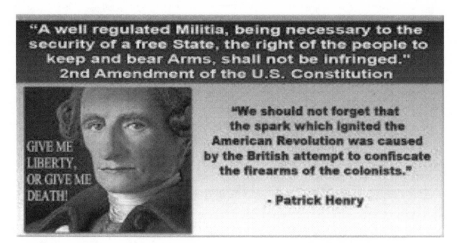

"A well regulated Militia, being necessary to the security of a free State, the right of the people to keep and bear Arms, shall not be infringed."
2nd Amendment of the U.S. Constitution

GIVE ME LIBERTY, OR GIVE ME DEATH!

"We should not forget that the spark which ignited the American Revolution was caused by the British attempt to confiscate the firearms of the colonists."

- Patrick Henry

Our Bill of Rights, our Constitution, and our freedoms hang on the preserving of the Second Amendment.

Why were the Fathers up in arms (pun intended) to secure this amendment? After all, the Constitution did have a clause regarding the militia. So why was Henry so irate? Read on!

Under the Articles of Confederation Article 6
"...but every State shall always keep up a well-regulated and disciplined militia, sufficiently armed and accoutered and shall provide and constantly have ready for use, in public stores, a due number of field pieces and tents, and a proper quantity of arms, ammunition and camp equipage."

Comment: Each state shall maintain its own militia and its weapons must be constantly ready for use. Constantly!

Now read the militia clauses in the Constitution Article 1, Section 8!

Clause 15: "The Congress shall have Power to provide for calling forth the Militia to execute the Laws of the Union, suppress Insurrections and repel Invasions.

Clause 16. "The Congress shall have Power to provide for organizing, arming, and disciplining, the Militia, and for governing such Part of them as may be employed in the Service of the United States, reserving to the States respectively, the Appointment of the Officers, and the Authority of training the Militia according to the discipline prescribed by Congress."

Comment: **All power is with the federal government**; they have the guns. They never have to authorize the militia to do anything.

Thus, the Anti- federalists could foresee there was no right to bear arms or have an existing militia under this new form of government!!

(Appendix XIX contains the amendments proposed to the Constitution by Virginia. The 17th amendment covers the right to bear arms.)

The war had started over the issue of gun control. General Gage had declared martial law in Boston in April of 1775 and required any man wanting to leave Boston had to turn in his muskets and flintlocks.

Over 2,400 were turned in and never returned!

The colonists were winning the Battle of Bunker Hill but had to retreat because they ran out of gunpowder. General Gage had seized Boston's arsenal. See **Appendix XVIII**. Gage's entire order is reproduced.

At this point, the reader may well ask what does the "right to bear arms" have to do with the premise of this book which is:

Are We a Christian Nation?

Harkening back to a previous Chapter, there was no greater authority than Jesus Christ who said that all men should be armed.

Alexander Hamilton further extolled:" The Supreme Being gave existence to man, together with the means of preserving and beautifying that existence. He...invested him with an inviable Right to personal liberty and personal safety."   40

"Do not think that I came to bring peace on the earth: I did not come to bring peace, but a sword."   *Mathew 10: 34*

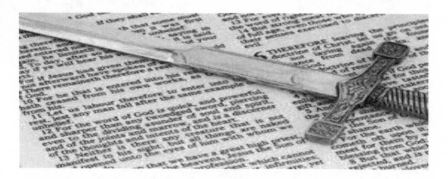

Since the right to self-defense is in fact a personal right that every American possess, the Second Amendment simply assured each citizen that he would be able to defend his life, family and/or property from an individual or government.

This amendment merely says in writing what God had already conferred on all of us.

Sir William Blackstone, an authoritative source of the common law for colonists and, therefore, a dominant influence on the drafters of the original Constitution and its Bill of Rights, set forth in his Commentaries the absolute rights of individuals as: personal security, personal liberty, and possession of private property, these absolute rights being protected by the individual's right to have and use arms for self-preservation and defense.

His treatise was the most influential writing upholding the 2nd amendment.

The following comments are found in" **Blackstone's Commentaries on the Law of England, 1765."**

As Blackstone observed, individual citizens were therefore entitled to exercise their "natural right of resistance and self-preservation, when the sanctions of society and laws are found insufficient to restrain the violence of oppression."

Clear in this statement is Blackstone's recognition that a standing army could imperil the exercise of an individual's absolute rights as well as by private individuals, a view supported by his observation that "Nothing ... ought to be more guarded against in a free state than making the military power ...a body too distinct from the people."

To prevent such an occurrence, Blackstone not only believed in the individual's right to have and use arms, but further believed that for its defense a nation should rely not on a standing army, but the citizen soldier. Plainly, for such a concept to be a reality, it was necessary that all able-bodied males possess and be capable of using arms.

George Tucker was a leader of the Annapolis Convention that led to the convening of the Constitutional Convention in 1787. He was law professor at College of William and Mary, a Justice on the Virginia Supreme court, and a federal judge under President Madison.

In his commentaries, he said the following:

"The right of the citizen is that of having arms for their defense. This is the natural right of resistance and self-preservation when the sanctions of society and laws are found insufficient to restrain the violence of oppression.

"To vindicate these rights, the citizens are entitled in the first place, to the regular administrating and free courses of justice in the courts of law, next, to the right of petitioning the government for redress of grievances, and lastly, to the right of having and using arms for self-preservation and Defense." [41]

Zephaniah Swift, author of America's first legal text in 1792 said:

"Self-defense, or self-preservation, is one of the first laws of nature, which no man ever resigned upon entering into society." [42]

"The right of self-defense is the first law of nature in most governments. It has been the study of rulers to confine this right within the narrowest limits possible.

" Whenever the right of the people to keep and bear arms is, under any color or pretext whatsoever, prohibited, liberty, if not already annihilated, is on the brink of destruction." [43]

William Rawle was offered a federal judgeship by George Washington.

He was a District Attorney in Philadelphia. In 1825 he published his "View on the Constitution." The text became a book in the U S Military Academy.

He said: "In the second amendment, it is declared that 'the right of the people to keep and bear arms shall not be infringed.' The prohibition is general.

"It was conceived to give the Congress no power to disarm the people, a flagitious flagrantly wicked attempt could only be made under some general pretense by a State legislature.

"But if, in any blind pursuit of inordinate power, either (the State or federal government) should attempt it, this Amendment may be appealed to as a restraint on both."   44

The following report restates the importance the 2nd amendment:

Report of the Subcommittee on the Constitution of the Committee, United States Senate, 97th Congress, Second session, February 1982. About Right to Bear Arms:

"The committee noted that the Founding Fathers, in contemplating the wording of the second amendment, they wanted to be sure the right to bear arms be an individual one, for private purposes, by rejecting wording that would have limited the keeping and bearing of arms to bearing 'for the common defense.

"The conclusion is thus inescapable that the history, content and wording of the Second Amendment to the Constitution of the United States, as well as its interpretation by every major commentator and court in the first half century after its ratification, indicates that what is protected is an individual right of a private citizen to own and carry firearms in a peaceful manner.

"For years, our government and some citizens take that position as they try to bend and twist both the Constitution and the Bill of Rights for their own purpose.

"The Founding Fathers were farsighted enough to see that this may well happen and thus addressed it quite frankly.'"   45

"…governing maxim in the interpretation of a statute is to discover the meaning of those who made it."   James Wilson   46

"Not only misinterpretation but even serious error can result when original meanings are ignored: in the lapse of two or three centuries, changes have taken place which…obscure the sense of the original languages.

"The effect of these changes is that wordage has now become a sense different from that which they had and thus present a wrong signification or false ideas. Whenever words are understood in a sense different from that which they had when introduced, mistakes may be very injurious. "
Noah Webster   47

"I entirely concur in the propriety of resorting to the sense in which the Constitution was accepted and ratified by the nation. What a metamorphosis would be produced in the code of the law if all of its ancient phraseology were to be taken in its modern sense."
James Madison   48

"On every question of construction, carry ourselves back to the time when the constitution was adopted, recollect the spirit manifested in the debates, and instead of trying what meaning may be squeezed out of the test, or invented against, to, conform to the probable one in which it was passed."   Thomas Jefferson   49

ARIZONA BILL OF RIGHTS MONUMENT

Chris Bliss, an Arizonan businessman, took on a project to erect a monument to the Bill of Rights.

He worked closely with several state Representatives and Senators to achieve this goal. This beautiful monument was built with private donations and no tax dollars involved. Each "Right" had its own stone.

It is located near the Arizona Capitol in Phoenix. Dedication was December 15, 2012 on "Bill of Rights" Day.

At the dedication ceremony, the Phoenix Mayor made a statement to the effect that our founding documents are "living breathing documents."

"Henry" said: "The Constitution ,as well as the Bill of Rights, as exemplified by this monument are not 'living and breathing,' they are **"cast in stone**."

"Henry" standing next to the 2nd Amendment stone.

What's next? The Bible is a living breathing document? No way.

The first true test on the 2nd amendment was decided by the United States Supreme Court in June 2008. In "**District of Colombia v. Heller**", by a vote of 5 to 4, the second amendment was upheld.

The dissenting Judges trotted out the old, biased, and completely bogus argument that the Founders meant that only a militia should have this right, and since we now have a National Guard, they are the only ones to be armed.

The colonists had just won a war against a standing army! The colonists were terrified of a standing army.

"If this Constitution passes, all our arms will be in Congress, who may or may not, decide to arm us. I predict if this measure passes there will not one musket be left in Virginia." Patrick Henry 50

This latter argument sadly and tragically was utilized during Katrina with devastating results.

In fact, what happened was exactly what Patrick Henry was referring to in the preceding quote.

In direct violation, people were stripped of their right to be armed.

Our own military in violation of the Constitution went house to house to enforce this rule.

Go to YouTube and click **NRA: The Untold Story of Gun Confiscation After Katrina." This will be very sobering.**

Henry said: "It is the great object that all men be armed."   51

"The Supreme Being...invested man with an inviable right to personal liberty and personal safety."   Alexander Hamilton   52

"The Constitution...should never be   construed to prevent the people of the United States from keeping their own arms." Samuel Adams 53

"And what country can preserve its liberties if its rulers are not warned from time to time that this people preserve the spirit of resistance? Let them take arms."   Thomas Jefferson 54

"To preserve liberty, it is essential that the whole body of the people always possess arms, and be taught alike, especially when young, how to use them."   Richard Henry Lee 55

"The advantage of being armed the American possess over the people of almost every other nation...(other)Governments are afraid to trust the people with arms."   James Madison 56

"A free people ought to be armed...No man should scruple or hesitate a moment to use arms in defense."   George Washington   57

"The Supreme power in America cannot enforce unjust laws by the sword because the whole body of the people are armed. Before a standing army can rule, the people must be disarmed, as they are in almost every kingdom in Europe."   Noah Webster   58

"When the resolution of enslaving America was formed in Great Britain, the British parliament was advised to disarm the people. But that they should not do it openly; but to weaken them and let them sink gradually." George Mason 59

What would have happened to the Colonies had the British prevailed?? Colonial Undersecretary William Knox drafted a plan entitled: **"What 's Fit to Be Done with America."'**

This was a plan to prevent any further rebellions in America. The plan called on the establishment of the Church of England in all the colonies, along a hereditary aristocracy.
.

 It would have kept a permanent standing army, along with the following :**"The Militia Laws should be repealed, and none suffered to be re-enacted. The Arms of all the People should be taken away...nor should any Foundry or manufactuary of Arms, Gun powder, or Warlike Stores, be ever suffered in America.**"

"A people who mean to continue free must be prepared to meet danger in person, not to rely upon the fallacious protection of armies."
John Randolph 60

Time after time through history, past and present, we have seen the draconian effects of gun control. Hitler murdered six million Jews after they were disarmed. The North Vietnamese murdered 2 million South Vietnamese, and the genocide in Rwanda took approximately 1 million lives. The Khmer Rouge murdered over 2 million of its countrymen. .

If we lose the right to bear arms, then there will be no protection to save the other amendments, and the attack against Christian America will be completed.

CHAPTER 11: WERE THE FOUNDING FATHERS DEISTS?

"Blessed are ye, when men shall revile you, and persecute you, and shall say all manner of evil against you falsely, for my sake· Rejoice, and be exceeding glad: for great is your reward in heaven: for so persecuted they the prophets which were before you."

Matthew 5: 11-12

This is probably the number one lie of Revisionist History.

Dr. Donald Lutz, a professor from the University of Houston, conducted a ten-year study of 15,000 documents from 1760 to 1805. They came up with approximately 3000 citations. The most quoted source of the Founder's comments was the Bible.

Lutz determined that 60% of all references were derived from the Bible.

They concluded that 94% of the ideas in our Constitution are based directly or indirectly from the Bible.

(The author did a great deal of research regarding Henry's "Give Me Liberty or Give Me Death" speech.

The speech is ten minutes in length. In his speech, Henry referred to God eight times and twenty-one statements that Henry made were directly or indirectly from the Bible.)

The internet is full of quotes of the Fathers, proving beyond an iota of doubt they were men of strong Christian faith.

As you read these following quotes which are but a few from thousands, you can see the utter nonsense of this revisionist lie.

"God who gave us life gave us liberty. And can the liberties of a nation be thought secure when we have removed their only firm basis a conviction in the minds of the people that these liberties are of the Gift of God."   Thomas Jefferson   61

"I have carefully examined the evidences of the Christian religion, and if was sitting as a juror upon its authenticity, I would unhesitatingly give my verdict in its favor, I can prove its truth as clearly as a Proposition ever submitted to the public."   Alexander   Hamilton   62

"I do declare to the whole world that we believe the Scriptures to contain a declaration of the mind and will of God in and to those ages in which they were written; being given forth by the Holy Ghost moving in the hearts of holy men of God; that they ought also to be read, believed, and fulfilled in our day."   William Penn   63

"The Holy Scripture can alone secure to society, order and peace. Bibles are strong entrenchments. Where they abound, men cannot pursue wicked ."   James McHenry   64

"The cause of America is in great measure the cause of all mankind. Where, say some is the King of America? I will tell you friend. He reigns above."   Thomas Paine   65

"I believe that there is only one living and true God, existing in three persons, the Father, the Son, and the Holy Ghost, the same in substance equal in power and glory."   Roger Sherman   66

"Without morals, a republic cannot subsist any length of time; they therefore who are decrying the Christian religion whose morality is so sublime and pure...are undermining the solid foundation of morals, the best security for the duration of free government."   Charles Carroll   67

"...of that Being in whose hands we are, who led our forefathers, as Israel of old, from their native land and planted them in a country flowing with all the necessaries and comforts of life."   Thomas Jefferson   68

"[Governments] should not give the rights essential to happiness... We claim them from a higher source: from the King of kings, and Lord of all the earth."   John Dickinson   69

"May the Supreme ruler of the world be pleased to establish and perpetuate these new foundations of liberty and glory. Thank God, my country is saved and by the smile of Heaven I am a free and independent Man."   John Hancock   70

"As to Jesus of Nazareth, my opinion of whom you particularly desire, I think the system of morals and His religion as He left them to us, the best the world ever saw or is likely to see."   Ben Franklin   71

"In gratitude, let us contemplate the blessings which have flowed from the unlimited grave and favor of offended Deity, that are still permitted to enjoy the first of Heaven's blessings: The Gospel of Jesus Christ that all nations may bow to the scepter of our Lord and Savior Jesus Christ and that the whole earth may be filled with his glory."
                                                                   Elbridge Gerry   72

"...that truth which verified the promises and predictions concerning Him and which exposed and corrected the various errors which had been imbibed respecting the Supreme Being, His attributes, and His and His laws."   John Jay   73

"I have sometimes thought there could not be a stronger testimony in favor of religion or against temporal enjoyments, even the most rational and manly, than for men who occupy the most honorable and gainful departments and [who] are rising in reputation and wealth, publicly to declare their satisfactoriness is by becoming fervent advocates in the cause of Christ; and I wish you may give in your evidence in this way."
                                                                   James Madison   74

"...hoping that through the meritorious death and passion of our Savior and Redeemer Jesus Christ to receive absolution and remission for all my sins."   George Mason   75

'The Gospel of Jesus Christ prescribes the wisest rules for just conduct in every situation of life... Nothing   but His blood will wash away my sins. [Acts 22:16]. I rely exclusively upon it. Come, Lord Jesus! Come quickly!"
                                                                   Benjamin Rush   76

"There is one only living and true God, existing in three persons, the Father, the Son, and the Holy Ghost, the same in substance, equal in power and glory.

"That the Scriptures of the Old and New Testaments are a revelation from God, and a complete rule to direct us how we may glorify and enjoy Him."   Roger Sherman   77

"Whoever is an avowed enemy of God, I scruple not to call him an enemy to his country."   John Witherspoon   78

" I conceive that we cannot better express ourselves than by humbly supplicating the Supreme Ruler of the world … by promoting and speedily bringing on that holy and happy period when the kingdom of our Lord and Savior Jesus Christ may be everywhere established, and all people everywhere willingly bow to the scepter of Him who is Prince of Peace."   Samuel Adams   79

"…with fasting and prayer, with penitent confession of our sins, and hope in His mercy through Jesus Christ, our Redeemer."
                                                Johnathan Trumball   80

"The Christian religion, in its purity, is the basis, or rather the source of all genuine freedom in government and I am persuaded that no civil government of a republican form can exist and be durable in which the principles of that religion have not a controlling influence."
                                                Noah Webster   81

"One of the beautiful boasts of our municipal jurisprudence is that Christianity is a part of the Common Law. There never has been a period   in which the Common Law did not recognize Christianity as lying at its foundations."   Joseph Story   82

"I desire to bless and praise the name of God most high for appointing me my birth in a land of Gospel Light where the glorious tidings of a Savior and of pardon and salvation through Him have been continually sounding in mine ears."   Robert Treat Paine   83

Now that the author has dealt with the number one lie of revisionist history, we turn to the second one.

The **Treaty of Paris** was signed on Sept 3rd, 1783. This was the official document ending the Revolutionary War.

During the authors presentations as Henry or Washington, there are often "protestors" on the fringes of the events holding various signs quoting   Article 11 which says in part:

> "The government of the United States is not in any sense founded upon the Christian religion."

They and the Deists offer this as "proof" that since this Treaty ended the war, it was a good time to make a definitive statement, for the last time, that we were not a Christian nation.

There's just one little problem they have. Joel Barlow added Articles 11 and 12 years later. Talk about Revisionist history!

The actual Treaty begins with this phrase: "In the name of the Holy and undivided Trinity…"   84

This is the last article in the actual Treaty.
Article 10 The solemn ratifications of the present treaty expedited in good and due form shall be exchanged between parties in the space of six months or sooner, if possible, to be computed from the day of the signatures of the present treaty.

In witness whereof we the undersigned, their ministers plenipotentiary, have in their name and in virtue of our full powers, signed with our hands the present definitive treaty and caused the seals of our arms to be affixed thereto.

Done at Paris, this third day of September in the year of our Lord, one thousand seven hundred and eighty-three.

JOHN ADAMS (SEAL)
BEN FRANKLIN (SEAL)
JOHN JAY (SEAL)

Below is a facsimile of Article 10 and directly under are the signatures John Adams, Benjamin Franklin, and John Jay. **There is no Article 11 and 12!!**

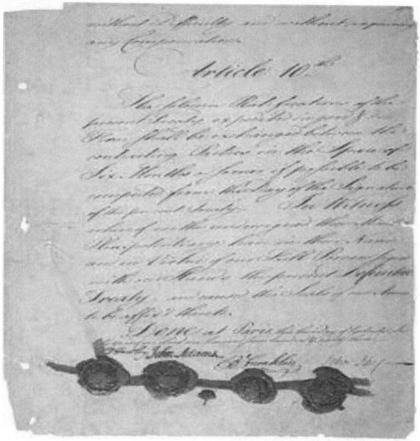

Appendix IX has the unaltered Treaty.

CHAPTER 12: THE HISTORY OF CHRISTIAN EDUCATION IN AMERICA'S PUBLIC- SCHOOL SYSTEM

"Train up a child in the way he should go, and when he is old, he will not depart from it."   Proverbs 22: 6

Satan knows the above Bible verse all too well.

John Adams said: "In vain are Schools, Academies, and Universities Instituted, if loose Principles and licentious habits are impressed upon Children in their early years."   85

Benjamin Franklin said: "Whoever shall introduce into public society the principles of primitive Christianity will change the face of the World."
86
Patrick Henry said: "The Bible is the most important book ever written."
87
The following is a great quote attributed to Abraham Lincoln but has not been substantiated by anyone. It is however, a very true statement regardless of the true author, as America's history has borne this out:

"The philosophy of the schoolroom in one generation will be the philosophy of the nation in the next."   88

The first common school system in America was established in 1647. The reader can certainly see the concerns that were already being expressed about the Bible not being a textbook in the classroom.

The legislature of Massachusetts enacted one such law: It is often Referred to as **"The Old Deluder Law."**

Text of the "Massachusetts General School Law of 1647."

"It being one chief project of that old deluder, Satan, to keep men from the knowledge of the Scriptures, as in former times by keeping them in an unknown tongue, so in these latter times by persuading from the use of tongues, that so that at least the true sense and meaning of the original might be clouded and corrupted with love and false glosses of saint-seeming deceivers; and to the end that learning may not be buried in the grave of our forefathers, in church and commonwealth, the Lord assisting our endeavors.

" It is therefore ordered that every township in this jurisdiction, after the Lord hath increased them to fifty households shall forthwith appoint one within their town to teach all such children as shall resort to him to write and read, whose wages shall be paid either by the parents or masters of such children, or by the inhabitants in general, by way of supply, as the major part of those that order the prudentials of the town shall appoint; provided those that send their children be not oppressed by paying much more than they can have them taught for in other towns.

"And it is further ordered, that when any town shall increase to the number of one hundred families or householders, they shall set up a grammar school, the master thereof being able to instruct youth as far as they may be fitted for the university, provided that if any town neglect the performance hereof above one year that every such town shall pay pounds to the next school till they shall perform this order."   89

"The England Primer" was our first major textbook.

 Considered the "little Bible of New England", it was the first successful and major textbook used in the colonies.

It has been considered the single most influential Christian textbook in history. Most scholars agree that most, if not all, of the Founding Fathers were taught to read and write using this volume which is unsurpassed to this day for its excellence of practical training and Christian worldview.

First published in 1690, the goal of the "Primer" was to combine the study of the Bible with the alphabet, vocabulary, and the reading of prose and poetry.

This is the book that introduced the children's prayer, "Now I lay me down to sleep," and which made the "Shorter Catechism" a staple of education for American children.

More than five million copies were sold in the nineteenth century alone.

Many of the sections of this book were based upon the King James version of the Bible. It embodied the dominant Puritan attitude and worldview of the day. Among the topics discussed are respect to parental figures, sin, and salvation.

While recognized by everyone for his dictionary, in 1783 Daniel Webster wrote a book entitled "**The Blue Back Speller**."

This book sold over 100 million copies.

Webster said: "In my view, the Christian religion is the most important and one of the first things in which all children, under a free government, ought to be instructed... No truth is more evident to mine than that the Christian religion must be the basis of any government intended to secure the rights and privileges of a free people."   90

The "**McGuffey Readers**" sold at least 120 million copies between 1836 and 1960. The author of the Readers William McGuffey had two passions. They were educating the young mind and preaching the gospel.

McGuffey attempted to give schools a curriculum that would instill Presbyterian Calvinistic beliefs and manners in their students. Some of his readings are still used today in the Home School curriculum.

Oh, yes, the Bible and Education were strictly entwined in our belief and educational system.

One hundred and six of the first one hundred and eight colleges in America were founded on the Christian faith and its main purpose was to graduate future Pastors!!

"Let the wise hear and increase in learning... " Proverbs 1:5

Yale University

All the charters and rule books for the students were similar to these:

HARVARD: "Let every Student be plainly instructed, and earnestly pressed to consider well, the main end of his life and studies is, to know God and Jesus Christ." Official Motto: "For Christ and the Church." 91

YALE: "Seeing God is the giver of all wisdom, every scholar, besides private or secret prayer, where all we are bound to ask wisdom, shall present morning and evening at public prayer in the hall at the accustomed hour..." 92

PRINCETON: "Cursed be all learning that is contrary to the cross of Christ." Official Motto is "Under God's Power She Flourishes."
93

It is obvious that the founders of our nation realized we needed a Christian philosophy of education.

Congress declared in the Northwest Ordinance of 1787 that Religion, morality, and knowledge, being necessary to good government and happiness of mankind, schools and the means of education shall I forever be encouraged.

Samuel Adams said: "Let divines and philosophers, statesmen and patriots, unite their endeavors...of inculcating in the minds of youth the fear and love of the Deity...instructing them in the art of self-government...in short,of leading them in the study and practice of exalted virtues of the Christian system." 94

If the reader is was born after 1962, you may have never **known that at one time in America we had daily prayer in our** classrooms, as well as prayer over the public- address system of High School, College, and professional sports events.

In 1946, the Dallas Independent School District published a New Testament Bible Study Curriculum. The Old Testament edition was published in 1954.

"Making the word of God of none effect through your tradition, which ye have delivered: and many such like things do ye"   Mark 17: 3

Fisher Ames: "Should not the Bible regain the place it once held as a schoolbook? Its morals are pure, its examples are captivating and noble… In no Book is there so good English, so pure and so elegant, and by teaching all the same they will speak alike, and the Bible will justly remain the standard of language as well of faith."   95

Ben Franklin: "A Bible and a newspaper in every house, a good school in every district-all studied and appreciated as they merit-are the principal and support of virtue, morality and civil liberty."   96

During the Revolutionary War, there was a shortage of Bibles.

The demand was so great to rely on God's word for faith and courage that the Continental Congress ordered 20,000 copies from Holland to fill this void and be distributed to the army.

Do you think our Congress would do such a thing today?

There are some states that allow "elective" Bible courses if enough students "request" them.

The problems we had in the 1950's was talking in class and chewing gum. Today its drugs, violence, and murder.

If you got punished at school, it was nothing compared to what awaited you at home.

With Bible and Prayer removed, you can see what the problems are we face today. How far we have drifted from the original intent of our Founding Fathers! You want to turn back our nation to God?

This Bible quote is a good place to start:

"I urge, then, first of all, that petitions, prayers, intercession and thanksgiving be made for all people— for kings and all those in authority, that we may live peaceful and quiet lives in all godliness and holiness."
I Timothy 2: 1-2

CHAPTER 13: CHRISTIAN ASPECTS OF OUR FLAG
NATIONAL ANTHEM AND PLEDGE

The story of our national treasures is unique within themselves. The author of these were men, and they all had the same first name: Francis. Two were attorneys and one was a Pastor.

OUR FLAG

"You have given a banner to those who fear you. It may be displayed because of the truth..."   Psalms 60:4

Washington commissions Betsy Ross to sew first American flag.

One of the fallacies of American history is that Betsy Ross designed the flag. The 2nd Continental Congress passed this Flag Resolution on June 14, 1777:

"Resolved: That the flag of the thirteen United States be thirteen stripes, alternate red and white; that the union be thirteen stars, white in a blue field, **representing a new constellation.**"

Frances Hopkinson was appointed the head of a committee to design the flag based upon the above criteria.

Hopkinson did most of the creative work and he lobbied to get full credit. It literally took an act of Congress to make the decision that he officially designed our first flag.

Nothing symbolized the Founding Fathers belief in the Christian aspects of the revolution and their dependence upon a Supreme Being, to champion their cause more than the American Flag.

The thirteen stripes represented the thirteen colonies. The red stripe stands for the blood that was and would be shed in the fight for independence, and the white stands for Christ. The blue background stands for Heaven.

The stars appear in the form of a constellation, which is seen in the heavenlies, symbolizing unity and purpose for the cause that would be undertaken. The significance of having a five-point star was that the star itself would be pointing directly to Heaven.

(In 2008, the author spoke at the National Convention of the Independent Flag Dealer Association of America. Not one person in an audience of 300 knew this.)

The colonists prayed that this new nation birthed on earth would also be a new nation birthed in heaven. In further proof of the colonist's prayers and beliefs, George Washington decreed that this pennant would fly on all naval vessels during the war.

"And I would place my cause before God."   Job 4:8

The white background stood for the purity of the cause.   The Evergreen tree represents strength and firmness, renewing itself each year. The tree points upwards to Heaven

The phrase "An Appeal to Heaven" shows the spiritual aspects of the war. The colonists knew they could not win this war without Heaven's guidance and direction.

OUR NATIONAL ANTHEM:
THE STAR-SPANGLED BANNER

During the War of 1812, British ships were attacking Ft. McHenry.

"Sing unto Him a new song..."　　　*Psalm 33:5*

Frances Scott Key peering over the morning mist and　.
The view from inside the Fort

A prominent American Doctor, as well as many soldiers, had been taken prisoner and were aboard the British flag-ship. On Sept. 13, 1814, Frances Scott Key, an attorney, rowed out to the command ship to negotiate a prisoner exchange.

He was successful, but the British would not let him leave the ship until the following morning. The British were going to commence a huge bombardment against the fort.

All through the night Key saw "the rockets' red glare and the bombs bursting through air giving proof that the flag was still there." (Bombs were not supposed to burst in the air, but a heavy rain had ruined much of the British arsenal aboard ship. God was protecting the Fort.)

The American prisoners were below deck and kept asking "is our flag still there?" In the morning, he could see that the flag was still flying, and the Fort was still in the hands of the Americans.

He sat down and composed a poem which he entitled "The Defence of Ft. McHenry." The words were written to a hymn : "To Anacreon In Heaven."

In 1898 the United States Navy recognized it for official use. In 1916, President Wilson approved it to be sung at military funerals.

It was not until March 3, 1931 that President Hoover signed it into Law as our National Anthem.

Did you ever wonder the source of our national motto?
Here is the fourth stanza of our National Anthem.

> "O, thus be it ever when freemen shall stand,
> Between their lov'd homes and the war's desolation;
> Blest with vict'ry and peace, may the heav'n-rescued land
> Praise the Pow'r that hath made and preserv'd us a nation!
> Then conquer we must, when our cause is just,
> **And this be our motto: "In God is our trust"**
> And the star-spangled banner in triumph shall wave"
> O'er the land of the free and the home of the brave!"

See **APPENDIX XVI** for the entire Anthem.

OUR PLEDGE OF ALLEGIANCE

"If a man makes a vow to the LORD or takes an oath to bind himself with a binding obligation, he shall not violate his word; he shall do according to all that proceeds out of his mouth." Numbers 30:2

In 1892, Frances Bellamy, a Baptist Preacher wrote the Pledge of Allegiance as part of a patriotic contest.

Until 1942 the correct way to do the pledge was to extend the right arm, palm upward, to the flag. When it was realized this was a similar sign as people gave in Nazi Germany, this immediately stopped. This was changed to placing the hand over the heart.

On June 14, 1942, on flag day, that Congress formally adopted the pledge. The phrase "under God" was added by President Eisenhower in 1954.

He stated: "in this way we are reaffirming the religious faith in America's heritage and future, in this way we shall constantly strengthen those spiritual weapons which will be our constant most powerful resource in peace and war.

"From this day forward, the millions of our schoolchildren will daily proclaim in every city and town, every village and rural schoolhouse, the dedication of our nation and our people to the Almighty."

This law also authorized "In God We Trust" to be put on all paper currency: Public Law 84-140 July 29, 1954.

National Defense Act of 2008 says:
SEC. 595. MILITARY SALUTE FOR THE FLAG DURING THE NATIONAL ANTHEM BY MEMBERS OF THE ARMED FORCES NOT IN UNIFORM AND BY VETERANS.

Section 301(b)(1) of title 36, United States Code, is amended :members of the Armed Forces and veterans who are present but not in uniform may render the military salute in the manner provided for individuals in uniform.

" lift up a standard over the peoples."   Isaiah 62: 10

The Reader is encouraged to read **Appendix XX** for Red Skelton's wonderful recitation of the Pledge. It was also done on national tv.

What the flag, the pledge, and our National Anthem have in common is the Christian heritage of America. How sad what has happened today.

This tribute to Veterans appears in many versions and the author has added the last three verses.

IT IS THE VETERAN

IT IS THE VETERAN, NOT THE REPORTER
WHO HAS GIVEN US FREEDOM OF THE PRESS

IT IS THE VETERAN, NOT THE POET
WHO HAS GIVEN US FREEDOM OF SPEECH

IT IS THE VETERAN, NOT THE CHURCH
WHO HAS GIVEN US FREEDOM OF RELIGION

IT IS THE VETERAN, NOT CIVIL RIGHTS
WHO HAS PROTECT THE RIGHT TO BEAR ARMS

IT IS THE VETERAN, NOT THE CAMPUS ORGANIZER
WHO HAS GIVEN US FREEDOM TO ASSEMBLE

IT IS THE VETERAN, NOT THE LAWYER
WHO HAS GIVEN US THE RIGHT TO A FAIR TRIAL

IT IS THE VETERAN, NOT THE POLITICAN
WHO PROTECTS OUR BILL OF RIGHTS

IT IS THE VETERAN, NOT THE TEACHER
WHO IS THE REASON YOU READ THIS IN ENGLSH

IT IS THE VETERAN, IT IS THE VETERAN, WHO KEEPS
AMERICA THE LAND OF THE FREE AND THE HOME
OF THE BRAVE

VIET NAM WAR MEMORIAL, WASHINGTON, D.C.

CHAPTER 14: LIFE IN AMERICA BEFORE 1962

"Go then, eat your bread in happiness...with a cheerful heart, for God has already approved your works."   *Eccles: 9: 7*

If the Reader has read this far, the author hopes that you are angry at how our true heritage has been stolen from us.

Before we look at today's America, let's review life prior to prayer and the Bible being removed from America's schools.

If you were born after 1962, you have grown up in an America very different from that of the author.

For those of us blessed to have been raised in the 40's and 50's, this may seem like a nostalgic trip down "memory lane."

It is important for those of who came along much later to see what you missed, and how you were robbed of a much happier, peaceful, prosperous, and religious time when values and virtues were of great importance.

The home and the church were the center of much activity. Christianity was thriving, and the Gospel was being preached and evangelism was exploding.

The author was absolutely blessed to be a teenager and college student during the fabulous 50's. This was by far the happiest decade of this past century. "Happy Days" on TV said it all.

In the 50's we had television shows such as "Father Knows Best," "My Three Sons," the "Brady Bunch," and "Leave It to Beaver." All shows emphasized traditional family values.

The Father was the head of the family, the children were respectful to him, and they had strong moral values.

In school, we began each day with prayer and the salute to the flag.

We proudly said the Pledge of Allegiance and didn't think twice after President Eisenhower added the words "under God."

At High Schools and Colleges across the nation, each sporting event began with prayer.

The author can vividly remember a 5th grade experience at Obadiah Knight Grade School in Dallas, Texas.

Someone (certainly not him) had misbehaved in penmanship class and the punishment, let me say that again, "the punishment" was to write one hundred times:

"For God so loved the world that He gave his only begotten Son, that whosoever should believeth in Him should not perish but have everlasting life." John 3: 16

The author was not a Christian at the time, but that is the only memorization he can remember learning in school from the 1st through 9th grade! Children are impressionable.

We mainly thought premarital sex was wrong and having an abortion was unthinkable. Girls that had sex were disrespected.

We had Christmas pageants at our schools.

Homosexuality and Lesbianism were not discussed.

In the school, there were no drugs. "Drugs" were what you got at the drug store. Minimal talk about evolution. And if we talked about it, was held in ridicule. Why? Because we were a Christian nation!

We just chewed gum and talked during class, played hooky, and wrote notes in class to our boyfriends and girlfriends.

We played out at night until we were whistled in. Does the Reader recognize these: "oly oly ox in free." "Red Rover Red Rover… Let_____come over.' "Green Light…. Red Light." "Simon says take___ steps"?

We had more friends and we were in better shape physically.

We knew our neighbors. No one locked their doors. People did not live together before they got married.

We studied American History in detail. We were taught love of country and respect for our country and service men and women.

Hollywood supported WWI, WWII, and the Korean "Conflict."

The movies of that era: "Twenty Seconds Over Tokyo," "Guadalcanal Diary," "The Longest Day," "Pork Chop Hill," "Sands of Iwo Jima," "Bridge on the River Kwai," and "The Longest Day" respected our military.

"It is the LORD who goes before you. He will be with you; he will not leave you or forsake you. Do not fear or be dismayed". Deut. 31:8

"Uncommon valor was a common virtue." Admiral Chester Nimitz
Marines raising flag on Iwo Jima, Feb. 23rd, 1945

The authors high school friends and college fraternity brothers served in the military. We felt it was our duty. We loved our country. We would not think of not serving. The author treasures his experience as a Captain in the United States Marine Corps.

When our Veterans came home from WWI, II and Korea there were huge welcoming home parades. America loved the servicemen.

They were respected, appreciated, and honored.

Draft dodgers were ill thought of and were very rare. Over 130 Hollywood actors served on active duty, many of them receiving high awards, several were wounded. Today, less than a handful ever served in the military.

"...each kept his weapon at his right hand."   *Neh. 4:23*

Charlton Heston said: (They will pry this) "from my cold dead hands."

The one actor who bridged the gap between "then and now" was Charlton Heston. He was in the military. He served as President of both the NRA and the Screen Actors Guild.

He was well respected and was awarded the Medal of Freedom by President George Bush. Sadly, he passed from the scene due to Alzheimer's and then died in 2008.

There were wholesome movies like "High Noon," "An American in Paris," "Gigi," My Fair Lady," "Blackboard Jungle." (There was almost a national faint when Rhett Butler gave his one-word expletive in "Gone With The Wind"!!)

In the movie industry, Christianity was upheld and respected. The industry respected the clergy. They were held in high esteem. There was no nudity, no simulated sex scenes, for the most part just good wholesome movies.

The question was not: "Do you go to church?" The question was: "Where do you go to church?" All my friends were churchgoers. Revivals were going on all the time.

God truly blessed our nation. We were protected, we were secure. Other nations respected us. We were financially strong, morally correct, and spiritual in nature. What a wonderful era that was indeed.

" lift up hands without anger or quarreling." Timothy 2: 8

"As iron sharpens iron, so one man sharpens another." Ps. 27:17

This was (and still is) a common scene in Texas where High School football is almost a religion. Many schools still pray in defiance of the Supreme Court.

CHAPTER 15: HOW TO DESTROY CHRISTIAN AMERICA

"For our struggle is not against flesh and blood, but against the rulers, against the authorities, against the powers of this world's darkness, and against the spiritual forces of evil in the heavenly Realms."   *Eph. 6:12*

The balance of this book is dedicated to exposing all the reasons why America has sunk to its current deplorable state.

As you will see, it is a well-designed plan and it is working very well.

"We have met the enemy and it is us."

It is indeed very sad that a country that so was blessed by God, that had been given so many freedoms, that have allowed evil men to gain public power and institute their own agendas to our detriment.

It may be hard for the Reader to accept the reasons for Americas decline.

It can in many instances be laid right at the feet of those of whom we have trusted to run our country.

SATAN'S PLAN

"Therefore, submit to God. Resist the devil and he will flee from You. Draw near to God and He will draw near to you.".

James 4: 7-8

THE FOLLOWING 17 POINTS WERE WRITTEN BY THE AUTHOR IN 2007. HOW IS SATANS PLAN WORKING?

If I were Satan and I wanted a World where Christianity is replaced by Humanism and a One World Religion and One World Government to be firmly established to usher in the Antichrist, I believe this would be my plan:

I have to completely destroy the strongest bastion of Christianity and the freest nation in the World. Therefore, America must go I can't do this overnight, so it must be done on a gradual but then accelerating basis. After all, my time is short!

1. Declare that it is illegal to read the Bible and to have prayer in the schools. This is by far the basic ground step Benjamin Rush, one of the Signors of the Declaration of Independence said: "The great enemy of the salvation of man never invented a more effectual means of extinguishing Christianity, than by declaring that it was improper to read the Bible at schools."

The absolute key is to capture the youth at an early age. I did this once before in Nazi Germany. I believe that if I can capture a youth's mind, I can capture his soul. If I can capture his soul, I can capture his destiny. If I can capture enough youth's destinies, I can control the future of the nation.

After all, Abraham Lincoln said "The philosophy of the schoolroom in one generation is the philosophy of the nation in the next." The Bible says "Train up a child in the way he should go, and when he is old he will not depart from it." I will use that verse for my own means.

I would introduce a program calling for MANDATORY "medical screening" of all students in public schools. Done under the guise of "helping" children with problems. Through psychological questioning I will set my parameters of who has what problem. This boggles my mind with the opportunities to control children.

Allow evolution, Humanism, Wiccanism, Islam, and New Age to be taught in the school. Preach tolerance, tolerance, tolerance, but of course Christianity will be excluded. Celebrate Halloween, but not Christmas.

2. Rewrite America's Christian heritage. This one will take some time, but some of the things I need to do are take Christ out of Christmas and make it a "Happy Holiday." Take God out of the pledge, remove God from America's national motto, take down the 10 Commandments wherever they may be found, remove the cross from state seals, remove prominent crosses from public view.

Portray the Founding Fathers as Deists don't teach America's heritage in seminary, so the Pastors are kept ignorant of their Christian background. If Pastors believe the lie of separation of church and state, so will their congregations.

My biggest challenge will be the buildings in Washington with all their references to God, but I am working on this one feverishly. America has toppled buildings and statues in other countries, haven't they?
I could probably get by with just sandblasting all the quotes on the walls. I would replace them with watered down or politically correct messages.

3. Rewrite or eliminate the history of the Christian foundation of America. Christopher Columbus, Mayflower Compact, Christian American Revolution. I.E., none happened, or it is not significant. Thomas Jefferson said: "Can the liberties of a nation be thought secure, when we have removed their only firm basis, a conviction in the minds of the people that those liberties are the gift of God?"

4. Attack the Family Unit. Ridicule the Father as the head of the Family. Promote the Mother as the true head. Use Hollywood, via television and movies to accomplish this. Do more and to remove children from the control of the family and give it to the socialistic public-school system. Continue to make it difficult for Godly teachers to be effective in this arena.

Hillary Clinton said, "It takes a village to raise a child." This line is right out of communist propaganda. I have succeeded in duping the free world that Communism is dead...and I have some beach front property in Hell to sell you. I well remember Nikkita Khrushchev's message: "The American people will themselves raise the flag of Communism!"

5. Muffle the clergy. This is another key area. But I have had great luck in the past with this one. Make "politically correct" instead of "morally correct" the churches motto. I would have the mainstream Pastors preach "prosperity, God is Love, Christians are tolerant" messages only. I would threaten to take away their tax-exempt status if they did not conform.

6. Completely disarm its populace. This one is tricky, but I am making headway. I have the Brady bunch working overtime on this one. This is working very well in the rest of the world. Violent crime is up over 40% in parts of Australia since they were disarmed. All I must do is manufacture a real crisis at the right time and then strike. I accomplished this in Nazi Germany; I believe I can make this work here as well.

7. Have a National Identity card to set in motion the machinery for monitoring every aspect of everyone's life. Next stop put that chip in a car and in the body. I am pleased to see this is happening on a grand scale with animals (families will not abandon their pets in times of crisis.)
8. Have a One World Government. Make America subservient to it. Place this machinery on American soil. Thomas Jefferson (who got the wrong city) said: "When all the nations in the world begin to gather in Washington, the government emanating from that will be more frightening than all of the governments up to that time."

9. Allow a flow of illegal aliens to cross the borders I can slip terrorists in with them. This will ultimately lead to a crisis and the populace will at some point cry out for help, a national Emergency will be called for. The President will call for martial law and suspend the Constitution. Fortunately, he already has this power.

10. Ship America's labor and material pool under the guise of a free trade agreement to foreign countries, so American works become unemployed, forced to live more and more in credit. This will encourage more bankruptcies, more distraught families, more cry for government control.

11.. Attack Christianity as bigotry and promote brotherhood of man (New Age) as the best choice. Use Hollywood to attack and slander Christianity on all aspects. In movies and television, make the Christian the murderer, the adulterer, the thief, etc. I know the Bible talks about 666 but I would condition America to believe this is but a fairy tale. Besides, once they realize it is the truth, it will be too late.

12. I would destroy the sanctity of life. I would promote abortion on demand. I would promote euthanasia as commonplace. (Remember the movie Logan's Run? Over 35? You are out of here!)

13. I would use Hollywood to promote violence, foul language, drug usage so that the youth would think it the norm, and this is what America is all about. If it feels good, do it.

14. I would have the Universities ridicule and attack capitalism, promote socialism as the better choice. I would teach the students to mistrust authority and put control in the hands of the few, the elite, the illumined ones.

15. I would gradually make America's military, and Constitution subservient to the United Nations. This will assist in taking away America's sovereignty and individualism and put them completely under control of a system where their fate is decided by other countries.

16. I need to weaken the military. I will close as many bases as possible. (This will be an excellent place to put those dissidents who ultimately would rebel against my master plan for America.)

I would put women in the military in combat roles. The sanctity of womanhood is thus diminished. Women and men in close contact will lead to extramarital affairs, pregnancies, divorce, etc.

17. Gradually have the judicial system become a complete runaway maverick institution, no matter the will of the people. Godless judges will overrule the will of the people all the time. The system will become a great tool for bringing down America. I will have these judges make their decisions based on international law rather than our own. They will ultimately toss the Constitution out the window.

As time goes by, I would probably think of other things to do as well. I believe if I could do all of this, America will decay from within and be ripe for a one world dictator and government to show them the true way to eternal peace!!

Yep, if I were Satan, that's what I would do.

"... For you yourselves are fully aware that the day of the Lord will come like a thief in the night. While people are saying, "There is peace and security," then sudden destruction will come upon them as labor pains come upon a pregnant woman, and they will not escape. But you are not in darkness, brothers, for that day to surprise you like a thief. For you are all children of light, children of the day. We are not of the night or of the darkness. ..."   *I Thessalonians 5: 1-2*

As of the date of this edition, here are but a few examples of how this plan is working:

Illegal Aliens flooding our country and getting free medical care.

Baker refusing to put an America flag on a cake.

A former Marine is not being allowed to attend his daughter's graduation because he refused to let her take a class at school on the Koran.

An Air Force Officer is reprimanded for saying "God" at a funeral.

A Pastor is arrested in his own home for having a prayer meeting.

Children are sent home from school due to Christian symbols on their clothing.

Christians in the military are being told to hide their faith.

Employees fired for having Christian symbols on their desk.

Pro football players sitting during National Anthem.

CHAPTER 16: SEPARATION OF CHURCH AND STATE

"There are...things that the Lord hates and cannot tolerate: a proud look, a lying tongue....a mind that thinks up wicked plan."
Proverbs 6: 18

The First Amendment says: "Congress shall make no law respecting an establishment of religion, prohibiting the free exercise thereof: or abridging the freedom of the press; or the right of the people peaceably to assemble, and to petition the Government for a Redress of grievances."

Supreme Court   Senate   House of Representatives

Does not appear to be a "separation of church and state" issue here!

We have Moses with the 10 Commandments, and our National Motto: "In God We Trust," occupying places of honor!

It is well established that America was founded upon Christian principles, and that all the major monuments in Washington D.C. have Scriptures from God's holy word.

We have had prayer in the schoolroom since the beginning of our country. There were Supreme Court cases clearly affirming Christianity in this nation, so where did this idea of "separation and church" come from?

To set the groundwork, we must lay the basis that the United States Supreme Court had historically established firmly that the United States of America was and always has been a Christian nation.

In 1799, '**Runkel v Winemiller**": "By our form of government, the Christian religion is the established religion and all sects and denominations of Christians are placed on the same equal footing."
97

In 1846, "**Charleston v Benjamin**": 'Christianity has reference to the principles of right and wrong...it is the foundation of those morals and manners upon which our society is formed: It is their basis. Remove this and they would fall..."   98

The "Bell Weather" case proving beyond any doubt that we are a Christian nation was **"Church of the Holy Trinity vs. United States"** which was decided in 1892.

This case clearly affirms we are a Christian nation, and the thought that prayer and the Bible were not appropriate for the classroom is absurd and would be laughable but for the fact that this case was somehow "lost in the minds" of the 1962 Court.

This case dealt on the surface with the issue that it was illegal to import foreign labor into the United States. The church had hired a Pastor from England.

The court went into a very strong discourse regarding Columbus, the Mayflower Compact, the preambles of the state constitutions, of Independence, William Penn's first charter of Virginia, etc. and concluded with this statement:

"There is no dissonance in these declarations. There is a universal language pervading them all, having one meaning. They affirm and reaffirm that this (America) is a religious nation.

"These are not individual sayings, declarations of private persons. They are organic utterances. They speak the voice of the entire people.

'Our law must be based upon the teachings of the Great Redeemer. It is impossible that it should be otherwise and, in this issue, and to this extent our institutions and civilizations are emphatically Christian. This is historically true.

"From the discovery of this continent to the present hour, there is a single voice making this affirmation...that this is a Christian nation, we are founded to legislate, propagate and secure Christianity.

"While because of a general recognition of this truth, the question seldom has been presented to the Courts."   99

In other words, it has always been assumed that we are a Christian nation founded on Christian principles. There is no real reason for the court to ever address this issue!!!

The Court then quoted two state Supreme Court cases and one previous United States Supreme Court case which clearly affirmed their reasoning.

"**People vs. Ruggles**" was an 1811 New York Supreme Court case dealing with a man who was distributing literature that said "Jesus was a bastard and his mother was a whore.'" He was arrested, fined $300 and imprisoned for six months.

The court basically said this was an attack against America, as America was a Christian nation.

The court specifically said: "The people of this state, in common with the people of this country, profess the general doctrines of Christianity as the rule of their faith and practice, and to scandalize the author of those doctrines in not only, in a religious point of view's extremely impious, but even in respect to the obligations due to society, is a gross violation of decency and good order."   100

"**Updegraph v. Commissioner**" was an 1824 Pennsylvania case in which the Court concluded: "Christianity, general Christianity...not Christianity with an established church and tithes and spiritual courts, but Christianity with liberty of conscience to all men...has always been part of the common law of Pennsylvania."   101

The Court then discussed an 1844 United States Supreme Court Case: "**Vidal vs. Girard's Executioners.**"

This case dealt with the legality of a Will where 7 million dollars had been left to a university with the stipulation that no teaching could come from the Bible.

The Court did uphold the validity of the Will but made a point to say:

"Why may not laymen instruct in the general principles of Christianity? We cannot overlook the blessing which such laymen by their conduct, as well as their instructions, many, nay must impart to their youthful pupils.

"Why may not the Bible and especially the New Testament, without note or comment be taught and read as a divine revelation…used as a textbook?

"Where else can the purest form of morality be found but, in the Bible and especially the New Testament?"   102

Could the true Christian basis of America be stated any clearer by 1892 United States Supreme Court decision?

In 1947, the Supreme Court in deciding "**Everson vs Board of Education**", for the first time ever in the annals of any justice system, brings up the phrase "separation of church and state."

The state of New Jersey was providing school buses to take students to both public schools as well as Catholic schools.

The Court upheld the decision that it was perfectly legal and not a breach of the First Amendment for the state to so do.

However, the court felt compelled to say, "The First Amendment has erected a wall of separation of church and state. The wall must be kept a high and impregnable. We could not approve the slightest breach."
                                                                    103
Really? Gee, when the author reads the First Amendment, he does not find the words "separation of church and state" in it.

"**Zorach v. Clausen**" was a 1952 case which dealt with students being allowed to leave school during the day to attend religious exercises. The Court ruled that it was all right to let the students leave class for this purpose.

The Supreme Court said:

"We are a religious people. Our institutions presuppose a religious being. We make room for a wide and variety of beliefs and creed as the spiritual needs of man deem necessary.

"We sponsor an attitude on the part of government that shows no partiality to any one group and that lets each flourish according to the zeal of its adherents and the appeal of its dogma.

"When the state encourages religious instruction or cooperates with religious authorities by adjusting the schedule of public events to sectarian needs, it follows the best of our traditions.

"For it then respects the religious nature of our people and accommodates the public service to their spiritual needs.

"To hold that it may not, would be to find in the Constitution a requirement that the government show a callous indifference to religious groups."

104

The onslaught removing God "legally" from our classroom and culture began in 1962, when the Court in **"Engle vs. Vitale**", by a vote of 6 to 1,said it was unconstitutional to have prayer in the classroom.

The state of New York had said that the following prayer could be voluntarily said in school each day:

"Almighty God, we acknowledge our dependence upon thee, and beg thy blessings upon us, our teacher and our courts."

Ten parents sued citing the First Amendment. They used the infamous "separation of church and state" argument.!!

Since the Judges in this case could not base taking prayer out of the classroom based upon any legal precedent, they had to manufacture one out of thin air.

Their decision was based upon a deliberate misinterpretation of a private letter that Thomas Jefferson wrote to the Danbury Baptist Convention. The Convention had written a letter to Jefferson on October 7,1801, expressing their concern about their religious freedoms.

At the time, they were being persecuted because they did not belong to the Congregationalist establishment in Connecticut.

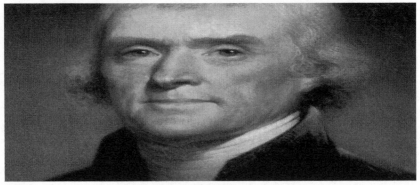
Thomas Jefferson

Jefferson wrote back a very short letter addressing the issue.

(Keep this in mind Reader. This was a private letter between the Baptists and Jefferson. There is nothing legal or legislative or law about this. It was merely a letter!)

"Believing with you that religion is a matter which lies solely between man and his God, that he owes account none other for his faith or his worship, that the legitimate powers of government reach actions only, and not opinions, I contemplate with sovereign reverence that at of the whole American people which declared that their legislature should "make no law respecting an establishment of religion, or prohibit the free exercise thereof, thus building a wall of separation of church and state."   105

Now, time out for a quick test on Wall Building 101:

Why did this castle build a wall around it? (keep enemy out.)

Why do prisons build a wall around it? (keep prisoners inside.)

Why did Communists build a wall in East Germany? (keep them in.)

By now you realize that walls are only built for one reason, and Jefferson clearly meant that Government was to stay out of religion.

Let's see what other comments Jefferson made that would refute what the court imputed to him:

"No power over the freedom of religion...is delegated to the United States by the Constitution."   106

"In matters of religion, I have considered that its free exercise is place by the Constitution independent on the powers of the federal government."
                                                                                                   107

"Our excellent Constitution...has not placed our religious rights under the power of any public functionary."   108

"I consider the government of the United States as interdicted by the Constitution from inter meddling with religious institutions."
                                                                                                   109
Prophetically, Jefferson wrote a letter to a friend in which he said:

"He who permits himself to tell a lie once, finds it much easier to do it a second and third time, till at length it becomes habitual; he tells lies without attending to it, and truths without the world believing him.

"The falsehood of tongue leads to that of the heart, and in time depraves all of its good dispositions."   110

This Court said that since the teacher, who is on the public pay roll, led the class, the state was basically financing the time for the prayer. This was a violation of "Jefferson's First Amendment."

Citing that "Jefferson had the sense of what Congress meant...Prayer in the public-school system breaches the Constitutional wall of separation between Church and State."   111

How could there be a breach in the Constitutional Wall since "separation of church and state" is not in the Constitution?

Justice Potter Stewart, the one dissenting vote blasted the ruling saying:

"It led not to true neutrality with respect to religion, but to the establishment of a religion of secularism." 112

Secularization: n.1. the social or political process of rejecting all forms of religious faith 2. the elimination of any religious elements with-in public education and other civic institutions.

The absolute irony to this whole charade is that Jefferson was not at the Constitution Convention, he was not present in Virginia where the Bill of Rights basically originated. He was serving as Ambassador to France.

In 1963, in "**School District of Abington v Schempp**", the Supreme Court removed the Bible from the classroom and the fight to remove God and Jesus Christ from America began in earnest. The vote was 8 to 1.

The state required that "at least ten verses from the Holy Bible [be] read, without comment, at the opening of each public school each school day."

Schempp specifically contended that the statute violated his and his family's rights under the First and Fourteenth Amendments.

Abbington court held that in organizing a reading of the Bible, the school was conducting "a religious exercise," and "that cannot be done without violating the 'neutrality' required of the State by the balance of power between individual, church and state that has been struck by the First Amendment." 113

In 1984, renowned Chief Justice William Rehnquist said:

"There is no historical foundation for the proposition that the framers intend to build the "wall of separation" that was constitutionalized in Everson…But the greatest injury of the "wall" notion is its mischievous diversion of judges from the actual intentions of the drafters of the Bill of Rights. No amount of repetitious errors can make the errors true.

The 'wall of separation between church and State' is a metaphor based on bad history...It should frankly be dissipated and abandoned....

It would come as much of a shock to those who drafted the Bill of Rights, as it will to many thoughtful Americans today, to learn that the Constitution, as construed by the majority prohibits...endorsing prayer.

George Washington himself, at the request of the very Congress which passed the Bill of Rights, proclaimed a day of 'public thanksgiving and prayer', to be observed by all acknowledging with grateful hearts the many and signal favors of Almighty God.

History must judge whether it was the Father of his country in 1789, or a majority of the Court today, which has strayed from the meaning of the Establishment Clause."   114

"The unassailable fortifications of your walls He will bring down, lay low and cast to the ground, even to the dust."   Isaiah 25:12

All Christians pray for the day when the wall is torn down.

The unasked question of the Elephant in the room:

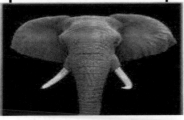

"Why in the face of these previous court decisions, and in complete defiance of the will of the American people, would this court have as its goal to remove the Bible and prayer from the classroom?"

Why would they manufacture this lie, and ignore all the preceding cases that had existed for over a hundred and fifty years before?

Five of the six judges who voted to remove prayer from the classrooms were Masons. The Chief Justice and one of the other four were 33rd degree Masons. (Vote was 6 to 1). They, along with two others voted to ban the Bible. (8-1).

It was hard for the author to come to terms regarding the Masons' involvement in all of this. His Father was a Mason.

The author refers the Reader to these books: "Beyond the Lodge Door," "Masonry Exposed," and "Brotherhood of Darkness" to become educated on the goals of this organization.

It is only at the 33rd degree level of Masonry that most Masons discover the truth about this organization.

"Beware of false prophets, who come to you in sheep's clothing but inwardly are ravenous wolves ."   *Matthew 7:15*

They do not worship Jesus but a "universal God." That is putting it mildly. It is much worse. Do your own research on Google to prove or disprove that statement.

This Supreme Court basically rewrote the history of America to set the stage to drive America into a one world government.

While the reader may question that last statement, it will become very clear in the next few Chapters.

In the last several years, the Judicial system in America has become a runaway freight train. States vote for traditional marriage and courts strike it down.

The vast Americans want prayer back in schools, want English as the official language, and are not in favor of abortion. Yet, the Judicial system goes against these.

It is apparent what Patrick Henry feared most would happen if the new Constitution would be adopted: no check and balance on the Court.

"I predict that if this measure passes (adoption of the Constitution), we will one day live under Judicial tyranny." (see **Appendix XII**)

FOOTNOTE: THE FOLLOWING WORDS: "SEPARATION, CHURCH, and STATE," ARE NOT IN THE CONSTITUTION!!!

Will the real Supreme Court stand up?   A little bit of humor

Or

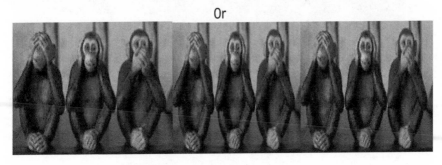

Hmmmmmmmm

CHAPTER 17: AMERICA'S PUBLIC-SCHOOL SYSTEM
SINCE 1962

"See to it that no one takes you captive by philosophy and empty deceit, according to human tradition, according to the elemental spirits of the world, and not according to Christ."   Colossians 2:8

Wichita Falls Senior High, Wichita Falls, Texas

America, as a nation, has sadly let the above quote become a reality.

This false "separation of church and state" doctrine has had a most negative impact on our public-school system and universities as well.

A few years ago, the author had the pleasure of portraying Patrick Henry at the Texas School District Police Chiefs Convention in Houston, Texas.

For several days, he interacted with police officers, whose duty station were public schools throughout the state of Texas.

This question was asked randomly: What are the reasons we are having problems in our schools? Why is your job necessary?

Without exception, **they said the main reason is that prayer and the Bible had been taken out of the classroom**.

As Benjamin Rush, one of the signors said:
"Mankind never invented a more effective method of extinguishing Christianity from a nation, than by declaring that it was improper to read the Bible in the classroom."   115

"Behold I stand at the door and knock."   *Rev.3: 20*

Supreme Court has you, ♥ , and the out of school.

The second most common reason the Police Chiefs gave was the diminishing role and influence of a Father presence. How sad. The attack against the family unit has been very successful.

Sadly, many teachers have gone to a liberal college, taught by liberal professors who are strongly socialistic.

This author has talked to several Christian schoolteachers who are so frustrated in their teaching, due to the curriculum and school board.

We have schools that now refuse to say the pledge because it contains the words "under God."

"The Declaration of Independence is banished from several schools because it contains the word "Creator."

Capture a youth's mind and you can capture his soul.
Capture his soul and you capture his destiny. Capture enough youth's destinies and you can change the destiny of that nation.

History is replete of the evils that this philosophy embodies.
Nazi Germany and Mao Tse tung are two such examples.

Many curriculums start with 1861 under the theory that what happened before is irrelevant.

The Reader is encouraged to check out school textbooks in his area and see what is being taught (or not taught.)

HARBINGER OF THINGS TO COME

The Author asks the Reader to look at this next discussion from "outside the box" and view it in the context of the continuing all-out attack on Christianity in America.

What one "sees" is not always "what is really going on." Perception versus Reality. Emotion verses Logic.

Schools and universities all over America are being deluged with demands to rename those that have Washington, Jefferson and other Founding Fathers in their name. Why? The stated reason is that they owned slaves.

Slavery is wrong, period. **This, however is a "red herring" and a "false flag."**

The real reason (in the Authors opinion) is that this is a continuing attack on the Christian aspects of the founding of America and particularly our Founding Fathers who were very strong Christians.

The author wonders how long before this statue of George Washington is removed from his alma mater: The University of Texas. Washington owned slaves. The Confederate statues have been removed.(Author attended Robert E Lee grade school in Dallas, Texas. It no longer has that name.)

In the Bible Belt, statues of strong Christians like Robert E Lee and "Stonewall" Jackson have been removed from schools and colleges allegedly for the slavery issue.

This is simply Revisionist History and removing all forms of Christianity from the public view. This is one other method to destroy our Christian heritage.

Why is all of this happening now? Satan knows his time is short.

In 2007, the National Park Service had the replica of the headstone of the Washington Monument so placed that the side that said "Laos Deo" was hidden from view. After 28,000 complaints it was resituated to make the words visible.

(The author has had this recurring vision for years: *He sees all the Bible verses on the landmark buildings in Washington D. C. being removed by acid baths*. He prays he is wrong.)

Praise God, Many schools all over America still have their annual "see you at the Pole" gathering.

"May my child trust God to meet all his or her needs." Philippians 4: 19

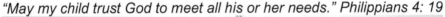

In 1952, the author was in the 9th grade. When he came to school one day, he saw that someone had cut down the flagpole. Instead of a student led prayer that morning, the School Principal did the prayer.

It was one of repentance, asking God to forgive the person or persons who had done such a thing. What an impression that has left the author all his life.

What would a School Principal do today under similar circumstances?

Consider the following:
A student in Texas lowered the Mexican flag that had been put on the school flagpole and raised the American flag. Result: Student suspended. What country do we live in?
(Following poem all over the Internet)

THE NEW SCHOOL PRAYER

Now I sit me down in school
Where praying is against the rule
For this great nation under God
Finds mention of Him very odd.

If Scripture now the class recites,
It violates the Bill of Rights,
Any anytime my head I bow
Becomes a Federal matter now

For praying in a public hall
'Might offend someone with no faith at all
In silence alone, we must meditate
God's name is prohibited by the state.

We're allowed to cuss and dress like freaks
And pierce our noses, tongues, and cheeks
They've outlawed guns, but FIRST the bible
To quote the Good Book makes me liable

So, Lord, this silent plea I make
Should I be shot:
My soul please take.   Amen

CHAPTER 18: THE CHURCH'S ROLE IN POLITICS

"It is a trustworthy statement: if any man aspires to the office of overseer it is a fine work he desires to do. An overseer must be above reproach."

Timothy 3: 12

Please study the above biblical quote, particularly the last sentence.

The "church" remains very silent on the issue of politics, more concerned about protecting its 501(3) exemption rather than speaking out on the issues that are dooming America.

The Bible does say that you should tithe....... however, nowhere does it say that you should do so to get an income tax deduction!!

Many Christians "sit out" politics and elections.

Some Pastors tell their flock that Politics is "dirty," and that Christians should not have anything to do with it. Several even advocate not even to participate in the election process.

This was not the intent of our Founding Fathers, who strongly believed that only Christians should be leaders of our nation.

In the early days of our country, you could not run for public office (or be appointed) unless you could pass a religious test.

This changed when our current Constitution went into effect.

Article 6, Section 3 of our Constitution says that no religious test shall be required to run for public office.

The Reader may find it interesting that every single state constitution refers to God it in its preamble!

These six State Constitutions require that you must believe in God, if you wish to run for public office. (Note that ministers are barred from holding office in Tennessee.)

Arkansas: Article 19, section 1: "No person who denies the being of a God shall hold any office in the civil departments of this State, nor be competent to testify as a witness in any Court."

Mississippi: Article 14, section 265: "No person who denies the existence of a Supreme Being shall hold any office in this State."

North Carolina: Article VI, section 8: "The following persons shall be disqualified for office: First, any person who shall deny the being of Almighty God…."

South Carolina: Article XVII, section 4: "No person who denies the existence of a Supreme Being shall hold any office under this Constitution."

Tennessee: Article IX, section 2: "No person who denies the being of God, or a future state of rewards and punishment, shall hold any office in the civil department of this state."

Note: Ministers are also barred from holding office, because they "ought not to be diverted from the great duties of their functions; therefore, no minister of the Gospel, or priest of any denomination whatever, shall be eligible to a seat in either House or the Legislature," Article IIX, section1.

Texas: Article 1, section 4: "No religious test shall ever be required as a qualification to any office, or public trust, in this State; nor shall anyone be excluded from holding office on account of his religious sentiments, provided he acknowledge the existence of a Supreme Being."

All of the colonies had a loyalty oath that you had to sign as well.

They were all very similar, but here is the oath for Delaware:

"Every person who shall be chosen a member of either house, or appointed to any office or place of trust...shall...make and subscribe the following declaration, to wit:

"I do acknowledge the Holy scripture of the Old and New testament to be given by divine inspiration. I do profess faith in God the Father, and in Jesus Christ His Only Son, and in the Holy Ghost, one God, blessed for evermore."   116

How many of our Congressman and Senators would sign that oath? The follow up question would be "do you really mean it?"

John Jay, our first Chief Justice of the United States Supreme Court so eloquently said:

"Providence has given to our people the choice of their rulers, and it is the duty and privilege of this Christian nation, for the people to select and prefer Christians to be their rulers."   117

James Madison, the Father of our Constitution said:

"We have staked the whole future of American civilization, not upon the power of government, far from it.

" We have staked the future of all of our political institutions upon the capacity of each and all of us to govern ourselves according to the Ten Commandments of God."   118

Charles Finney, a great minister and leader in America's Second Great Awakening, would shout from the rooftops what he said in 1835:

"The church must take right ground in regard to politics. God Cannot sustain this free and blessed country which we love and pray for unless the church will take right ground.

"Politics are a part of a religion in such a country as this, and Christians must do their duty to the country as a part of their duty to God. He will bless or curse this nation according to the course they take."
119

Benjamin Rush said:

"When you become entitled to exercise the of voting for public officers, let it be impressed on your mind that God commands you to choose for rulers, just men who will rule in the fear of God.

"The preservation of republican form of government depends on the faithful discharge of this duty, if the citizens neglect their duty, and place unprincipled men in office, the government will soon be corrupted.

"The only foundation for a republic is to be laid in Religion. Without this there can be no virtue, and without virtue there can be no liberty, and liberty is the object and life of all republican governments."   120

Patrick Henry said "Bad men cannot make good citizens. It is when people forget God that tyrants forge their chains. A vitiated state of morals, and corrupted public conscience, is incompatible with freedom.

"No free government, or the blessings of liberty, can be preserved to any people but by a firm adherence to justice, moderation, temperance, frugality, and virtue: and by a frequent recurrence to fundamental principles."   121

John Adams even went further as he described the role of the church in politics:

"The Holy Ghost carries on the whole Christian system in this earth, not a baptism, not a marriage, not a sacrament can be administered but by the Holy Ghost...

"THERE IS NO AUTHORITY CIVIL OR RELGIOUS. THERE CAN BE NO LEGITIMATE GOVERNMENT BUT WHAT IS ADMINISTERED BY THE HOLY GHOST. THERE CAN BE NO SALVATION WITHOUT."
                                                                                    122

Alex de Tocqueville, a great, renowned, and well respected French political philosopher toured America in1830 to seek the source of America's greatness.

" For what man knows the things of a man except the spirit of the man which is in him?"   *I Corinthians 2: 11*

Alex de Tocqueville

In his book, "Democracy in America," he made the following observations:

"On my arrival in the United States the religious aspect of the country was the first thing that struck my attention; and the longer I stayed there, the more I perceived the great political consequences from this new state of things....In the United States the influence of religion is not confined to the manners, but it extends to the intelligence of the people...

"Christianity, therefore, reigns without obstacle, by universal consent: The Americans combine the notions of Christianity   and of liberty so intimately in their minds, that it is impossible to make them conceive the one without the other.

"I sought for the key to the greatness and genius of America in her commodious harbors and her ample fields, it was not there...in her rich mines...it was not there ...in her vast world commerce, it was not there.

"Not until I went to the churches of America and her pulpits aflame with righteousness, did I understand the secret of her genius and power. America is great because she is good and if America ever ceases to be good, America will cease to be great."   123

If he visited out churches today, he would not be able to make the same observations. What do you think, dear reader, would be his observations now?

"God just wants to love and bless you," "Touchy feely," "Yoga," "Meditation," and "Praying in the dark." Oh yes, New Age is alive and well in the "church."

It is a rare Pastor who will address the issues of abortion, the attacks against the traditional marriage unit, speak on patriotism, ask the congregation if there is sin in their life and that maybe, just perhaps, that is why they are having difficult challenges in their life?

The church does not want to hear the message that this book expounds.

Among dozens of personal examples this one stands out. The author was referred to a church that had a congregation of over a thousand. He had a very strong referral, so much so, that the Pastor himself took the call.

After going into much detail about the historical, educational, and relevant message to today's events, the reaction of congregations the message, referring him to my website with dozens of referrals, he politely said:

"That is nothing that my church would be interested in." How about your Pastor? *Is he blind as to what is happening?*

What is the role of your church in waking up its congregation about the attack against Christian America? Instead of "standing on the promises," many churches are just "sitting on the premises."

As FDR once said: "The only thing we have to fear is fear itself."

Author's definition of FEAR is

FALSE... EVIDENCE... APPEARING... REAL

What is frightening is that the "church" was effectively silenced by the Nazis during WWII. Those Pastors who did speak out were imprisoned.

The most common statement that the author gets from a church Pastor is: "Please do not talk about church and state."

Ironically, this question comes up during Q and A and so he can answer it. After the service, the Pastor thanks him for the education.

Congress of the United States publicly declared 1983 the national "Year of the Bible."

 The bipartisan document known as Public Law 97-280, was signed on October 4, 1982 by Speaker of the House Thomas P. O'Neill, President of the Senate - Pro Tempore Strom Thurmond, and President of the United States Ronald Reagan.

It reads as follows:

"WHEREAS the Bible, the Word of God, has made a unique contribution in shaping the United States as a distinctive and blessed nation and people;

"WHEREAS deeply held religious convictions springing from the Holy Scriptures led to the early settlement of our Nation;

"WHEREAS Biblical teachings inspired concepts of civil government that are contained in our Declaration of Independence and Constitution of the United States;

"WHEREAS Presidents Washington, Jackson, Lincoln, and Wilson--paid tribute to the surpassing influence of the Bible in our country's development, as in the words of President Jackson that the Bible is "the Rock on which our Republic rests";

"WHEREAS the history of our Nation clearly illustrates the value of voluntarily applying the teachings of the Scriptures in the lives of individuals, families, and societies; WHEREAS this Nation now faces great challenges that will test this Nation as it has never been tested before; and

"WHEREAS that renewing our knowledge of and faith in God through Holy Scripture can strengthen us as a nation and a people:

"NOW,

"THEREFORE, be it Resolved by the Senate and House of Representatives of the United States of America in Congress, That the President is authorized and requested to 1983 as a national "Year of the Bible" in recognition of both the formative influence the Bible has been for our Nation, and our national need to study and apply the teachings of the Holy Scriptures."

Would our current Congress issue such a document today?

CHAPTER 19: THE WAR AGAINST CHRISTIAN AMERICA

"But Jesus knew their thoughts and said to them: "Every kingdom divided against itself is brought to desolation, and every city or house divided against itself will not stand".   Matthew 12: 25

America lost its innocence in 1962 when we took prayer out of the school, and then in 1963 the Bible was removed. America has been on a downhill slope ever since. Here is what happened the rest of the decade:

President John F. Kennedy was assassinated in 1963, his brother Robert in 1968. Malcom X is killed in 1965 and Martin Luther King in 1968.

In 1964 we get involved in the Viet Nam War. A decade later we leave South Viet Nam in disgrace; it falls to the North Vietnamese. We lose over 50,000 dead and hundreds of thousands wounded emotionally and/or physically and over a thousand "unaccounted for."

We now lead the world in divorce, bankruptcies, abortion, and we are now a debtor nation.

There are number of entities that are contributing to the decline of America and this next coverage is by no means a complete list.

Start playing even closer attention to your television, movies, news casts, etc.

Christians and Conservatives, except in a few rare exceptions, are the bad guys and gals.

AUTHORS NOTE: From 1982 to 1986 the author spent one week a month in Hollywood, in his profession as a Certified Financial Planner. His clients were all in "postproduction": film and sound editing. Many won Academy Awards.

Not one client or potential client was a Christian! The author mentions this because it gives credence to his comments on Hollywood.

"But among you there must not be even a hint of sexual immorality, or of any kind of impurity, or of greed, because these are improper for God's holy people."   *Ephesians 5:3*

In 1951," Quo Vadis" was nominated for 8 Academy Awards. In1956, " Moses" won 6 Academy Awards, and in 1959, "Ben Hur" won 11 Academy Awards. (The latter two starred Charlton Heston. Where have we seen his name before?)

These were strong Christian oriented movies. Now let's fast forward roughly five decades.

A 1999 film, "American Beauty", is nominated for several Oscars.

The plot of this movie is the result of the breakdown in the morals of Hollywood since Bible and Prayer have been banished from schools.

It is the story of two families that are next door neighbors. There was not one "beautiful" thing in this movie.

Family number one:

Husband is fired from his job, has incriminating information on his boss and blackmails him for $60,000 and gets a great severance package.

He develops a crush on his daughter's teen-age girlfriend, and it is only when he finds out that she is a virgin at the last minute, that prevents him from committing statutory rape.

His wife has an affair with a Realtor.

Their daughter poses nude in front of her bedroom window, so the next-door neighbor's son of family number two can take pictures of her.

Family number two:

Husband is a Marine Corps Officer who is gay. His wife is comatose and spaced out in every scene.

The father terrorizes his son. His son is a drug dealer who supplies husband number one with drugs, (and possibly his own mother, though that is simply implied).

The movie ends when the Marine makes a pass at the neighbor's husband and is rejected by him. The Marines mentally sick wife murders the neighbor (honor killing in defense of her husband, thus ending the movie on a high note!)

What a disgusting picture attacking all we used to whole dear: the sanctity of marriage, the military, abstinence, no use of drugs, high morals.

"American Beauty" won these major Oscars at the 72nd annual Academy Awards ceremony, winning in five categories: Best Picture, Best Director, Best Actor, Best Original Screenplay, and Best Cinematography.

As Hollywood goes, so does the influence on our younger generation.

This next quote is # 6 on the **Illuminati** plan to destroy America:

"……. To encourage, and eventually **legalize the use of drugs** and **make pornography an "art-form"**, which will be widely accepted and, eventually, become quite commonplace."

The entire Illuminati plan is in **Appendix XV.**

Now the "f" word is used in movies and television. It is so commonplace that it is disgusting. How low this industry has sunk? Late night television is rampant on HBO with disgusting sex.

We have "Sex in The City," "Desperate Housewives," "Real Sex," "King of Queens," "Two and a Half Men," et cetera.

Most movies and TV shows portray Christians in an unfavorable light. The clergy is often held to ridicule as well.

Christians are portrayed as adulterers, bigots, drunkards, thieves, murderers, or a combination of them. They are laughed at, held up to ridicule and mocked severely.

Our military is now degraded in movies such as" Apocalypse Now," "Full Metal Jacket," "The Deer Hunter," "Born on the 4th of July," and particularly in "Platoon." The latter won an Oscar for Best Picture in 1986. Our servicemen are portrayed as murderers. Shame on you Hollywood.

Hollywood has and will play a lead role in the bringing down of America. Movies are full of profanity, nudity, and drugs.

Hollywood has a double standard when it comes to Christianity and the Academy Awards. Let's look at what happened to an Oscar nomination for "Best Song."

In 2016, the song "Alone but not Alone" from the movie by the same name was nominated for an Academy Award.

Almost immediately the song was declared ineligible because the song had been "lobbied for" on the internet.

All nominations for awards have always been subject to "being lobbied" for and none of them were ever disqualified. Talk about hypocrisy.

ROLE OF NEWS MEDIA

"Do not spread a false report......" Exodus 23:1

We do not have a free press in America. We have a press that is free to write what they want, talk about what they want, and to slant the truth any way they want.

They basically "self-censor." They report by "omission" so that the public does not often hear both sides of a conflict.

The great preponderance of well-known TV newscasters are members of the Council of Foreign Relations. (CFR's)

.Ask Google for a list of its current members and you will be shocked
.Council of Foreign Relations will be discussed later in book.

Many will not wear the American flag, and they are all very liberal. During election year, it is obvious that they always back one liberal candidate, portray he/she in a very favorable light and report only what would be beneficial to "their" candidate.

So, the American people are spoon fed, and most just take what's on the spoon without any thought. Owners are also CFR's and except for some small-town newspapers you are going to have the bias.

The only true Christian bastion left is" talk radio' and the internet. There is much "afoot" on how to control these with "equal time" to offset their bias.

Talk about the pot calling the kettle black. or as they say in the south, "that dog won't hunt." So, to get news from a Christian perspective, the talk radio is about it.

Alex Jones, Rush Limbaugh, Michael Savage, Sean Hannity are among the very few conservative talk radio show hosts.

As far as television, we only have a few diehards left who are not afraid to be bold and speak the truth: Hal Lindsay, Jack Van Impe, and John Hagee come to mind.

FOX News is one of the few conservative news media that attempts to be middle of the road.

AMERICAN CIVIL LIBERTIES UNION

"Rejoice and be glad, because great is your reward in heaven, for in the same way they persecuted the prophets who were before you."
Matthew 5:12

The name itself is an oxymoron. The author believes Its true name should be :THE ANTI CHRISTIAN LIBERTIES UNION.

This group is a socialistic anti-Christian, anti-American organization which wields an unbelievable amount of power.

Roger Baldwin was the founder and for 30 years the Executive Director of the ACLU.

Prior to his death in 1981, this top official socialist liberal leader wrote in the Harvard University yearbook:

"I am for socialism, disarmament, and ultimately for abolishing the State itself as an instrument of violence and compulsion.

" I seek the social ownership of property, the abolition of the propertied class (read: wealthy) and sole control of those who produce wealth."
124
The author will let the reader decide what sole control is. Sounds like something out of the French Revolution and the Communist Manifesto.

Wake up America, this is a highly financed, highly profiled arm of those who would drive American into a one world government.

The ACLU has sued to have declared unconstitutional: the tax-exempt status of churches and synagogues, employment of chaplains by Congress, prisons, and the armed services; all displays of nativity scenes on public properties, removal of scriptural references on public monuments and buildings, the singing of "Silent Night" in the classroom and of course the words "under God" in the Pledge of Allegiance.

They go into community after community and intimidate them into removing any plaques and signs relating to Christianity from public view.

Strangely, the ACLU has no problem with the Koran, Wiccanism, Halloween, New Age Exercises, Islam etc. being allowed in the public-school system.

They continue to fight against the Bible being used in the classroom.

THE ENEMY WITHIN

This is "politically incorrect." There is a maxim: "a picture is worth a thousand words."

The author believes the next three pictures stand completely on their own and that a four-page Chapter could not express his concerns any better.

What about "separation of church and state" issue?

The following picture was taken in Dearborn, Michigan Note the words:

"Down with USA"

CHAPTER 20: NEW WORLD ORDER, COUNCIL ON FOREIGN RELATIONS, ILLUMINATI AND AGENDA 21, BILDERBERGERS, TRILATERALISTS

This may be the hardest Chapter for the Reader to grasp and understand, **only** if he/she has not heard of any of these organizations. The author has studied these sinister groups since 1961.

Everything in this Chapter can be found on the internet.

(Please click on https://cfrmedia.wordpress.com/ to read chart.)

The chart gives strong support to the author's thesis **that all of these organizations have the same ultimate goal: the destruction of America as we know it, and to drive us into the ungodly government under the United Nations.**

Note the heavy involvement of the news media which the vast majority supports the goals of all of these organizations.

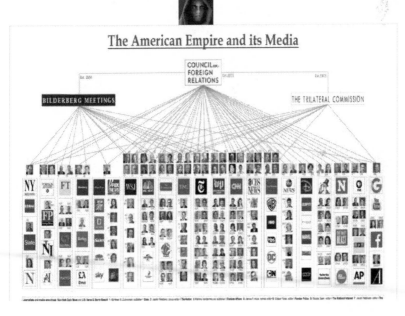

The first attempt to snare America into a world government was the League of Nations. This organization was the precursor to the United Nations and failed badly in its goal thanks to the foresight of wise Congressman who would not let America join.

The One Worlders did not give up. This was accomplished in 1948 when the United Nations came to America.

The Rockefellers donated the land to house the United Nations.

NEW WORLD ORDER
COUNCIL ON FOREIGN RELATIONS

"So that Godless men should not rule, nor be snares of the people"
Job 34:30

The Council on Foreign Relations, and other organizations such as the Bilderbergers, and the Illuminati all basically have the same motive, and that is simply to force America and every other free nation into a One World Government under the banner of the United Nations.

The CFR's Study No. 7, published November 25, 1959, openly declared its true purpose: "...building a New International Order [which] must be responsive to world aspirations for peace, [and] for social and economic change...an international order [code for world government] ...including states labeling themselves as 'Socialist".

One could safely say that a nutshell descriptor of the CFR is to bring about a New World Order through the manipulation of U.S. foreign n policy and relations and through international economic Interdependence."

Nations of the world will be forced into regions, much like the ongoing but constantly denied plan to make Mexico, United States, and Canada a new region called The North American Union.

"Woe to those who enact evil statutes and to those who constantly record unjust decisions."　　　　　　　　Isaiah 10: 1

Since when does the American flag fly at the same level??

Goal of the one Worlders: merge all three countries into one. Check it on Google. Why else is there no real effort to stop the influx of illegal immigrants?

Here are the words of David Rockefeller who donated the land in New York to house this anti-Christian organization.

"We are grateful to the New York Times... It would have been impossible for us to develop our plan for the world if we had been subjected to the lights of publicity during those years...The supranational sovereignty of an intellectual elite and world bank is sure preferable to the nation's auto determination practiced in past centuries."　　　125

"Some even believe we are part of a secret cabal working against the best interests of the United States, characterizing my family and me as 'internationalists' and of conspiring with others around the world to build a more integrated global political and economic structure -- one world, if you will. If that's the charge, I stand guilty, and I am proud of it."　　125

"Do not participate in the unfruitful deeds of darkness, but instead even expose them; for it is disgraceful even to speak of the things which are done by them in secret."   *Ephesians 5: 11-12*

Our dollar bill has the phrase:" Novus Ordo Seclorum", meaning a "New Order for the Ages." It also has the occultic symbol of the "all seeing eye."

Woodrow Wilson once said "Some of the biggest men in the United States, in the field of commerce and manufacture, are afraid of something. They know that there is a power somewhere so organized, so subtle, so watchful, so interlocked, so complete, so pervasive, that they had better not speak above their breath when they speak in condemnation of it."   127

Henry Kissinger said:

"The New World Order cannot happen without U.S. **participation, as we are the most significant single component. Yes, there will be a New World Order, and it will force the United States to change its perceptions.**"   128

President George H. Bush mentioned it on **September 11,1990** during a speech to a joint session of Congress.

THIS WAS OUR FIRST 911 WARNING

He said, "we are entering a New World Order...We will from this point forward dedicate ourselves to the sacred shrines of the United Nations."

129

(There is nothing sacred about the United Nations goals for America)

In the same speech, he mentioned a "thousand points of light," a well-known New Age phrase. Be aware that the religion of Christianity is not compatible at all with New Age.

All the above organizations are dedicated to taking away America's sovereignty and driving America into a One World Government, ala the United Nations.

How determined are they?

Arthur Schlesinger, Jr:

"We are not going to achieve a new world order without paying for it in blood as well as in words and money."   130

As you read their goals and philosophies, you will begin to understand why America is being driven into the New World Order and the tool will be the United Nations.

They want abolition of private party, complete disarmament of all citizens, a direct tax on all individuals for their support, all national governments will be subservient to them.

A leaflet about the United Nations Meditation Room written under the direction of Dag Hammarskjöld stated that the eerie lodestone altar within it: '**is dedicated to the God whom man worships under many names and in many forms**.' Quoted in R.K. Spenser's The Cult of the All-Seeing Eye. (Christian Book Club of America, 1962), p.9.]

The preceding quote sounds like a New Age (or name your own God) Mantra being put forth. The prayer room bears this out.

"Thou shalt have no other gods before me Thou shalt not make unto thee any graven image, or any likeness of any thing that is in heaven above, or that is in the earth beneath, or that is in the water under the earth."   *Exodus 20: 3-4*

Does the above look like any "prayer room" the Reader has ever seen?

ILLUMINATI AND AGENDA 21

The **Illuminati** is another sinister organization that is dedicated to the destruction of America. Agenda 21 is their master plan.

"Woe to those who deeply hide their plans from the LORD, And whose deeds are done in a dark place, And they say, "Who sees us?" "Who knows us?"   *Isaiah 29: 15*

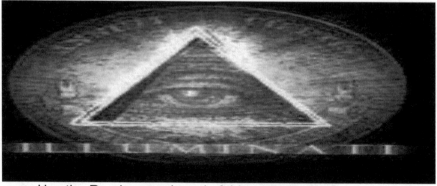

Has the Reader ever heard of this organization?

AUTHOR STRONGLY RECOMMENDS YOU READ APPENDIX XVI FOR THEIR AGENDA 21 GOALS. YOU WILL BE SHOCKED!

"A day of wrath is that day, a day of distress and anguish, a day of ruin and devastation, a day of darkness and gloom, a day of and the darkness." <u>Zephaniah 1:15</u>

These are the first five :

1. To establish a One World Government/New World Order with a **unified church and monetary system** under their direction. The One World Government began to set up its church in the 1920: s and 30: s, for they realized the need for a religious belief inherent in mankind must have an outlet and, therefore, set up a "church" body to channel that belief in the direction they desired.

2. To bring about the utter **destruction of all national identity and national pride**, which was a primary consideration if the concept of a One World Government was to work.

3. To engineer and bring about the destruction of religion, and more especially, the Christian Religion, with the one exception, their own creation, as mentioned above.

4. To establish the ability to control of each and every person through means of mind control and what Zbignew Brzezinski called techonotronics, which would create human-like robots and a system of terror which would make Felix Dzerzinhski's Red Terror look like children at play.

5. To bring about the end to all industrialization and the production of nuclear generated electric power in what they call "the post-industrial zero-growth society.

It is all about "sustainable development."

The goal of Agenda 21 is very scary. It deals with confiscating all your assets, eliminating people to have more social order.

Population needs to be controlled. People will live, eat, work in the same building, private land will be gone, steps will be taken to eliminate vehicles.

No, the author is not making this up. It is a United Nations brainchild and President George Bush Sr. signed us up for it. President Clinton and President Obama endorsed it. President Trump does not.

Agenda 21 affects every single person living in the world.

(A chill should go through you when you read this.)

The following statements are all over the internet in basically the same format. The author has taken them from American Policy Center, articles by Kathleen Margardt, Ron Taylor, and others.

" Effective execution of humans, unlike anything the world has ever experienced" Agenda 21: The Earth Summit Strategy to Save Our Planet (Earth press, 1993). Emphases – DR.

"We must make this place an insecure and inhospitable place for Capitalists and their projects – we must reclaim the road and plowed lands, halt dam construction, tear down existing dams, free shackled rivers and return to wilderness millions of tens of millions of acres or presently settled land." Dave Foreman, Earth First

"economic development as we know it cannot be sustained… Sustainable development, therefore, is a program of action for local and global economic reform – a program that has yet to be fully defined."
Local Agenda 21 Planning Guide, published by ICLEI, 199

"The development can be achieved; however, there is growing consensus that it must be accomplished at the local level if it is ever to be achieved on a global basis."
The Local Agenda 21 Planning Guide, published by ICLEI, 1996."

"Land...cannot be treated as an ordinary asset, controlled by
 individuals and subject to the pressures and inefficiencies of the Private
land ownership is also a principal instrument of accumulation and
concentration of wealth, therefore contributes to social injustice."
From the report from the 1976 UN's Habitat I Conference.

"Private land use decisions are often driven by strong economic
incentives that result in several ecological and aesthetic
consequences...The key to overcoming it is through public policy..."
Report from the President's Council on Sustainable Development
page 112.

"Current lifestyles and consumption patterns of the affluent
middle class – involving high meat intake, use of fossil fuels, appliances,
home and work air conditioning, and suburban housing are not
sustainable."
Maurice Strong, Secretary General of the UN's Earth Summit, 1992.

No private residences. Collectiveness style of living .Animals freely run
everywhere. No vehicles.

"We need a new collaborative decision process that leads to better
decisions, more rapid change, and more sensible use of human, and
financial resources   in achieving our goals." Report from the President's
Council on Sustainable Development. Individual rights will need to be
sacrificed." Harvey Ruvin, Vice Chairman, ICLEI The Wildlands Project

"Now the Holy Spirit tells us clearly that in the last times some will turn away from the true faith; they will follow deceptive spirits and teachers."   *I Timothy 4:1*

Pope Francis

Pope Francis, Head of the Catholic Church, spoke before the United Nations on September 25, 2015.

He said: "The agenda for Sustainable Development at the World Summit, which opens today, is an important sign of hope." "Hope" for what?

At various times, he has said that atheists can go to Heaven! Check it out on Google. This is an example of the "living breathing Bible" and/or "progressive Christianity" frame of mind.

He also signed a pact with the Muslim World that there should be no diversity in religion. Is he serious???? It is true. Check it out.

Two of our leading Fathers, George Washington and Thomas Jefferson prophetically foresaw the dangers of becoming involved in foreign interests.

Harking back to Washington's warning of foreign entanglements, lets read what Jefferson had to say about this subject.

"Determined as we are to avoid, if possible, wasting the energies of our people in war and destruction, we shall avoid implicating ourselves with the powers of Europe, even in support of principles which we mean to pursue.

"They have so many other interests different from ours, that we must avoid being entangled in them.

"We believe we can enforce these principles as to ourselves by peaceable means, now that we are likely to have our public councils detached from foreign views.

"Nothing but the failure of every peaceable mode of redress, nothing but dire necessity, should force us from the path of peace which would be our wisest pursuit, to embark in the broils and contentions of Europe and become a satellite to any power there."   131

The author highly recommends that you study and educate others to the true philosophies and goals of the United Nations.

The John Birch Society's lifelong mission is to get the United States out of the United Nations, and to get the United Nations out of the United States.

The picture below shows how transparent the United Nations is in "showcasing" one of their major goals:

THE ELIMINATION OF PRIVATE OWNERSHIP OF GUNS.

"No man can enter into a strong man's house, and spoil his goods, except he will first bind the strong man; and then he will spoil his house."
Mark 3:27

This statute is a direct affront to our 2nd Amendment.

The following review article by **Stephen Lendman** was originally published on Global Research in June 2009.

" His book, "The True Story of the Bilderberg Group," was published in 2005 and is now updated in a new 2009 edition. He states that in 1954, "the most powerful men in the world met for the first time" in Oosterbeek, Netherlands, "debated the future of the world," and decided to meet annually in secret.

They called themselves the Bilderberg Group with a membership representing a who's who of world power elites, mostly from America, Canada, and Western Europe with familiar names like David Rockefeller, Henry Kissinger, Bill Clinton, Gordon Brown, Angel a Merkel, Alan Greenspan, Ben Bernanke, Larry Summers, Tim Geithner, Lloyd Blankfein, George Soros, Donald Rumsfeld, Rupert Murdoch, other heads of state, influential senators, congressmen and parliamentarians, Pentagon and NATO brass, members of European royalty, selected media figures, and invited others – some quietly by some accounts like Barack Obama and many of his top officials.

In all cases participants are adherents to One World Order governance run by top power elites.

Host governments provide overall security to keep away outsiders.

"The Facts on the Trilateral Commission Reveal That David Rockefeller and Other Elite ... Want Global Government Tyranny.

"The Trilateral Commission is international and is intended to be the vehicle for multinational consolidation of the commercial and banking interests by seizing control of the political government of the U.S." - Sen. Barry Goldwater

When looking at the facts on the Trilateral Commission, it's important to understand that it was set up as a front for the exact same goals of the Council on Foreign Relations.

The Trilateral Commission is another tool used by the leaders of the CFR shadow government.

The world's elite utilizes secretive organizations such as the Committee of 300 structure, the CFR, the Bilderberg Society, and the Trilateral Commission to further its ultimate goal of global domination.

Although all these groups play a part in the movement toward a One World Government, the facts on the Trilateral Commission all lead us more specifically to the Council on Foreign Relations."

Canada Free Press, November 3, 2007

BOTTOM LINE: EVERY ORGANIZATION IN THIS CHAPTER IS A NON-CHRISTIAN ORGANIZATION DESIGNED TO TAKE AWAY AMERICAS INDEPENDENT SOVERIGNTY. THE NEWS MEDIA IS HEAVILY INVOLVED IN THIS PROCESS.

A very popular song of our era is "IMAGINE" by the late John Lennon.
It reached number one on several music charts.

Lennon goes on to say, imagine there is:

No reason to kill   No Hell   No country
    or die for

No Heaven   No religion   No possesions

   In this authors opinion, this song is a tribute to the New World Order,
Council on Foreign Relations, Agenda 21, and the Illuminati.

Everyone will live as one happy family in the brotherhood of man.
When the author shows the words to people, their attitude about the
song changes immediately.

Google CFR, Trilateralists, etc. and be prepared to be shocked at the
prominent Americans who belong to these organizations dedicated to
ending America's place as a world leader, reducing us to a 3rd World
Country, and shoving us into the arms of The New World Order.

**Now, keep in mind what you have learned in this Chapter and
RELATE it to George Washington's' Farewell Address in the
next Chapter. The author believes you will concur that his warning
and prophecy is for today's America.**

CHAPTER 21: GEORGE WASHINGTON'S PROPHETIC FAREWELL ADDRESS

".. If there is a prophet among you, I, the LORD, shall make Myself known to him in a vision, I shall speak with him in a dream."
Numbers 12:1

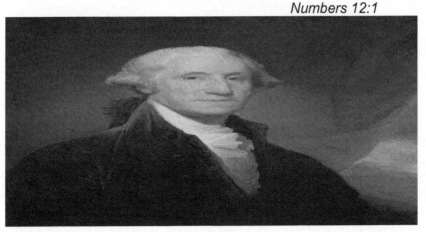

Washington did not give his Farewell Address in person. Instead, he released it to all the major newspapers in the states.

What is interesting is that he asked for input from both Alexander Hamilton and James Madison. His concern was that he was too negative in what was to be his final communication with the American people.

There is no question that he must have had some prophetic vision as he prepared his "Farewell Address." At the time of this message America was safe, secure, highly Christian, and very stable. We were not under attack either spiritually or physically.

We were a morally sound country, and yet he felt to touch on aspects that concerned him about the future.

In this authors opinion, Washington had incredible insight as to the danger of involvement with other countries. Current history is proving him correct.

While several of his main points are included here, you are encouraged to go **Appendix XIV** and read the entire Address.

"I shall carry it to my grave my vows that heaven may continue to you the choicest tokens of its beneficence; that your union and brotherly affection may be perpetual; that the free Constitution, which is the work of your hands, may be sacredly maintained; that its administration in every department may be stamped with wisdom and virtue; that, in fine, the happiness of the people of these States, under the auspices of liberty, may be made complete by so careful a preservation and so prudent a use of this blessing as will acquire to them the glory of recommending it to the applause, the affection, and adoption of every nation which is yet a stranger to it.

"Of all the dispositions and habits which lead to political prosperity, religion and morality are indispensable supports.

'In vain would that man claim the tribute of patriotism, who should labor to subvert these great pillars of human happiness, these firmest props of the duties of men and citizens.

'The mere politician, equally with the pious man, ought to respect and to cherish them.

"A volume could not trace all their connections with private and public felicity. Let it simply be asked: Where is the security for property, for reputation, for life, if the sense of religious obligation desert the oaths which are the instruments of investigation in courts of justice?

"And let us with caution indulge the supposition that morality can be maintained without religion. Whatever may be conceded to the influence of refined education on minds of peculiar structure, reason, and experience both forbid us to expect that national morality can prevail in exclusion of religious principle.

'As avenues to foreign influence in innumerable ways, such attachments are particularly alarming to the truly enlightened and independent patriot, the great rule of conduct for us in regard to foreign nations is in extending our commercial relations, to have with them as little political connection as possible.

"So far as we have already formed engagements let them be fulfilled with perfect good faith. Here let us stop.

"Europe has a set of primary interests which to us have none; or a very remote relation. Hence, she must be engaged in frequent controversies, the causes of which are essentially foreign to our concerns.

"Hence, therefore, it must be unwise in us to implicate ourselves by artificial ties in the ordinary vicissitudes of her politics, or the ordinary combinations and collisions of her friendships or enmities.

'Against the insidious wiles of foreign influence believe me, fellow-citizens, the jealousy of a free people ought to be constantly awake, since history and experience prove that   foreign influence is one of the most baneful foes of republican government.

"Excessive partiality for one foreign nation and excessive dislike of another cause those whom they actuate to see danger only on one side and serve to veil and even second the arts of influence on the other.

"In the portion of the foreign world. there can be no greater error than to expect or calculate upon real favors from nation to nation. It is an illusion, which experience must cure, which is a just pride."

As the Reader may recall, both Columbus and Washington had visions of America being invaded by another country.

GEORGE WASHINGTON'S THIRD VISION

"Again, I heard the mysterious voice saying, 'Son of the Republic, look and learn.' At this the dark, shadowy angel placed a trumpet to his lips and blew three distinct blasts; and taking water from the ocean, he sprinkled it on Europe, Asia, and Africa.

"Then my eyes beheld a fearful scene. From each of these countries arose thick black clouds that were soon joined into one; and throughout this mass there gleamed a dark red light be which I saw hordes of armed men, who, moving with the cloud, marched by land and sailed by sea to America, which country was enveloped in the volume of cloud.

'And I dimly saw these vast armies devastate the whole country and burn the villages, towns, and cities that I had beheld springing up." As my ears listened to the thundering of the cannon, the slashing of swords, and the shouts and cries of millions in mortal combat, I again heard the mysterious voice saying, 'Son of the Republic, look and learn.

"When the voice had ceased, the dark angel placed his trumpet once more to his mouth and blew a long and fearful blast. Instantly a light as of a thousand suns shone down from above me and pierced and broke into fragments the dark cloud which enveloped America. At the same moment the angel upon whose head still shown the word 'Union' and who bore our national flag in one hand and a sword in the other descended from the heavens attended by legions of white spirits.

"These immediately joined the inhabitants of America, who I perceived were well-nigh overcome, but who, immediately taking courage again, close dup their broken ranks and renewed the battle. Again, amid the fearful noise of the conflict I heard the mysterious voice saying, 'Son of the Republic, look and learn.'

'As the voice ceased, the shadowy angel for the last time dipped water from the ocean and sprinkled it upon America. Instantly the dark cloud rolled back, together with the armies it had brought, leaving the inhabitants of the land victorious.

"Then once more, I beheld the villages, towns, and cities springing up where I'd seen them before, while the bright angel, planting the azure standard he had brought in the midst of them, cried with a loud voice:

'While the stars remain, and the heavens send down dew upon the earth, so long shall the Union last.'

"And taking from his brow the crown on which blazoned the word 'Union,' he placed it upon the standard while the people ,kneeling down said "Amen ."The scene instantly began to fade and dissolve, and I, at last, saw nothing but the rising, curling vapor I had at first beheld.

'This also disappeared, and I found myself once more gazing upon the mysterious visitor, who in the same voice I had heard before said: 'Son of the Republic, what you have seen is thus interpreted.

'Three great perils will come upon the Republic. The most fearful is the third, but in this greatest conflict the whole world united shall not prevail against her.

"Let every child of the Republic learn to live for his God, his land, and the Union.'

'With these words the vision vanished, and I started from my seat and felt that I had seen a vision wherein had been shown me the birth, progress, and destiny of the United States."

"Such, my friends," said the venerable narrator, "were the words I heard from Washington's own lips, and America will do well to profit by them."

(Under Revisionist History, hundreds of quotes of the Founding Fathers have been dismissed including this vision of Washington. It was first formally printed in 1862 and is based on written comments from a soldier in Washington s army. There are several sources under Google.)

In light in what is happening in America at the time of the writing of this book, the author feels this last vision is in fact going to be a reality, whether Washington or someone else had the vision. To be forewarned, is to be forearmed.

CHAPTER 22: THE BATTLE TO SAVE CHRISTIAN AMERICA

"But I have this against you. You have forgotten your first love.
Remember the heights from which you have fallen. Repent and do
the deeds you did at first or I am coming quickly, and I will remove
your lamp stead from its post."   *Revelation 2:4*

"Then Jesus wept"
John 11:35

The author believes that Jesus may well weep when he looks down
at this country that has been so blessed.

A country founded by Godly men and a nation birthed to serve and
glorify Him....and a nation that has so turned its back on Him.

With God, prayer, and the Bible relentlessly being removed from
public life, we see an America in disarray. Pornography flourishes,
abortion on demand, teenage pregnancies and violence are at an
all-time high.

Drugs are rampant, our divorce rate is as high in Christian families as
they are in non-Christian. Personal bankruptcies continue to increase.

America is now a debtor nation, and we have lost the respect of much
of the free world.

As this book goes to press America is plagued by earthquakes, floods,
mortgage foreclosures, bankruptcies, an economy in disarray and
legislation against Biblical precepts.

What other calamities may fall our once great America, if we do not
return God to the important place He once had in this land?

The author truly believes that America is in a spiritual battle for its very own existence. We are ignoring all the warning signs.

Except for notables such as John Hagee, the late Dr. James Kennedy, (the author had the pleasure of ministering at his church), Jack Van Impe, Charles Stanley, and James Dobson, the "church" is a silent non-entity.

As previously mentioned, "name it and claim it," "praying in the dark," "visualization exercises," and "chanting" are infiltrating our churches.

"For a time is coming when people will no longer listen to sound and wholesome teaching. They will follow their own desires and will look for teachers who will tell them whatever their itching ears want to hear They will reject the truth and chase after myths." 2 Timothy 4:3-4

"For false messiahs and false prophets will rise up and perform great signs and wonders so as to deceive, if possible, even God's chosen ones." Matthew 24: 24

What should have been a huge "wake-up" call came on Sept 11, 2001: The destruction of the Twin Towers I n New York City.

THIS WAS OUR SECOND 911. WILL THERE BE A THIRD?

"Thus, says the Lord GOD: 'A disaster, unique disaster, behold it is coming!'" Ezekiel: 7:8

Note what appears to be the Devil in the preceding photos.

The author is convinced that it was not a coincidence that this tragic event happened on a day whose number "911" is known by all Americans as a cry for help.

(Remember, our first "911" was greeted with a yawn.)

Many of the pictures taken that fateful day, purport to show the Devil. Is this a coincidence as well? The author does not so believe.

There was one brief shiny spiritual moment when there was a huge upsurge in church attendance. Sadly, this only lasted a short time.

What new disaster must befall our country before we turn back to God?

The author believes God may have had America in mind with the following passages from *Jeremiah18: 7-12*

"7 At what instant I shall speak concerning a nation, and concerning a kingdom, to pluck up, and to pull down, and to destroy it;

8 If that nation, against whom I have pronounced, turn from their evil ways, I will repent of the evil that I thought to do unto them.

9 And at what instant I shall speak concerning a nation, and concerning a kingdom, to build and to plant it;

10 If it do evil in my sight, that it obey not my voice, then I will repent of the good, wherewith I said I would benefit them.

11 Now therefore go to, speak to the men of Judah, and to the inhabitants of Jerusalem, saying, thus saith the Lord; Behold, I frame evil against you, and devise a device against you: return ye now everyone from his evil way, and make your ways and your doings good.

12 But they will say "No use! We will follow our own devices; each one of us will behave according to the stubbornness of his evil heart!"

ISRAEL IS OUR ALLY

"Do not forsake your friend or your fathers' friend. " Prov. 27:11

Israel is America's future. We have always been its staunchest ally and have done so in the face of formidable opposition. Several Jews were very active during the American Revolution.

One such man was **Haym Solomon**. He was a financial broker. He helped convert the French loans into ready cash by selling bills of exchange for Robert Morris, the Superintendent of Finance.

In this way, he aided the Continental Army and was possibly, along with Morris, the prime financier of the American side during the American Revolution. He was a member of the "Sons of Liberty."

He even personally loaned money to many prominent Americans. He was instrumental in obtaining financing for Washington's army. He was arrested several times as a spy and was sentenced to die but managed to escape.

On March 25th, 1975, in time for the bicentennial, the United State Post Office issued a commemorative postage stamp which honored him as **a** Revolutionary War hero. It depicted him seated at a desk.

The front side of the stamp has the words *"Financial Hero".* And, for only the second time in 143 years of U.S. stamps, a message appeared on the back of this stamp, reading:

"Businessman and broker Haym Salomon was responsible for raising most of the money needed to finance the American Revolution and later to save the new nation from collapse. "

Christians and all of Americans for that matter, have a very selfish, self-motivated reason to want Israel to survive and prosper and that is simply that Jews are God's chosen people. Period, exclamation point!

Israel became a new nation in May of 1948, thus fulfilling the last prophecy that had to occur before Jesus returns.

The Bible is full of warnings of dire consequences for those who are against Israel.

"For the nation and kingdom that will not serve you shall perish; those nations shall be utterly laid waist."   *Isaiah 60:12*

"Comfort my people, says your God. Speak tenderly to Jerusalem, and cry to her that her war, fare is ended, that her iniquity is pardoned, that she has received from the LORD's hand double for all her sins."
                                                                Isaiah 40: 1
" A voice cries: 'the wilderness prepares the way of the LORD; make straight in the desert a highway for our God.' "   *Isaiah 40: 4*

'Every valley shall be lifted, and every mountain and hill be made low; the uneven ground shall become level, and the rough places a plain.

And the glory of the LORD shall be revealed, and all flesh shall see it together, for the mouth of the LORD has spoken."   *Isaiah 40:5*

JEDIDIAH MORSE WARNING FOR AMERICA?

Jedidiah Morse (1761–1826) was pastor of the First Congregational Church in Charlestown, Mass., 1789–1819, and a staunch defender of orthodoxy within the Congregational church.

The author believes the following is a message for **America** today.

In 1799 he made these remarks when he was preaching at a Massachusetts church:

"*Our* danger are of two kinds, those that affect our religion and those that affect our government. They are, however, so closely allied that they cannot, with propriety, be separated.

"The foundations which supports the interest of Christianity, are also necessary to support a free and equal government like our own.

"In all those countries where there is little or no religion, or a very gross and corrupt one...there you will find, with scarcely a single exception, arbitrary and tyrannical governments, gross ignorance and wickedness, and deplorable wretchedness among the people.

"To the Kindly influence of Christianity, we owe to that degree of civil freedom, and political and social happiness which mankind now enjoy.

"In proportion as the genuine effects of Christianity are diminished in any nation, either through unbelief, or the corruption of its doctrines, or the neglect of its institutions: in the same proportion, will the people of that nation recede from the blessings of genuine freedom, and approximate the miseries of despotism.

"I hold this to be a truth confirmed by experience.

"If so, it follows, that all efforts made to destroy the foundations of our holy religion, ultimately tend to the subversion also of our political freedom and happiness.

"Whenever the pillars of Christianity shall be overthrown, our present republican forms of government, and all the blessing's which flow from them, must fall with them."   132

"Communities are dealt with in this world by the wise and just Ruler of the Universe. He rewards or punishes them according to their general character."   Samuel Adams 133

"As nations cannot be rewarded or punished in the next world, so they must be in this. By an inevitable chain of causes and effect, Providence punishes national sins by national calamities."

George Mason   134

As our nation is sliding increasingly into an amoral abyss, the question becomes "Where is God?"

As previously mentioned, Pastors are arrested for having Bible in their homes. Bibles are removed from Hospitals; Chaplains no longer welcome in some facilities.

Sex books replace Gideon's Bibles in hotel/motel rooms. Banished from just about everywhere, He still has his hand on this country. But for how long I wonder. Why is He letting these things happen you ask?

The National Defense Act of 2017 contains a provision that allows for "indefinite confinement" of American citizens **without a trial.**

"The Lord himself will fight for you."   *Exodus 14: 14*

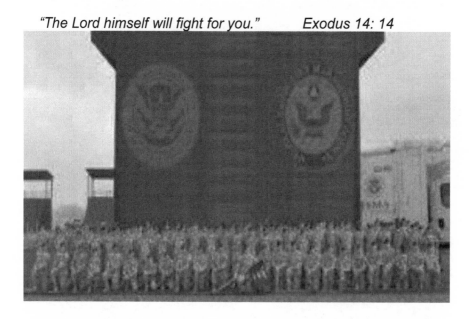

Why the need for "watch towers" and barbed wire? **Why are the uniforms different from America's Armed Forces?**

Former Governor Jesse Ventura did his own research and reported that he saw hundreds of coffins being transported to one of these camps.

WHY THE NEED FOR COFFINS? WHY WAS THEIR EXISTENCE DENIED FOR ALLTHOSE YEARS? MORE IMPORTANTLY, WHAT IS THE REAL REASON FOR THEM?

Reader, do your own research on this and based upon how the Holy Spirit leads you, take whatever precautionary steps you feel is necessary to protect you and your family. Utilize Google in your search.

"But it was because of the false brethren secretly brought in, who had sneaked in to spy out our liberty which we have in Christ Jesus, in order to bring us into bondage."   135

John Adams: "Have you ever found in history; One Single example of a nation thoroughly corrupted that was ever restored to virtue?" 136

Robert Schuller: "Tough times never last, but tough people do."
                                                                                137
Edmund Burke: "The only way for evil men to prosper is for good men to do nothing."   138

Benjamin Franklin: "those who would give up a little bit of liberty for temporary freedom deserve neither."   139

Thomas Jefferson:" And what country can preserve it's liberties if their rulers are not warned from time to time that their people preserve the spirit of resistance? **The tree of liberty must be refreshed from time to time with the blood of patriots and tyrants.**   140

Are you willing to die for your faith, rather than denounce it, so you may live longer? All Christians, including the author may face that question someday.

The author believes that Psalms 11 is prophetic for what Christians will be going through during these end times:

In the LORD put I my trust: how say ye to my soul, Flee as a bird to your mountain?

2 For, lo, the wicked bend their bow, they make ready their arrow upon the string, that they may privily shoot at the upright in heart.

3 If the foundations be destroyed, what can the righteous do?

4 The LORD is in his holy temple, the LORD's throne is in heaven: his eyes behold, his eyelids try, the children of men.

5 The LORD trieth the righteous: but the wicked and him that loveth violence his soul hateth.

6 Upon the wicked he shall rain snares, fire and brimstone, and an horrible tempest: this shall be the portion of their cup.

7 For the righteous LORD loveth righteousness; his countenance doth behold the upright.

Reader, be comforted by *Psalms 23 : 4,6*

4Even though I walk through the valley of the shadow of death I will fear no evil, for you are with me; your rod and your staff, they comfort me.

6Surely goodness and mercy shall follow me the rest of my life and I will dwell in the house of the Lord forever."

CHAPTER 23: FIGHT TO SAVE AMERICA

The author firmly believes the solution to this problem is to put prayer, the Bible and Jesus Christ, back in the classrooms of the United States of America. God still holds out the olive branch:

"if my people, who are called by my name, will humble themselves, pray and seek my face and turn from their wicked ways then I will heal their call from Heaven, and I will heal their land". 2 Chronicles 7:14

Let's examine the above Bible verse.

IF
We know something big is coming when a passage begins with "IF".

MY PEOPLE, WHO ARE CALLED BY MY NAME
He is talking about Christians: people who have accepted Jesus as their Lord and Savior.

WILL HUMBLE THEMSELVES
Webster defines "HUMBLE" s lowering one's esteem of themselves. In this case, meaning not putting ourselves first. (Pride goeth before the fall.)

PRAY, AND SEEK MY FACE
He is calling us to get on our knees and truly seek His Will.

AND TURN FROM THEIR WICKED WAYS
Ouch. We say we are Christians, but we need to ask for forgiveness for our not always being obedient to His word.

THEN I WILL HEAR THEIR CALL FROM HEAVEN,
If we do all the above, then Jesus says he will listen or hear us.

AND I WILL HEAL THEIR LAND

Does America as a nation have a need for healing? Reader, how do you answer that question?

The often-lamentable cry : "I am only person. What can I do?"

GOD IS LOOKING FOR

The Reader may or may not be thinking this: "God cannot use me. If you knew the things I have done." Stop right now.

We are all sinners and God has always used a sinner in a mighty way.

Throughout history, God has chosen men to do an extreme act of courage. In each case, all had at least one major sin.

Remember the story of Gideon. He was hiding in a wine vat, trembling with fear.

Then he hears God's voice: "Thy great and mighty warrior." Gideon questions God at length doubting that it was really Him.

Gideon goes from being a coward to a mighty man of God.

David is a mere shepherd boy, armed only with a sling shot and five stones he kills the "giant of giants": Goliath.

There were thousands of soldiers in the Israeli army who were afraid to face him. But one brave lad did.

This is the same David who had an affair when he was King and made sure the husband lost his life in battle. Thus he was a defacto murderer.

Moses killed an Arab. Yet Moses led the people to the promised

Land and he wrote the 10 Commandments.

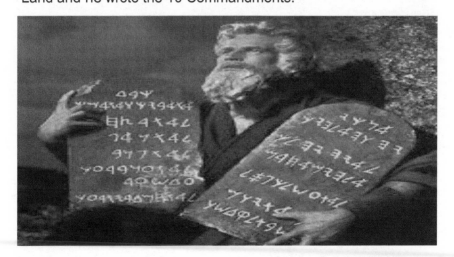

Paul persecuted Christians and held Stephen's cloak when he was being stoned. But God used him to become a teacher and write numerous books in the Bible!

While the author's website, hurleypatriot.org, has under "Your Role" numerous suggestions, here are but a few:

1. Become a precinct chairman.

2. Become a volunteer on a Christian's staff who is running for election.

3. Run for your school board, attend school board meetings, examine the curriculum, you may be shocked.

4. Become educated and volunteer to speak at Rotary, Optimists and Kiwanis clubs.

5. Give your Pastor a copy of this book, encourage him to become better informed.

6. Teach a class at your church on our American Heritage.

7. Pray like you have never prayed before.

8. Take your children out of public schools and send them to Charter schools or Home School them.

Be comforted by *Psalms 9: 7-16*

7A thousand may fall at your side,
And ten thousand at your right hand;
But it shall not come near you.
[88] Only with your eyes shall you look,
And see the reward of the wicked.

[9] Because you have made the LORD, who is my refuge,
Even the Highest, your dwelling place,

[10] No evil shall befall you, Nor shall any plague come near your

[11] For He shall give His angels charge over you, To keep you in all your ways.

[12] In their hands they shall bear you up, Lest you dash your foot against a stone.

[13] *You shall tread upon the lion and the cobra,*
The young lion and the serpent you shall trample underfoot

[14] *"Because he has set his love upon Me, therefore I will deliver him ;*
I will set him on high, because he has known My name.

[15] *He shall call upon Me, and I will answer him, I will be with him in*
trouble; will deliver him and honor him.

[16] *With long life I will satisfy him And show him My salvation.*

REMEMBER THE ALAMO

" We are hard pressed on every side, but not crushed; perplexed,
not in despair; persecuted, but not abandoned; struck down, but not
destroyed."   *2nd Corinthians 4: 8*

Almost everyone has heard the phrase "Remember the Alamo."

The founding of The Republic of Texas in many ways parallels
that of the founding of America. They rebelled against an
unjust tax system and had to deal with gun control.

Texas is of course now part of the United States (though most
Texans would dispute that.)

The Texicans (as they were called then) were in a war with Mexico to
gain their independence. They had been rebelling against a very
unjust tax system imposed by the government of Mexico.

The revolution began in 1836 and the most memorable event in the fight for freedom was a siege that occurred at a Catholic diocese near the town of San Antonio called The Alamo.

These Texans were made up in large numbers by an influx of people from Tennessee, the most notable being Davy Crockett who had served in the United States Congress.

There were 187 defenders in the Alamo pitted against the Mexican army under General Santa Ana who had over 2000 soldiers.

Santa Ana had issued an order for immediate and unconditional surrender or all the defenders would be put to death. He kept his word, just as Texans who had surrendered at previous battles were also put to death.

Travis's last letter for help as gone down in history as one of the most patriotic documents dealing with fighting for liberty.

"Fellow citizens and compatriots;
Fellow citizens, I am besieged, by a thousand or more of the Mexicans under Santa Anna. I have sustained a continual Bombardment and cannonade for 24 hours and have not lost a man. The enemy has demanded a surrender at discretion, otherwise, the garrison are to be put to the sword, if the fort is taken.

"I have answered the demand with a cannon shot, and our flag still waves proudly from the walls. **I shall never surrender or retreat**. Then, **I call on you in the name of Liberty, of patriotism & everything dear to the American character,** to come to our aid, with all dispatch. The enemy is receiving reinforcements daily and will no doubt increase to three or four thousand in four or five days.

"If this call is neglected, **I am determined to sustain myself as long as possible and die like a soldier who never forgets what is due to his own honor & that of his country. _Victory or Death_.**
William Barret Travis
Lt. Col. Commanding

"P.S. The Lord is on our side. When the enemy appeared in sight, we had not three bushels of corn. We have since found in deserted houses 80 or 90 bushels and got into the walls 20 or 30 head of Beeves."

At the "moment of truth" Travis gathered all of the forces under his command and drew the infamous **"line in the sand."**

He asked that those who wished to stay and fight and thus help delay the Mexican forces from pursuing General Sam Houston to step across the line. All but one did.

"Be on the alert, stand firm in the faith, act like men, be strong."
I Corinthians 16: 13

"Line in the Sand" James Muir Artist www.jamesmuir.com

Santa Ana and his army crushed the Texans. Every defender was killed. This was a classic case of "winning the battle" but "losing the war." Santa Ana lost 700 men during this 14-day siege, and it gave Sam Houston time to regroup and organize his main army.

On April 21, 1836, (in the "shot heard round Texas") Houston routed Santa Ana at the Battle of San Jacinto with a loss of only two men and Texas became an independent nation. **What can the reader learn from the story about The Alamo?**

The lesson is that in similar incidents throughout history, a minority of brave men were willing to take a stand for what they believed in, fought and gave their lives so that others could be free .**One day we may all be asked to step across a "line in the sand."**

PLEA FROM THE PAST ©

DR LANCE HURLEY

I WAS THINKING OF OUR FOREFATHERS THE OTHER DAY
I BEGAN TO PONDER, WHAT WOULD THEY SAY?

WHAT WOULD THEY SAY WE HAVE DONE WITHT THEIIR VISION
AS CHRISTIAN AMERICA COMES UNDER ATTACK AND DERISION?

I SEE THEM ASSEMBLED: WASHINGTON, JEFFERSON, AND THE
REST.THEIR MOOD IS   SOMBER, SAD, AND DISTRESSED

THEIR CLOTHES ARE TATTERED, THEY STAND FIRM AND PROUD
THEY NOW BEGIN TO SPEAK, SO ELOQUENTLY AND LOUD

HEAR OUR PLEA! THEY CRY OUT AS WITH ONE VOICE
CHRISTIAN AMERICA, YOU NOW HAVE A CHOICE!

WE FOUGHT AGAINST TYRANNY TO BE FREE! NOT A SLAVE
TO RAISE A FLAG OF FREEDOM THAT O'ER YOUR LAND WOULD
ALWAYS WAVE!

WITH A STRONG FAITH IN GOD, THE SUPREME HEAD OF OUR
LAND,   WE WROTE THE CONSTITUTION WITH HIS LOVING,
GUIDING HAND!

FOR OVER 200 YEARS THE SACRIFICES, HARDSHIPS AND
PRICES WE PAID,
ENSURED AMERICA WOULD ALWAYS BE THE LAND OF THE FREE
AND THE BRAVE.

BUT IN NINETEEN SIXTY-TWO, SIX MEN MADE A DECISION
THAT HAS TURNED YOUR NATION INTO ONE WITH MUCH
DIVISION!

"SEPARATION OF CHURCH AND STATE;" THESE EVIL MEN DID
PROCLAIM,
 THIS WOULD BE THE NEW LAW OF THE LAND, MUCH TO YOUR
SHAME!

THIS BALD-FACED LIE, BASED ON JEFFERSON'S LETTER, NOT
YOUR CONSTITUTION;
HAS STRUCK AND RENDERED THE VERY FABRIC OF AMERICA'S
CHRISTIAN INSTITUTION.

THE ACLU HAS TAKEN UP A MISSION WITH UTMOST GLEE
TO REMOVE ALL MENTION OF GOD FROM AMERICA'S HISTORY!

THE ATTACK AGAINST THE TEN COMMANDMENTS AND THE
PLEDGE OF ALLEGIANCE,
SHOWS THAT THE DEVIL AND HIS LEGIONS HATE AMERICA WITH
A VENGENANCE

LINCOLN SAID THE TEACHINGS IN A CLASSROOM IN ONE
GENERATION
WOULD BECOME THE PHILOSOPHY IN THE FUTURE OF THAT
SCHOOL'S NATION

THE BIBLE AND PRAYER BANISHED FROM ANY GOVERNMENT
SCHOOL,
REMOVAL OF ALL THINGS "CHRISTIAN" HAS BECOME THE NEW
GOLDEN RULE.

THE DECLARATION OF INDEPENDENCE, UPON WHICH OUR
REVOLUTION WAS BASED;
DUE TO ITS MENTION OF GOD, FROM MANY CLASSROOMS NOW
ERASED.

TAKING CHRIST OUT OF CHRISTMAS, YULETIDE SCENES
FORBIDDEN,
IT IS CLEAR SATAN'S AGENDA NO LONGER IS HIDDEN.

AS EVIL MEN CONTINUE TO REMOVE GOD FROM YOUR DAILY
LIFE,
YOU AS A NATION LABOR UNDER STRESS AND STRIFE!

YOU HAVE BECOME A WORLD LEADER IN ABORTIONS, DRUGS,
PORNOGRAPHY, AND DIVORCE.
CAN YOU HEAR OUR VOICES PLEADING: WAKE UP!
TAKE ACTION, CHANGE YOUR COURSE!

HAVE YOU FORGOTTEN AMERICAS MOTTO: "IN GOD WE
TRUST"?
OR ARE YOU NOW TOO FOCUSED ON GREED, PRIDE AND
 LUST?

YOUR VISION GONE, YOU ARE BECOMING LESS THAN A SLAVE
 IN THIS, THE LAND OF THE FREE AND THE HOME OF THE
BRAVE!

YOUR LEADERS ARE PUSHING YOU INTO THE NEW WORLD
ORDER
WHERE BETWEEN AMERICA, CANADA, AND MEXICO WILL BE
 NO BORDER.

AMERICAS SACRED CONSTITUTION, THE SUPREME LAW OF
 THE LAND
WILL BE BUT A FOOTNOTE IN HISTORY, MERELY WRITTEN ON
THE SAND.

PASTORS RETREAT FROM THE GODLY TENANTS OFTHEIR
SECT
AFRAID TO BE BOLD, FOR FEAR OF BEING POLITICALLY
INCORRECT

 FIGHT TO KEEP GOD IN AMERICA, PLEASE HEAR OUR CRY!
TO STAY GOD'S ANGRY JUDGEMENT, IT IS NOW DO OR DIE.

HOW LONG WILL GOD WAIT, AS YOU TREMBLE, WATCH, TOO
AFRAID TO FIGHT?
AS TYRANTS TRAMPLE YOUR GOD GIVEN FREEDOM'S MUCH
TO SATAN'S DELIGHT!

CHRISTIAN AMERICA, ARISE FROM YOUR SLUMBER, PRAY AND
FIGHT!
SO YOU CAN KEEP THE TORCH OF FREEDOM BURNING BRIGHT!

YOUR CAUSE IT IS JUST, TOO CONQUER YOU MUST
OR AMERICA, AS A NATION WILL WITHER AND RUST!

THE FUTURE OF AMERICA IS UP TO YOU CHRISTIAN SOLDIER
WILL YOU STAND WITH YOUR BROTHERS, SHOULDER TO
SHOULDER?

OUR PRAYERS ARE WITH YOU IN THIS UNCERTAIN TIME
IT IS AN UPHILL BATTLE......ONE YOU MUST CLIMB!

THE TIME HAS COME TO TAKE ACTION, TO BE BOLD AND BRAVE
IF THE FREEDOM OF AMERICA, YOU WISH TO SAVE!

GOD WILL GUIDE, LOVE AND PROTECT YOU FROM HARM
AS YOU TAKE AN ACTIVE ROLE IN SOUNDING THE ALARM!

THE FUTURE OF YOUR AMERICA WILL DEPEND ON WHAT YOU DO
STAND AND WATCH OR GET IN THE FIGHT......IT IS UP TO YOU!

THE CHOICE IS YOURS: WILL YOUR CHILDREN BE FREE OR LIVE A
SLAVE?
IN THIS, THE LAND OF THE FREE AND THE HOME OF THE BRAVE!

THEIR WORDS WERE SOMBER, THEY RANG IN MY EARS
I STOOD THERE IN AWE WITH MY EYES FULL OF TEARS

AS THEY LEFT ME TO REFLECT ON THEIR ANGUISHED CRY
I HEARD ONE LAST QUESTION, AS I WAVED GOODBYE

WHEN YOU STAND BEFORE JESUS CHRIST ON JUDGEMENT DAY

WHAT IS IT ABOUT YOUR LIFE THAT YOU WILL WANT HIM TO SAY?
THAT YOU SAT ON THE SIDELINES, TREMBLING WITH
FRIGHT

OR THOU GOOD AND FAITHFUL SERVANT

YOU FOUGHT THE GOOD FIGHT?

WINSTON CHURCHILL

Churchill was Prime Minister of Great Britain during WWII.
Via radio he encouraged his countrymen to remain vigilant, to stay
the course and fight the good fight against a merciless Godless enemy.

"Since we have such a hope, we are very bold..." II Cor. 3: 12

These are excerpts from some of his famous speeches during that time:

"We shall fight them on the beaches, we shall fight on the landing
grounds, we shall fight in the fight fields and in the streets, we shall fight
in the hills; we shall never surrender." House of Commons, 04/01/1940

"Never give in; never give in; never, never, never, never--in nothing great
or small, large or petty--never give in except to convictions of honor and
good sense. Never yield to force; never yield to the apparently over
whelming might of the enemy." Harrow School 10/28/1940

"If you will not fight, when your victory can be achieved without
bloodshed, if you will not fight when your victory will be sure and so
costly, you may come to the moment when you will have to fight with all
the odds against you and only a precarious chance for survival.

"There may be a worse case: **You may have to fight when there is no
chance for victory, because it is better to perish than to live as
slaves.**" 142

EDMUND BURKE

The Author closes with words of wisdom not from a Founding Father, but from a member of King George III's Parliament!!

"The words of a wise man are gracious..." Eccl.10: 12

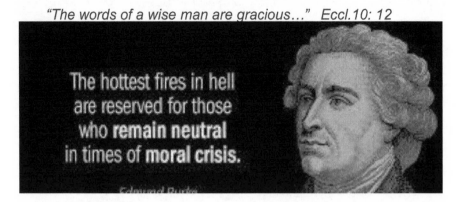

The hottest fires in hell are reserved for those who **remain neutral** in times of **moral crisis.**

Edmund Burke, who served in Parliament from 1766 to 1794, is well known for some famous quotes. Among them are:

"Nobody made a greater mistake than he who did nothing because he could only do little."

"All tyranny needs to gain a foothold is for people of good conscience remain silent."

"The people never give up their liberties but under some delusion."

"Nothing .turns out to be more oppressive than a feeble government."

"Those who don't know history, are doomed to repeat it."

There are two sayings the author remembers from childhood:

"When the going gets tough the tough get going." "If it is to be, it is up to me."

God said that he would have spared Sodom and Gomorrah if He could but find one righteous man. One righteous man. Didn't happen. **How about you? Are you that righteous man/woman?**

FIRST STEP TO COMPLETE FREEDOM

"It was for your freedom that Christ died, stand firm and never again be subject to a yoke of slavery." Gal. 5: 1

The author has discussed at great length the price our Founding Fathers paid to give us the freedoms of security that we have and enjoy today.

Now it is time to pay homage to the original founding fathers: a ragtag group of fishermen, storekeepers, a doctor, et cetera who were led by an itinerant preacher/carpenter.

All but one of these died horrible deaths, and he died an outcast on a deserted island. They paid the ultimate price so that we could have the freedom of eternal life with Jesus in Heaven.

This is my last question: Have you accepted Jesus Christ as your Lord and Savior?

If not, do not let this moment go by before making the most important decision that you will ever make in your life.

Jesus died on the cross, and the blood he shed on Calvary was to wash away your sins. Yes, your sins and for all of mankind.

The Bible tells us that *"For all have sinned and fallen short of the glory of the Lord." Romans 3:23*

God does not want you to die and go to Hell for eternity. He wants you to reign in Heaven with Him.

"But the gift of God is eternal life through Jesus Christ our Lord."
Romans 6: 23.

"If you will confess with thy mouth the Lord Jesus, and shalt believe in thine heart that god raised him from the dead, thou shalt be saved   … For whosoever shall call upon the name of the Lord shall I be saved."   *Romans 10: 9,10,13.*

Lord Jesus, I confess to you that I am a sinner.

I know that you died for me, that the blood you shed washed away my sins. I now call upon you to forgive my sins and ask you to come into my heart and save me.

I accept you as my Lord and Savior and from this day on I will follow you.   I make this promise willingly and without any reservation.

Thank you, Jesus, for dying for me. I will now my live for you.

Signed   Date

If you accepted Jesus as your Lord and Savior, please drop me a line at Lhurley55@gmail.com and let me know.   I want to hear from you. Dr. Hurley

APPENDIX I

DECLARATION OF COLONIAL RIGHTS: RESOLUTIONS OF THE FIRST CONTINENTAL CONGRESS OCTOBER 14, 1774

[Following the Boston Tea Party and the adoption of the Intolerable Acts, delegates gathered on September 5, 1774, at Philadelphia, in what was to become the First Continental Congress

Every colony but Georgia was represented.

They voted on September 6 to appoint a committee "to state the rights of the Colonies in general, the several instances in which these rights are violated or infringed, and the means most proper to be pursued for obtaining a restoration of them" (Journals of the Continental Congress, 1774-1789, Washington, 1904, I, 26).

Joseph Galloway (173l -1803), a Philadelphia merchant and lawyer, led a conservative attempt to unite the colonies within the Empire.

He had served as speaker of the Pennsylvania Assembly from 1776 to 1774. In the war, Galloway supported the British cause and after 1778 became spokesman for the Loyalists in England.

In the First Continental Congress the more radical delegates thrust aside Galloway's proposal and on October 14 adopted instead, by unanimous action, the Declaration of Colonial Rights reproduced here.

The first draft of these resolutions was written by Major John Sullivan (1740-95), delegate from New Hampshire, lawyer, major of the New Hampshire militia, major general in the Continental Army, judge, and eventually governor of his state.

Before they dissolved, on October 26, the members voted to meet again in the same city on May 10, 1775, "unless the redress of grievances ... be obtained before that time."

The Congress met according to adjournment, and resuming the consideration of the subject under debate -- came into the following resolutions:

Whereas, since the close of the last war, the British Parliament, claiming a power of right to bind the people of America, by statute in all cases whatsoever, hath in some acts expressly imposed taxes on them, and in others, under various pretenses, but in fact for the purpose of raising a revenue, hath imposed rates and duties payable in these colonies, established a board of commissioners, with unconstitutional powers, and extended the jurisdiction of courts of admiralty, not only for collecting the said duties, but for the trial of causes merely arising within the body of a county.

And whereas, in consequence of other statutes, judges, who before held only estates at will in their offices, have been made dependent upon the crown alone for their salaries, and standing armies kept in times of peace:

And it has lately been resolved in Parliament, that by force of a statute, made in the thirty-fifth year of the reign of King Henry the Eighth, colonists may be transported to England, and tried there upon accusations for treasons, and misprisions, or concealments of treasons committed in the colonies; and by a late statute, such trials have been directed in cases therein mentioned.

And whereas, in the last session of Parliament, three statutes were made; one, entitled "An act to discontinue, in such manner and for such time as are therein mentioned, the landing and discharging, lading, or shipping of goods, wares and merchandise, at the town, and within the harbor of Boston, in the province of Massachusetts Bay, in North America"; another, entitled "

An act for the better regulating the government of the province of the Massachusetts Bay in New England"; and another, entitled

"An act for the impartial administration of justice, in the cases of persons questioned for any act done by them in the execution of the law, or for the suppression of riots and tumults, in the province of the Massachusetts Bay, in New England.

And another statute was then made, "for making more effectual provision for the government of the province of Quebec, etc."
All which statutes are impolitic, unjust, and cruel, as well as unconstitutional, and most dangerous and destructive of American rights.

And whereas, assemblies have been frequently dissolved, contrary to the rights of the people, when they attempted to deliberate on grievances; and their dutiful, humble, loyal, and reasonable petitions to the crown for redress have been repeatedly treated with contempt by His Majesty's ministers of state:

The good people of the several colonies of New Hampshire, Massachusetts Bay, Rhode Island, and Providence Plantations, Connecticut, New York, New Jersey, Pennsylvania, Newcastle, Kent and Sussex on Delaware, Maryland, Virginia, North Carolina, and South Carolina, justly alarmed at these arbitrary proceedings of Parliament and administration, have severally elected, constituted, and appointed deputies to meet and sit in General Congress, in the city of Philadelphia, to obtain such establishment, as that their religion, laws, and liberties may not be subverted:

Whereupon the deputies so appointed being now assembled, in a full and free representation of these colonies, taking into their most serious consideration, the best means of attaining the ends aforesaid, do, in the first place, as Englishmen, their ancestors in like cases have usually done, for asserting and vindicating their rights and liberties, declare,

That the inhabitants of the English Colonies in North America, by the immutable laws of nature, the principles of the English constitution, and the several charters or compacts, have the following rights:

Resolved, N.C.D. _1. That they are entitled to life, liberty, and property, and they have never ceded to any sovereign power whatever, a right to dispose of either without their consent.

Resolved, N.C.D. 2. That our ancestors, who first settled these colonies, were, at the time of their emigration from the mother country, entitled to all the rights, liberties, and immunities of free and natural-born subjects, within the realm of England.
, N.C.D. 3. That by such emigration they by no means forfeited, surrendered, or lost any of those rights, but that they were, and their descendants now are, entitled to the exercise and enjoyment of all such of them, as their local and other circumstances enable them to exercise and enjoy.

Resolved that government, is a right in the people to participate in their legislative council: and as the English colonists are not represented, and from their local and other circumstances, cannot properly be represented in the British Parliament, they are entitled to a free and exclusive power of legislation in their several provincial legislatures, where their right of representation can alone be preserved, in all cases of taxation and internal polity, subject only to the negative of their sovereign, in such manner as has been heretofore used and accustomed. But, from the necessity of the case, and a regard to the mutual interest of both countries, we cheerfully consent to the operation of such acts of the British Parliament, as are bona fide, restrained to the regulation of our external commerce, for the purpose of securing the commercial advantages of the whole empire to the mother-country, and the commercial benefits of its respective members; excluding every idea of taxation, internal or external, for raising a revenue on the subjects in America, without their consent.

Resolved, N.C.D. 5. That the respective colonies are entitled to the common law of England, and more especially to the great and inestimable privilege of being tried by their peers of the vicinage, according to the course of that law.

Resolved, 6. That they are entitled to the benefit of such of the English statutes as existed at the time of their colonization; and which they have, by experience, respectively found to be applicable to their several local and other circumstances.

Resolved, N.C.D. 7. That these His Majesty's colonies, are likewise entitled to all the immunities and privileges granted and confirmed to them by royal charters or secured by their several codes of provincial laws.

Resolved, N.C.D. 8. That they have a right peaceably to assemble, consider of their grievances, and petition the king; and that all prosecutions, prohibitory proclamations, and commitments for the same are illegal.

Resolved, N. C. D. 9 That the keeping of standing armies in the colonies, in times of peace, without the consent of the legislature is against the law. And rendered essential by the English constitution, that the constituent branches of the legislature be independent of each other; that, therefore, the exercise of the legislative power in several colonies, by a council appointed, during pleasure, by the crown, is unconstitutional, dangerous, and destructive to the freedom of American legislation.

All and each of which the aforesaid deputies, in behalf of themselves and their constituents, do claim, demand, and insist on, as their indubitable rights and liberties; which cannot be legally taken from them, altered or abridged by any power whatever, without their own consent, by their representatives in their several provincial legislatures.

violations of the foregoing rights, which, from an ardent desire, that harmony and mutual intercourse of affection and interest may be restored, we pass over for the present, and proceed to state such acts and measures as have been adopted since the last war, which demonstrate a system formed to enslave America.
Resolved, N.C.D. That the following acts of Parliament are infringements and violations of the rights of the colonists; and that the repeal of them is essentially necessary to restore harmony between Great Britain and the American colonies, viz.:

The several acts of 4 Geo. 3, Ch. 15, and Ch. 34. -- 5 Geo. 3, Ch. 25. - 6 Geo. 3, Ch. 52. -- 7 Geo. 3, Ch. 41, and Ch. 46. -- 8 Geo. 3, Ch. 22, which impose duties for the purpose of raising a revenue in America, extend the powers of the admiralty courts beyond their ancient limits, deprive the American subject of trial by jury, authorize the judges' certificate to indemnify the prosecutor from damages, that he might otherwise be liable to, requiring oppressive security from a claimant of ships and goods seized, before he shall be allowed to defend his property, and are subversive of American rights.

Also the 12 Geo. 3, Ch. 24, entitled "An act for the better securing His Majesty's dockyards, magazines, ships, ammunition, and stores," which declares a new offense in America, and deprives the American subject of a constitutional trial by a jury of the vicinage, by authorizing the trial of any person, charged with the committing any offense described in the said act, out of the realm, to be indicted and tried for the same in any shire or county within the realm.

Also, the three acts passed in the last session of Parliament, for stopping the port and blocking up the harbor of Boston, for altering the charter and government of the Massachusetts Bay, and that which is entitled "An act for the better administration of justice," etc.

Also, the act passed in the same session for establishing the Roman Catholic religion in the Province of Quebec, abolishing the equitable system of English laws, and erecting a tyranny there, to the great danger, from so total a dissimilarity of religion, law, and government of the neighboring British colonies, by the assistance of whose blood and treasure the said country was conquered from France.
Also, the act passed in the same session for the better providing suitable quarters for officers and soldiers in His Majesty's service in North America.

Also, that the keeping a standing army in several of these colonies, in time of peace, without the consent of the legislature of that colony in which such army is kept, is against law.
To these grievous acts and measures, Americans cannot submit, but in hopes that their fellow-subjects in Great Britain will, on a revision of them, restore us to that state in which both countries found happiness and prosperity, we have for the present only resolved to pursue the following peaceable measures:

Resolved, unanimously, that from and after the first day of December next, there be no importation into British America, from Great Britain or Ireland of any goods, wares or merchandise whatsoever, or from any other place of any such goods, wares or merchandise.

1st. To enter a nonimportation, nonconsummation, and nonexportation agreement or association. 2. To prepare an address to the people of Great Britain, and a memorial to the inhabitants of British America, and 3. To prepare a loyal address to His Majesty; agreeable to resolutions already entered into.

APPENDIX II

A DECLARATION BY THE REPRESENTATIVES OF THE UNITED COLONIES OF NORTH AMERICA, NOW MET IN CONGRESS AT PHILADELPHIA, SETTING FORTH THE CAUSES AND NECESSITIES OF THEIR TAKING UP ARMS ADOPTED BY THE SECOND CONTINENTAL CONGRESS' MAY 1775

If it was possible for men, who exercise their reason to believe, that the divine Author of our existence intended a part of the human race to hold an absolute property in, and an unbounded power over others, marked out by his infinite goodness and wisdom, as the objects of a legal domination never rightfully resistible, however severe and oppressive, the inhabitants of these colonies might at least require from the parliament of Great-Britain some evidence, that this dreadful authority over them, has been granted to that body.

But a reverence for our Creator, principles of humanity, and the dictates of common sense, must convince all those who reflect upon the subject, that government was instituted to promote the welfare of mankind, and ought to be administered for the attainment of that end.

The legislature of Great-Britain, however, stimulated by an inordinate passion for a power not only unjustifiable, but which they know to be peculiarly reprobated by the very constitution of that kingdom, and desperate of success in any mode of contest, where regard should be had to truth, law, or right, have at length, deserting those, attempted to effect their cruel and impolitic purpose of enslaving these colonies by violence, and have thereby rendered it necessary for us to close with their last appeal from reason to arms. −

Yet, however blinded that assembly may be, by their intemperate rage for unlimited domination, so to sight justice and the opinion of mankind, we esteem ourselves bound by obligations of respect to the rest of the world, to make known the justice of our cause.

Our forefathers, inhabitants of the island of Great-Britain, left their native land, to seek on these shores a residence for civil and religious freedom. At the expense of their blood, at the hazard of their fortunes, without the least charge to the country from which they removed, by unceasing labour, and an unconquerable spirit, they effected settlements in the distant and unhospitable wilds of America, then filled with numerous and warlike barbarians. -- Societies or governments, vested with perfect legislatures, were formed under charters from the crown, and an harmonious intercourse was established between the colonies and the kingdom from which they derived their origin.

The mutual benefits of this union became in a short time so extraordinary, as to excite astonishment. It is universally confessed, that the amazing increase of the wealth, strength, and navigation of the realm, arose from this source; and the minister, who so wisely and successfully directed the measures of Great-Britain in the late war, publicly declared, that these colonies enabled her to triumph over her enemies. --Towards the conclusion of that war, it pleased our sovereign to make a change in his counsels. -- From that fatal movement, the affairs of the British empire began to fall into confusion, and gradually sliding from the summit of glorious prosperity, to which they had been advanced by the virtues and abilities of one man, are at length distracted by the convulsions, that now shake it to its deepest foundations. -- The new ministry finding the brave foes of Britain, though frequently defeated, yet still contending, took up the unfortunate idea of granting them a hasty peace, and then subduing her faithful friends.

These devoted colonies were judged to be in such a state, as to present victories without bloodshed, and all the easy emoluments of statuteable plunder. -- The uninterrupted tenor of their peaceable and respectful behaviour from the beginning of colonization, their dutiful, zealous, and useful services during the war, though so recently and amply acknowledged in the most honourable manner by his majesty, by the late king, and by parliament, could not save them from the meditated innovations. –

Parliament was influenced to adopt the pernicious project, and assuming a new power over them, have in the course of eleven years, given such decisive specimens of the spirit and consequences attending this power, as to leave no doubt concerning the effects of acquiescence under it.

They have undertaken to give and grant our money without our consent, though we have ever exercised an exclusive right to dispose of our own property; statutes have been passed for extending the jurisdiction of courts of admiralty and vice-admiralty beyond their ancient limits; for depriving us of the accustomed and inestimable privilege of trial by jury, in cases affecting both life and property; for suspending the legislature of one of the colonies; for interdicting all commerce to the capital of another; and for altering fundamentally the form of government established by charter, and secured by acts of its own legislature solemnly confirmed by the crown; for exempting the "murderers" of colonists from legal trial, and in effect, from punishment; for erecting in a neighboring province, acquired by the joint arms of Great-Britain and America, a despotism dangerous to our very existence; and for quartering soldiers upon the colonists in time of profound peace. It has also been resolved in parliament, that colonists charged with committing certain offences, shall be transported to England to be tried.

But why should we enumerate our injuries in detail? By one statute it is declared, that parliament can "of right make laws to bind us in all cases whatsoever." What is to defend us against so enormous, so unlimited a power?

Not a single man of those who assume it, is chosen by us; or is subject to our control or influence; but, on the contrary, they are all of them exempt from the operation of such laws, and an American revenue, if not diverted from the ostensible purposes for which it is raised, would actually lighten their own burdens in proportion, as they increase ours.

We saw the misery to which such despotism would reduce us. We for ten years incessantly and ineffectually besieged the throne as supplicants; we reasoned, we remonstrated with parliament, in the most mild and decent language.
Administration sensible that we should regard these oppressive measures as freemen ought to do, sent over fleets and armies to enforce them. The indignation of the Americans was roused, it is true; but it was the indignation of a virtuous, loyal, and affectionate people.
A Congress of delegates from the United Colonies was assembled at Philadelphia, on the fifth day of last September. We resolved again to offer a humble and dutiful petition to the King and addressed our fellow-subjects of Great-Britain.

We have pursued every temperate, every respectful measure; we have even proceeded to break off our commercial intercourse with our fellow subjects, as the last peaceable admonition, that our attachment to no nation upon earth should supplant our attachment to liberty. -- This, we flattered ourselves, was the ultimate step of the controversy: but subsequent events have shewn, how vain was this hope of finding moderation in our enemies.

Several threatening expressions against the colonies were inserted in his majesty's speech; our petition, tho' we were told it was a decent one, and that his majesty had been pleased to receive it graciously, and to promise laying it before his parliament, was huddled into both houses among a bundle of American papers, and there neglected.

The lords and commons in their address, in the month of February, said, that "a rebellion at that time actually existed within the province of Massachusetts-Bay; and that those concerned with it, had been countenanced and encouraged by unlawful combinations and engagements, entered into by his majesty's subjects in several of the other colonies; and therefore they besought his majesty, that he would take the most effectual measures to inforce due obediance to the laws and authority of the supreme legislature." –

Soon after, the commercial intercourse of whole colonies, with foreign countries, and with each other, was cut off by an act of parliament; by another several of them were intirely prohibited from the fisheries in the seas near their coasts, on which they always depended for their sustenance; and large reinforcements of ships and troops were immediately sent over to general Gage.
Fruitless were all the entreaties, arguments, and eloquence of an illustrious band of the most distinguished peers, and commoners, who nobly and strenuously asserted the justice of our cause, to stay, or even to mitigate the heedless fury with which these accumulated and unexampled outrages were hurried on. -- equally fruitless was the interference of the city of London, of Bristol, and many other respectable towns in our favor.

Parliament adopted an insidious manoeuvre calculated to divide us, to establish a perpetual auction of taxations where colony should bid against colony, all of them uninformed what ransom would redeem their lives; and thus, to extort from us, at the point of the bayonet, the unknown sums that should be sufficient to gratify, if possible to gratify, ministerial rapacity, with the miserable indulgence left to us of raising, in our own mode, the prescribed tribute. What terms more rigid and humiliating could have been dictated by remorseless victors to conquered enemies? in our circumstances to accept them, would be to deserve them.

Soon after the intelligence of these proceedings arrived on this continent, general Gage, who in the course of the last year had taken possession of the town of Boston, in the province of Massachusetts Bay, and still occupied it a garrison, on the 19th day of April, sent out from that place a large detachment of his army, who made an unprovoked assault on the inhabitants of the said province, at the town of Lexington, as appears by the affidavits of a great number of persons, some of whom were officers and soldiers of that detachment, murdered eight of the inhabitants, and wounded many others.

From thence the troops proceeded in warlike array to the town of Concord, where they set upon another party of the inhabitants of the same province, killing several and wounding more, until compelled to retreat by the country people suddenly assembled to repel this cruel aggression. Hostilities, thus commenced by the British troops, have been since prosecuted by them without regard to faith or reputation. –

The inhabitants of Boston being confined within that town by the general their governor, and having, in order to procure their dismission, entered into a treaty with him, it was stipulated that the said inhabitants having deposited their arms with their own magistrate, should have liberty to depart, taking with them their other effects.

.They accordingly delivered up their arms, but in open violation of honour, in defiance of the obligation of treaties, which even savage nations esteemed sacred, the governor ordered the arms deposited as aforesaid, that they might be preserved for their owners, to be seized by a body of soldiers; detained the greatest part of the inhabitants in the town, and compelled the few who were permitted to retire, to leave their most valuable effects behind.

By this perfidy wives are separated from their husbands, children from their parents, the aged and the sick from their relations and friends, who wish to attend and comfort them; and those who have been used to live in plenty and even elegance, are reduced to deplorable distress.

The general, further emulating his ministerial masters, by a proclamation bearing date on the 12th day of June, after venting the grossest falsehoods and calumnies against the good people of these colonies, proceeds to "declare them all, either by name or description, to be rebels and traitors, to supersede the course of the common law, and instead thereof to publish and order the use and exercise of the law martial." --

His troops have butchered our countrymen, have wantonly burnt Charlestown, besides a considerable number of houses in other places; our ships and vessels are seized; the necessary supplies of provisions are intercepted, and he is exerting his utmost power to spread destruction and devastation around him.

We have received certain intelligence, that general Carleton], the governor of Canada, is instigating the people of that province and the Indians to fall upon us; and we have but too much reason to apprehend, that schemes have been formed to excite domestic enemies against us. In brief, a part of these colonies now feels, and all of them are sure of feeling, as far as the vengeance of administration can inflict them, the complicated calamities of fire, sword, and famine.

We are reduced to the alternative of chusing an unconditional submission to the tyranny of irritated ministers, or resistance by force. -- The latter is our choice. –

- We have counted the cost of this contest and find nothing so dreadful as voluntary slavery. -- Honour, justice, and humanity, forbid us tamely to surrender that freedom which we received from our gallant ancestors, and which our innocent posterity have a right to receive from us. We cannot endure the infamy and guilt of resigning succeeding generations to that wretchedness which inevitably awaits them, if we basely entail hereditary bondage upon them.

Our cause is just. Our union is perfect. Our internal resources are great, and, if necessary, foreign assistance is undoubtedly attainable. -- We gratefully acknowledge, as signal instances of the Divine favour towards us, that his Providence would not permit us to be called into this severe controversy, until we were grown up to our present strength, had been previously exercised in warlike operation, and possessed of the means of defending ourselves.

With hearts fortified with these animating reflections, we most solemnly, before God and the world, declare, that, exerting the utmost energy of those powers, which our beneficent Creator hath graciously bestowed upon us, the arms we have been compelled by our enemies to assume, we will, in defiance of every hazard, with unabating firmness and perseverence, employ for the preservation of our liberties; being with one mind resolved to die freemen rather than to live slaves.

Lest this declaration should disquiet the minds of our friends and fellow-subjects in any part of the empire, we assure them that we mean not to dissolve that union which has so long and so happily subsisted between us, and which we sincerely wish to see restored. - Necessity has not yet driven us into that desperate measure or induced us to excite any other nation to war against them. –

We have not raised armies with ambitious designs of separating from Great-Britain and establishing independent states. We fight not for glory or for conquest. We exhibit to mankind the remarkable spectacle of a people attacked by unprovoked enemies, without any imputation or even suspicion of offence.

They boast of their privileges and civilization, and yet proffer no milder conditions than servitude or death. In our own native land, in defence of the freedom that is our birthright, and which we ever enjoyed till the late violation of it -- for the protection of our property, acquired solely by the honest industry of our fore-fathers and ourselves, against violence actually offered, we have taken up arms.

We shall lay them down when hostilities shall cease on the part of the aggressors, and all danger of their being renewed shall be removed, and not before.

With an humble confidence in the mercies of the supreme and impartial Judge and Ruler of the Universe, we most devoutly implore his divine goodness to protect us happily through this great conflict, to dispose our adversaries to reconciliation on reasonable terms, and thereby to relieve the empire from the calamities of civil war.

APPENDIX III

"I AM AN AMERICAN"

Virginia delegate George Mason stated of Patrick Henry's speech:
"He is by far the most powerful speaker I ever heard. Every word he says not only engages but commands the attention, and your passions are no longer your own when he addresses them. ... He is, in my opinion, the first man upon this continent, as well in abilities as public virtues. ... Had he lived in Rome about the time of the first Punic War ... Mr. Henry's talents must have put him at the head of that glorious commonwealth."

When the members assembled the second morning of the First Continental Congress in 1774, and the Secretary had called the roll and read the minutes, there was a pause. Members from various and distant provinces were personal strangers. Some had been instructed what to do, and others had been left free to act according to their own judgments, and the circumstances. No one seemed willing to take the first step in business. No one seemed to have determined what measure first to propose.

The silence was becoming painful, when a grave-looking man, apparently about forty years of age, with unpowdered hair, a thin face, not very powerful in person, and dressed in a plain dark suit of "minister's gray," arose. "Then," said Mr. White, who was present, "I felt a regret that a seeming country parson should so far have mistaken his talents and the theatre for their display."

His voice was musical, and as he continued to speak, he became more animated, and his words more eloquent. With alternate vigor and pathos, he drew a picture of the wrongs which the colonies had suffered by acts of the Parliament.

He said that all the governments in America were dissolved; that the colonies were in a state of nature. He believed that the Congress then in session was the beginning of a long series of congresses; and speaking to the undecided question about voting, he declared his great concern, for their decision would form a precedent.

He favored representation according to population; and in reference to the objection that such representation would confer an undue weight of influence upon some of the larger provinces, he said, with words that prophesied of a nation: "British oppression has effaced the boundaries of the several colonies; the distinctions between Virginians, Pennsylvanians and New Englanders are no more. I am not a Virginian, but an American."

His speech drew the earnest attention of the whole House; and when he sat down the question went from lip to lip, "Who is he?" A few who knew the speaker replied, "It is Patrick Henry of Virginia."

There was now no hesitation. The bold-spirited man, who electrified the continent with his burning words in stamp-act times, was now there to lead in a revolt. He had uttered the sentiment of union and nationality that warmed the hearts of all present, when he exclaimed: "I am not a Virginian, but an American."

 It was the text of every patriotic discourse thereafter; and from that hour the Congress went forward with courage and vigor in the work assigned them.

They determined that the voting should be done by colonies, each colony having one vote, because they had no means for ascertaining the importance of each in population, wealth, and trade. It is estimated that the aggregate population at that time, including five hundred thousand blacks and excluding Indians, was about two million six hundred thousand.

OUR COUNTRY was published in 1877 as a "Household History For all Readers." This article is an excerpt from the second volume of the book in which the author, Benson J. Lossing, chronicles the American Revolution from 1760 until early 1800.

APPENDIX IV

VIRGINA STAMP ACT RESOLVES

Patrick Henry, at a meeting of the Virginia House of Burgesses, proposed seven resolutions against the Stamp Act. The first four resolutions were adopted and passed by the House of Burgesses.

The Fifth resolution was repealed on the second day of the debates. Though resolutions six and seven were never passed by the House, all seven were widely reported in the colonial press, giving the impression that all passed the Virginia Assembly.

The following four resolves were adopted by the House of Burgesses on May 30, 1765:

Resolved, that the first adventurers and settlers of His Majesty's colony and dominion of Virginia brought with them and transmitted to their posterity, and all other His Majesty's subjects since inhabiting in this His Majesty's said colony, all the liberties, privileges, franchises, and immunities that have at any time been held, enjoyed, and possessed by the people of Great Britain.

The colonists aforesaid are declared entitled to all liberties, privileges, and immunities of denizens and natural subjects to all intents and purposes as if they had been abiding and born within the Realm of England.

Resolved, that the taxation of the people by themselves, or by persons chosen by themselves to represent them, who can only know what taxes the people are able to bear, or the easiest method of raising them, and must themselves be affected by every tax laid on the people, is the only security against a burdensome taxation, and the distinguishing characteristic of British freedom, without which the ancient constitution cannot exist.

Resolved, that His Majesty's liege people of this his most ancient and loyal colony have without interruption enjoyed the inestimable right of being governed by such laws, respecting their internal policy and taxation, as are derived from their own consent, with the approbation of their sovereign, or his substitute; and that the same has never been forfeited or yielded up, but has been constantly recognized by the kings and people of Great Britain.

The following version of the much-debated fifth resolution (which was not adopted) was found with Patrick Henry's will:

Resolved, therefor that the General Assembly of this Colony have the only and exclusive Right and Power to lay Taxes and Impositions upon the inhabitants of this Colony and that every Attempt to vest such Power in any person or persons whatsoever other than the General Assembly aforesaid has a manifest Tendency to destroy British as well as American Freedom.

The Virginia Assembly did not pass the following two resolutions, but were reported in several newspapers:

Resolved, That His Majesty's liege people, the inhabitants of this Colony, are not bound to yield obedience to any law or ordinance whatever, designed to impose any taxation whatsoever upon them, other than the laws or ordinances of the General Assembly aforesaid.

Resolved: That any person who shall, by speaking or writing, assert or maintain that any person or persons other than the General Assembly of this Colony, have any right or power to impose or lay any taxation on the people here, shall be deemed an enemy to His Majesty's Colony.

Source: John Pendleton Kennedy, ed., Journals of the House of Burgesses of Virginia, 1761-1765 (Richmond, Va., 1907).

APPENDIX V

PATRICK HENRY 'GIVE ME LIBERTY OR DEATH" SPEECH

MR. PRESIDENT: No man thinks more highly than I do of the patriotism, as well as abilities, of the very worthy gentlemen who have just addressed the House. But different men often see the same subject in different lights; and, therefore, I hope it will not be thought disrespectful to those gentlemen if, entertaining as I do, opinions of a character very opposite to theirs, I shall speak forth my sentiments freely, and without reserve. This is no time for ceremony.

The question before the House is one of awful moment to this country.

For my own part, I consider it as nothing less than a question of freedom or slavery; and in proportion to the magnitude of the subject ought to be the freedom of the debate. It is only in this way that we can hope to arrive at the truth and fulfil the great responsibility which we hold to God and our country.

Should I keep back my opinions at such a time, through fear of giving offence, I should consider myself as guilty of treason towards my country, and of an act of disloyalty toward the majesty of heaven, which I revere above all earthly kings.

Mr. President, it is natural to man to indulge in the illusions of hope. We are apt to shut our eyes against a painful truth and listen to the song of that siren till she transforms us into beasts. Is this the part of wise men, engaged in a great and arduous struggle for liberty?

Are we disposed to be of the number of those who, having eyes, see not, and, having ears, hear not, the things which so nearly concern their temporal salvation?

For my part, whatever anguish of spirit it may cost, I am willing to know the whole truth; to know the worst, and to provide for it.

I have but one lamp by which my feet are guided; and that is the lamp of experience. I know of no way of judging of the future but by the past.

And judging by the past, I wish to know what there has been in the conduct of the British ministry for the last ten years, to justify those hopes with which gentlemen have been pleased to solace themselves, and the House?

Is it that insidious smile with which our petition has been lately received? Trust it not, sir; it will prove a snare to your feet. Suffer not yourselves to be betrayed with a kiss. Ask yourselves how this gracious reception of our petition comports with these war-like preparations which cover our waters and darken our land. Are fleets and armies necessary to a work of love and reconciliation? Have we shown ourselves so unwilling to be reconciled, that force must be called in to win back our love?

Let us not deceive ourselves, sir. These are the implements of war and subjugation; the last arguments to which king's resort. I ask, gentlemen, sir, what means this martial array, if its purpose be not to force us to submission? Can gentlemen assign any other possible motive for it? Has Great Britain any enemy, in this quarter of the world, to call for all this accumulation of navies and armies? No, sir, she has none.

They are meant for us; they can be meant for no other. They are sent over to bind and rivet upon us those chains which the British ministry have been so long forging. And what have we to oppose to them? Shall we try argument? Sir, we have been trying that for the last ten years.

Have we anything new to offer upon the subject? Nothing. We have held the subject up in every light of which it is capable; but it has been all in vain. Shall we resort to entreaty and humble supplication? What terms shall we find which have not been already exhausted? Let us not, I beseech you, sir, deceive ourselves. Sir, we have done everything that could be done, to avert the storm which is now coming on.

We have petitioned; we have remonstrated; we have supplicated; we have prostrated ourselves before the throne and have implored its interposition to arrest the tyrannical hands of the ministry and Parliament.

Our petitions have been slighted; our remonstrance's have produced additional violence and insult; our supplications have been disregarded; and we have been spurned, with contempt, from the foot of the throne. In vain, after these things, may we indulge the fond hope of peace and reconciliation.

There is no longer any room for hope.

If we wish to be free² if we mean to preserve inviolate those inestimable privileges for which we have been so long contending²if we mean not basely to abandon the noble struggle in which we have been so long engaged, and which we have pledged ourselves never to abandon until the glorious object of our contest shall be obtained, we must fight! I repeat it, sir, we must fight! An appeal to arms and to the God of Hosts is all that we have left.

They tell us, sir, that we are weak; unable to cope with so formidable an adversary. But when shall we be stronger? Will it be the next week, or the next year? Will it be when we are totally disarmed, and when a British guard shall be stationed in every house? Shall we gather strength by irresolution and inaction?

Shall we acquire the means of effectual resistance, by lying supinely on our backs, and hugging the delusive phantom of hope, until our enemies shall have bound us hand and foot? Sir, we are not weak if we make a proper use of those means which the God of nature hath placed in our power.

Three millions of people in such a country as that which we possess, are invincible by any force which our enemy can send against us. Besides, sir, we shall not fight our battles alone.

There is a just God who presides over the destinies of nations; and who will raise up friends to fight our battles for us. The battle, sir, is not to the strong alone; it is to the vigilant, the active, the brave.

Besides, sir, we have no election. If we were base enough to desire it, it is now too late to retire from the contest. There is no retreat but in submission and slavery! Our chains are forged! Their clanking may be heard on the plains of Boston!
The war is inevitable²and let it come! I repeat it, sir, let it come. It is in vain, sir, to extenuate the matter.

Gentlemen may cry, Peace, Peace but there is no peace. The war has begun! The next gale that sweeps from the north will bring to our ears the clash of resounding arms!

Our brethren are already in the field! Why stand we here idle? What is it that gentlemen wish? What would they have? Is life so dear, or peace so sweet, as to be purchased at the price of chains and slavery? Forbid it, Almighty God! I know not what course others may take; but as for me, give me liberty or give me death!

St John's Episcopal Church
Virginia House of Burgesses, March 23, 1775

AUTHORS NOTE: I WAS BLESSED TO PARTICIPATE IN AN ACTUAL REENACTMENT OF THE EVENT AT ST JOHNS EPISCOPAL CHURCH.

I WAS THE CHURCH PASTOR AND DID HAVE SOME SPEAKING LINES.

APPENDIX VI
VIRGINIA' S DECLARATION OF RIGHTS

On May 15, 1776, the Virginia Convention "resolved unanimously that the delegates appointed to represent this colony in General Congress be instructed to propose to that respectable body to declare the United Colonies free and independent states . . . [and] that a committee be appointed to prepare a DECLARATION OF RIGHTS and . . . plan of government." R. H. Lee's resolution of June 7, 1776, implemented the first of these resolutions and precipitated the appointment of the committee to draw up the Declaration of Independence; the second proposal was carried out by the framing of Virginia's first state constitution, of which this declaration was an integral part. It is notable for containing an authoritative definition of the term *militia* in Section 13.

As passed, the Virginia Declaration was largely the work of George Mason; the committee and the Convention made some verbal changes and added Sections 10 and 14. This declaration served as a model for bills of rights in several other state constitutions and was a source of the French Declaration of the Rights of Man and of the Citizen, though its degree of influence upon the latter document is a highly controversial question. The reference to "property" in Section I may be compared with the use of the word by John Locke, its omission by Thomas Jefferson from the second paragraph of the Declaration of Independence, and its use in the Constitution, Amendments V and XIV.

George Mason (1725-92), one of Virginia's wealthiest planters, a neighbor and friend of Washington, is best remembered for his part in drafting the Virginia constitution of 1776. In 1787 he was a leader in the Federal Convention. Refusing to sign the completed document, Mason, along with Patrick Henry and others, opposed its ratification in the Virginia Convention **good** people of Virginia, assembled in full and free convention; which rights do pertain to them and their posterity, as the basis and foundation of government.

SECTION I. That all men are by nature equally free and independent and have certain inherent rights, of which, when they enter into a state of society, they cannot, by any compact, deprive or divest their posterity; namely, the enjoyment of life and liberty, with the means of acquiring and possessing property, and pursuing and obtaining happiness and safety.

SEC. 2. That all power is vested in, and consequently derived from, the people; that magistrates are their trustees and servants and at all times amenable to them.

SEC. 3. That government is, or ought to be, instituted for the common benefit, protection, and security of the people, nation, or community; of all the various modes and forms of government, that is best which is capable of producing the greatest degree of happiness and safety and is most effectually secured against the danger of maladministration; and that, when any government shall be found inadequate or contrary to these purposes, a majority of the community hath an indubitable, inalienable, and indefeasible right to reform, alter, or abolish it, in such manner as shall be judged most conducive to the public weal.

SEC. 4. That no man, or set of men, are entitled to exclusive or separate emoluments or privileges from the community, but in consideration of public services; which, not being descendible, neither ought the offices of magistrate, legislator, or judge to be hereditary.

SEC. 5. That the legislative and executive powers of the state should be separate and distinct from the judiciary; and that the members of the two first may be restrained from oppression, by feeling and participating the burdens of the people, they should, at fixed periods, be reduced to a private station, return into that body from which they were originally taken, and the vacancies be supplied by frequent, certain, and regular elections, in wh ich all, or any part, of the former members, to be again eligible, or ineligible, as the laws shall direct.

SEC. 6. That elections of members to serve as representatives of the people, in assembly, ought to be free; and that all men, having sufficient evidence of permanent common interest with, and attachment to, the community, have the right of suffrage and cannot be taxed or deprived of their property for public uses without their own consent, or that of their representatives so elected, nor bound by any law to which they have not, in like manner, assented for the public good.

SEC. 7. That all power of suspending laws, or the execution of laws, by any authority, without consent of the representatives of the people, is injurious to their rights and ought not to be exercised.

SEC. 8. That in all capital or criminal prosecutions a man hath a right to demand the cause and nature of his accusation, to be confronted with the accusers and witnesses, to call for evidence in his favor, and to a speedy trial by an impartial jury of twelve men of his vicinage, without whose unanimous consent he cannot be found guilty; nor can he be compelled to give evidence against himself; that no man be deprived of his liberty, except by the law of the land or the judgment of his peers.

SEC. 9. That excessive bail ought not to be required, nor excessive fines imposed, nor cruel and unusual punishments inflicted.

SEC. 10. That general warrants, whereby an officer or messenger may be commanded to search suspected places without evidence of a fact committed, or to seize any person or persons not named, or whose offense is not particularly described and supported by evidence, are grievous and oppressive and ought not to be granted.

SEC. 11. That in controversies respecting property, and in suits between man and man, the ancient trial by jury is preferable to any other and ought to be held sacred.

SEC. 12. That the freedom of the press is one of the great bulwarks of liberty and can never be restrained but by despotic governments.

SEC. 13. That a well-regulated militia, or composed of the body of the people, trained to arms, is the proper, natural, and safe defense of a free state; that standing armies, in time of peace, should be avoided as dangerous to liberty; and that in all cases the military should be under strict subordination to, and governed by, the civil power.

SEC. 14. That the people have a right to uniform government; and, therefore, that no government separate from or independent of the government of Virginia ought to be erected or established within the limits thereof.

SEC. 15. That no free government, or the blessings of liberty, can be preserved to any people, but by a firm adherence to justice, moderation, temperance, frugality, and virtue, and by frequent recurrence to fundamental principles.

SEC. 16. That religion, or the duty which we owe to our Creator, and the manner of discharging it, can be directed only by reason and conviction, not by force or violence; and therefore all men are equally entitled to the free exercise of religion, according to the dictates of conscience; and that it is the mutual duty of all to practice Christian forbearance, love, and charity toward each other.

APPENDIX VII

DECLARATION OF INDEPENDENCE

The Unanimous Declaration of the Thirteen United States of America

When, in the course of human events, it becomes necessary for one people to dissolve the political bands which have connected them with another, and to assume among the powers of the earth, the separate and equal station to which the laws of nature and of nature's God entitle them, a decent respect to the opinions of mankind requires that they should declare the causes which impel them to the separation.

We hold these truths to be self-evident, that all men are created equal, that they are endowed by their Creator with certain unalienable rights, that among these are life, liberty and the pursuit of happiness. That to secure these rights, governments are instituted among men, deriving their just powers from the consent of the governed.

That whenever any form of government becomes destructive to these ends, it is the right of the people to alter or to abolish it, and to institute new government, laying its foundation on such principles and organizing its powers in such form, as to them shall seem most likely to effect their safety and happiness. Prudence, indeed, will dictate that governments long established should not be changed for light and transient causes; and accordingly, all experience hath shown that mankind are more disposed to suffer, while evils are sufferable, than to right themselves by abolishing the forms to which they are accustomed.

But when a long train of abuses and usurpations, pursuing invariably the same object evinces a design to reduce them under absolute despotism, it is their right, it is their duty, to throw off such government, and to provide new guards for their future security. —

Such has been the patient sufferance of these colonies; and such is now the necessity which constrains them to alter their former systems of government.

The history of the present King of Great Britain is a history of repeated injuries and usurpations, all having in direct object the establishment of absolute tyranny over these states. To prove this, let facts be submitted to a candid world.

He has refused his assent to laws, the most wholesome and necessary for the public good.

He has forbidden his governors to pass laws of immediate and pressing importance, unless suspended in their operation till his assent should be obtained; and when so suspended, he has utterly neglected to attend to them.

He has refused to pass other laws for the accommodation of large districts of people, unless those people would relinquish the right of representation in the legislature, a right inestimable to them and formidable to tyrants only. He has called together legislative bodies at places unusual, uncomfortable, and distant from the depository of their public records, for the sole purpose of fatiguing them into compliance with his measures.

He has dissolved representative houses repeatedly, for opposing with manly firmness his invasions on the rights of the people.

He has refused for a long time, after such dissolutions, to cause others to be elected; whereby the legislative powers, incapable of annihilation, have returned to the people at large for their exercise; the state remaining in the meantime exposed to all the dangers of invasion from without, and convulsions within.

He has endeavored to prevent the population of these states; for that purpose, obstructing the laws for naturalization of foreigners; refusing to pass others to encourage their migration hither and raising the conditions of new appropriations of lands.

He has obstructed the administration of justice, by refusing his assent to laws for establishing judiciary powers. He has made judges dependent on his will alone, for the tenure of their offices, and the amount and payment of their salaries.

He has erected a multitude of new offices, and sent hither swarms of officers to harass our people and eat out their substance.

He has kept among us, in times of peace, standing armies without the consent of our legislature.

He has affected to render the military independent of and superior to civil power.

He has combined with others to subject us to a jurisdiction foreign to our constitution, and unacknowledged by our laws; giving his assent to their acts of pretended legislation:

For quartering large bodies of armed troops among us: For protecting them, by mock trial, from punishment for any murders which they should commit on the inhabitants of these states:

For cutting off our trade with all parts of the world: For imposing taxes on us without our consent:

For depriving us in many cases, of the benefits of trial by jury: For transporting us beyond seas to be tried for pretended offenses:

For abolishing the free system of English laws in a neighboring province, establishing therein an arbitrary government, and enlarging its boundaries to render it at once an example and fit instrument for introducing the same absolute rule in these colonies
:
For taking away our charters, abolishing our most valuable laws, and altering fundamentally the forms of our governments:

For suspending our own legislatures and declaring themselves invested with power to legislate for us in all cases whatsoever. out of his protection and waging war against us.

He has plundered our seas, ravaged our coasts, burned our towns, and destroyed the lives of our people.

He is at this time transporting large armies of foreign mercenaries to complete the works of death, desolation and tyranny, already begun with circumstances of cruelty and perfidy scarcely paralleled in the most barbarous ages, and totally unworthy of the head of a civilized nation.

He has constrained our fellow citizens taken captive on the high seas to bear arms against their country, to become the executioners of their friends and brethren, or to fall themselves by their hands.

He has excited domestic insurrections amongst us and has endeavored to bring on the inhabitants of our frontiers, the merciless Indian savages, whose known rule of warfare, is undistinguished destruction of all ages, sexes and conditions. In every stage of these oppressions we have petitioned for redress in the humblest terms: our repeated petitions have been answered only by repeated injury. A prince, whose character is thus marked by every act which may define a tyrant, is unfit to be the ruler of a free people.

Nor have we been wanting in attention to our British brethren. We have warned them from time to time of attempts by their legislature to extend an unwarrantable jurisdiction over us.

We have reminded them of the circumstances of our emigration and settlement here. We have appealed to their native justice and magnanimity, and we have conjured them by the ties of our common kindred to disavow these usurpations, which, would inevitably interrupt our connections and correspondence. They too have been deaf to the voice of justice and of consanguinity. We must, therefore, acquiesce in the necessity, which denounces our separation, and hold them, as we hold the rest of mankind, enemies in war, in peace friends.

We, therefore, the representatives of the United States of America, in General Congress, assembled, appealing to the Supreme Judge of the world for the rectitude of our intentions, do, in the name, and by the authority of the good people of these colonies, solemnly publish and declare, that these united colonies are, and of right ought to be free and independent states; that they are absolved from all allegiance to the British Crown, and that all political connection between them and the state of Great Britain, is and ought to be totally dissolved; and that as free and independent states, they have full power to levey war, conclude peace, contract alliances, establish commerce, and to do all other acts and things which independent states may of right do.

And for the support of this declaration, with a firm reliance on the protection of Divine Providence, we mutually pledge to each other our lives, our fortunes and our sacred honor.

APPENDIX VIII   ARTICLES OF CONFEDERATION

To all to whom these Presents shall come, we the undersigned Delegates of the States affixed to our Names send greeting. The Articles of Confederation and perpetual Union between the states of New Hampshire, Massachusetts-bay Rhode Island and Providence Plantations, Connecticut, New York, New Jersey, Pennsylvania, Delaware, Maryland, Virginia, North Carolina, South Carolina, and Georgia.

Article I
The Stile of this Confederacy shall be "The United States of America".

Article II
Each state retains its sovereignty, freedom, and independence, and every power, jurisdiction, and right, which is not by this Confederation expressly delegated to the United States, in Congress assembled.

Article III
The said States hereby severally enter into a firm league of friendship with each other, for their common defense, the security of their liberties, and their mutual and general welfare, binding themselves to assist each other, against all force offered to, or attacks made upon them, or any of them, because of religion, sovereignty, trade, or any other pretense whatever.

Article IV
The better to secure and perpetuate mutual friendship and intercourse among the people of the different States in this Union, the free inhabitants of each of these States, paupers, vagabonds, and fugitives from justice excepted, shall be entitled to all privileges and immunities of free citizens in the several States; and the people of each State shall free ingress and regress to and from any other State, and shall enjoy therein all the privileges of trade and commerce, subject to the same duties, impositions, and restrictions as the inhabitants thereof respectively, provided that such restrictions shall not extend so far as to prevent the removal of property imported into any State, to any other State, of which the owner is an inhabitant; provided also that no imposition, duties or restriction shall be laid by any State, on the property of the United States, or either of them. If any person guilty of, or charged with, treason, felony, or other high misdemeanor in any State, shall flee from justice, and be found in any of the United States, he shall, upon demand of the Governor

or executive power of the State from which he fled, be delivered up and removed to the State having jurisdiction of his offense. Full faith and credit shall be given in each of these States to the records, acts, and judicial proceedings of the courts and magistrates of every other State.

Article V
For the most convenient management of the general interests of the United States, delegates shall be annually appointed in such manner as the legislatures of each State shall direct, to meet in Congress on the first Monday in November, in every year, with a power reserved to each State to recall its delegates, or any of them, at any time within the year, and to send others in their stead for the remainder of the year.

No State shall be represented in Congress by less than two, nor more than seven members; and no person shall be capable of being a delegate for more than three years in any term of six years; nor shall any person, being a delegate, be capable of holding any office under the United States, for which he, or another for his benefit, receives any salary, fees or emolument of any kind.

Each State shall maintain its own delegates in a meeting of the States, and while they act as members of the committee of the States. assembled, each State shall have one vote.

Freedom of speech and debate in Congress shall not be impeached or questioned in any court or place out of Congress, and the members of Congress shall be protected in their persons from arrests or imprisonments, during the time of their going to and from, and attendence on Congress, except for treason, felony, or breach of the peace.
No State, without the consent of the United States in Congress assembled, shall send any embassy to, or receive any embassy from, or enter into any conference, agreement, alliance or treaty with any King, Prince or State; nor shall any person holding any office of profit or trust under the United States, or any of them, accept any present, emolument, office or title of any kind whatever from any King, Prince or foreign State; nor shall the United States in Congress assembled, or any of them, grant any title of nobility.
No two or more States shall enter any treaty, confederation or alliance whatever between them, without the consent of the United States in Congress assembled, specifying accurately the purposes for which the same is to be entered, and how long it shall continue. No State shall lay any imposts or duties, which may interfere with any stipulations in

treaties, entered by the United States in Congress assembled, with any King, Prince or State, in pursuance of any treaties already proposed by Congress, to the courts of France and Spain.

No vessel of war shall be kept up in time of peace by any State, except such number only, as shall be deemed necessary by the United States in Congress assembled, for the defense of such State, or its trade; nor shall any body of forces be kept up by any State in time of peace, except such number only, as in the judgement of the United States in Congress assembled, shall be deemed requisite to garrison the forts necessary for the defense of such State; but every State shall always keep up a well-regulated and disciplined militia, sufficiently armed and accoutered, and shall provide and constantly have ready for use, in public stores, a due number of filed pieces and tents, and a proper quantity of arms, ammunition and camp equipage.

No State shall engage in any war without the consent of the United States in Congress assembled, unless such State be actually invaded by enemies, or shall have received certain advice of a resolution being formed by some nation of Indians to invade such State, and the danger is so imminent as not to admit of a delay till the United States in Congress assembled can be consulted; nor shall any State grant commissions to any ships or vessels of war, nor letters of marque or reprisal, except it be after a declaration of war by the United States in Congress assembled, and then only against the Kingdom or State and the subjects thereof, against which war has been so declared, and under such regulations as shall be established by the United States in Congress assembled, unless such State be infested by pirates, in which case vessels of war may be fitted out for that occasion, and kept so long as the danger shall continue, or until the United States in Congress assembled shall determine otherwise.

Article VII
When land forces are raised by any State for the common defense, all officers of or under the rank of colonel, shall be appointed by the legislature of each State respectively, by whom such forces shall be raised, or in such manner as such State shall direct, and all vacancies shall be filled up by the State which first made the appointment.

Article VIII
All charges of war, and all other expenses that shall be incurred for the common defense or general welfare, and allowed by the United States in

Congress assembled, shall be defrayed out of a common treasury, which shall be supplied by the several States in proportion to the value of all land within each State, granted or surveyed for any person, as such land and the buildings and improvements thereon shall be estimated according to such mode as the United States in Congress assembled, shall from time to time direct and appoint.

The taxes for paying that proportion shall be laid and levied by the authority and direction of the legislatures of the several States within the time agreed upon by the United States in Congress assembled.

Article IX
The United States in Congress assembled, shall have the sole and exclusive right and power of determining on peace and war, except in the cases mentioned in the sixth article—of sending and receiving ambassadors—entering into treaties and alliances, provided that no treaty of commerce shall be made whereby the legislative power of the respective States shall be restrained from imposing such imposts and duties on foreigners, as their own people are subjected to, or from prohibiting the exportation or importation of any species of goods or commodities whatsoever—of establishing rules for deciding in all cases, what captures on land or water shall be legal, and in what manner prizes taken by land or naval forces in the service of the United States shall be divided or appropriated—of granting letters of marque and reprisal in times of peace— appointing courts for the trial of piracies and felonies commited on the high seas and establishing courts for receiving and determining finally appeals in all cases of captures, provided that no member of Congress shall be appointed a judge of any of the said courts.

The United States in Congress assembled shall also be the last resort on appeal in all disputes and differences now subsisting or that hereafter may arise between two or more States concerning boundary, jurisdiction or any other causes whatever; which authority shall always be exercised in the manner following.
 Whenever the legislative or executive authority or lawful agent of any State in controversy with another shall present a petition to Congress stating the matter in question and praying for a hearing, notice thereof shall be given by order of Congress to the legislative or executive authority of the other State in controversy, and a day assigned for the appearance of the parties by their lawful agents, who shall then be directed to appoint by joint consent, commissioners or judges to constitute a court for hearing and determining the matter in question: but

if they cannot agree, Congress shall name three persons out of each of the United States, and from the list of such persons each party shall alternately strike out one, the petitioners beginning, until the number shall be reduced to thirteen; and from that number not less than seven, nor more than nine names as Congress shall direct, shall in the presence of Congress be drawn out by lot, and the persons whose names shall be so drawn or any five of them, shall be commissioners or judges, to hear and finally determine the controversy, so always as a major part of the judges who shall hear the cause shall agree in the determination: and if either party shall neglect to attend at the day appointed, without showing reasons, which Congress shall judge sufficient, or being present shall refuse to strike, the Congress shall proceed to nominate three persons out of each State, and the secretary of Congress shall strike in behalf of such party absent or refusing; and the judgement and sentence of the court to be appointed, in the manner before prescribed, shall be final and conclusive; and if any of the parties shall refuse to submit to the authority of such court, or to appear or defend their claim or cause, the court shall nevertheless proceed to pronounce sentence, or judgement, which shall in like manner be final and decisive, the judgement or sentence and other proceedings being in either case transmitted to Congress, and lodged among the acts of Congress for the security of the parties concerned: provided that every commissioner, before he sits in judgement, shall take an oath to be administered by one of the judges of the supreme or superior court of the State, where the cause shall be tried, 'well and truly to hear and determine the matter in question, according to the best of his judgement, without favor, affection or hope of reward': provided also, that no State shall be deprived of territory for the benefit of the United States.

All controversies concerning the private right of soil claimed under different grants of two or more States, whose jurisdictions as they may respect such lands, and the States which passed such grants are adjusted, the said grants or either of them being at the same time claimed to have originated antecedent to such settlement of jurisdiction, shall on the petition of either party to the Congress of the United States, be finally determined as near as may be in the same manner as is before presecribed for deciding disputes respecting territorial jurisdiction between different States. The United States in Congress assembled shall also have the sole and exclusive right and power of regulating the alloy and value of coin struck by their own authority, or by that of the respective States—fixing the standards of weights and measures throughout the

United States—regulating the trade and managing all affairs with the Indians, not members of any of the States, provided that the legislative right of any State within its own limits be not infringed or violated—establishing or regulating post offices from one State to another, throughout all the United States, and exacting such postage on the papers passing through the same as may be requisite to defray the expenses of the said office—appointing all officers of the land forces, in the service of the United States, excepting regimental officers—appointing all the officers of the naval forces, and commissioning all officers whatever in the service of the United States—making rules for the government and regulation of the said land and naval forces, and directing their operations.

The United States in Congress assembled shall have authority to appoint a committee, to sit in the recess of Congress, to be denominated 'A Committee of the States', and to consist of one delegate from each State; and to appoint such other committees and civil officers as may be necessary for managing the general affairs of the United States under their direction—to appoint one of their members to preside, provided that no person be allowed to serve in the office of president more than one year in any term of three years; to ascertain the necessary sums of money to be raised for the service of the United States, and to appropriate and apply the same for defraying the public expenses—to borrow money, or emit bills on the credit of the United States, transmitting every half-year to the respective States an account of the sums of money so borrowed or emitted—to build and equip a navy—to agree upon the number of land forces, and to make requisitions from each State for its quota, in proportion to the number of white inhabitants in such State; which requisition shall be binding, and thereupon the legislature of each State shall appoint the regimental officers, raise the men and cloath, arm and equip them in a solid-like manner, at the expense of the United States; and the officers and men so cloathed, armed and equipped shall march to the place appointed, and within the time agreed on by the United States in Congress assembled. But if the United States in Congress assembled shall, on consideration of circumstances judge proper that any State should not raise men, or should raise a smaller number of men than the quota thereof, such extra number shall be raised, officered, cloathed, armed and equipped in the same manner as the quota of each State, unless the legislature of such State shall judge that such extra number cannot be safely spread out in the same, in which case they shall raise, officer, cloath, arm and equip as many of such extra number as they judge can be safely spared. And the officers and men so cloathed, armed, and equipped, shall march to the place appointed, and within the time agreed on by the United States in Congress assembled.

The United States in Congress assembled shall never engage in a war, nor grant letters of marque or reprisal in time of peace, nor enter into any treaties or alliances, nor coin money, nor regulate the value thereof, nor ascertain the sums and expenses necessary for the defense and welfare of the United States, or any of them, nor emit bills, nor borrow money on the credit of the United States, nor appropriate money, nor agree upon the number of vessels of war, to be built or purchased, or the number of land or sea forces to be raised, nor appoint a commander in chief of the army or navy, unless nine States assent to the same: nor shall a question on any other point, except for adjourning from day to day be determined, unless by the votes of the majority of the United States in Congress assembled.

The Congress of the United States shall have power to adjourn to any time within the year, and to any place within the United States, so that no period of adjournment be for a longer duration than the space of six months, and shall publish the journal of their proceedings monthly, except such parts thereof relating to treaties, alliances or military operations, as in their judgement require secrecy; and the yeas and nays of the delegates of each State on any question shall be entered on the journal, when it is desired by any delegates of a State, or any of them, at his or their request shall be furnished with a transcript of the said journal, except such parts as are above excepted, to lay before the legislatures of the several States.

Article X
The Committee of the States, or any nine of them, shall be authorized to execute, in the recess of Congress, such of the powers of Congress as the United States in Congress assembled, by the consent of the nine States, shall from time to time think expedient to vest them with; provided that no power be delegated to the said Committee, for the exercise of which, by the Articles of Confederation, the voice of nine States in the Congress of the United States assembled be requisite.

Article XI
Canada acceding to this confederation, and adjoining in the measures of the United States, shall be admitted into, and entitled to all the

advantages of this Union; but no other colony shall be admitted into the same, unless such admission be agreed to by nine States.

Article XII
All bills of credit emitted, monies borrowed, and debts contracted by, or under the authority of Congress, before the assembling of the United States, in pursuance of the present confederation, shall be deemed and considered as a charge against the United States, for payment and satisfaction whereof the said United States, and the public faith are hereby solemnly pledged.

Article XIII
Every State shall abide by the determination of the United States in Congress assembled, on all questions which by this confederation are submitted to them. And the Articles of this Confederation shall be inviolably observed by every State, and the Union shall be perpetual; nor shall any alteration at any time hereafter be made in any of them; unless such alteration be agreed to in a Congress of the United States and be afterwards confirmed by the legislatures of every State.

And Whereas it hath pleased the Great Governor of the World to incline the hearts of the legislatures we respectively represent in Congress, to approve of, and to authorize us to ratify the said Articles of Confederation and perpetual Union. Know Ye that we the undersigned delegates, by virtue of the power and authority to us given for that purpose, do by these presents, in the name and in behalf of our respective constituents, fully and entirely ratify and confirm each and every of the said Articles of Confederation and perpetual Union, and all and singular the matters and things therein contained:

And we do further solemnly plight and engage the faith of our respective constituents, that they shall abide by the determinations of the United States in Congress assembled, on all questions, which by the said Confederation are submitted to them. And that the Articles thereof shall be inviolably observed by the States we respectively represent, and that the Union shall be perpetual
In Witness whereof we have hereunto set our hands in Congress.

Done at Philadelphia in the State of Pennsylvania the ninth day of July in the Year of our Lord One Thousand Seven Hundred and Seventy-Eight, and in the Third Year of the independence of America. Agreed to by Congress 1775

APPENDIX IX   DEFINITIVE TREATY OF PEACE 1783
In the name of the most holy and undivided Trinity.

It having pleased the Divine Providence to dispose the hearts of the most serene and most potent Prince George the Third, by the grace of God, king of Great Britain, France, and Ireland, defender of the faith, duke of Brunswick and Lunebourg, arch- treasurer and prince elector of the Holy Roman Empire etc., and of the United States of America, to forget all past misunderstandings and differences that have unhappily interrupted the good correspondence and friendship which they mutually wish to restore, and to establish such a beneficial and satisfactory intercourse , between the two countries upon the ground of reciprocal advantages and mutual convenience as may promote and secure to both perpetual peace and harmony; and having for this desirable end already laid the foundation of peace and reconciliation by the Provisional Articles signed at Paris on the 30th of November 1782, by the commissioners empowered on each part, which articles were agreed to be inserted in and constitute the Treaty of Peace proposed to be concluded between the Crown of Great Britain and the said United States, but which treaty was not to be concluded until terms of peace should be agreed upon between Great Britain and France and his Britannic Majesty should be ready to conclude such treaty accordingly; and the treaty between Great Britain and France having since been concluded, his Britannic Majesty and the United States of America, in order to carry into full effect the Provisional Articles above mentioned, according to the tenor thereof, have constituted and appointed, that is to say his Britannic Majesty on his part, David Hartley, Esqr., member of the
Parliament of Great Britain, and the said United States on their part,

John Adams, Esqr., late a commissioner of the United States of America at the court of Versailles, late delegate in Congress from the state of Massachusetts, and chief justice of the said state, and minister plenipotentiary of the said United States to their high mightinesses the States General of the United Netherlands;
Benjamin Franklin, Esqr., late delegate in Congress from the state of Pennsylvania, president of the convention of the said state, and minister plenipotentiary from the United States of America at the court of Versailles;

John Jay, Esqr., late president of Congress and chief justice of the state of New York, and minister plenipotentiary from the said United States at the court of Madrid; to be plenipotentiaries for the concluding and signing the present definitive treaty; who after having reciprocally communicated their respective full powers have agreed upon and confirmed the following articles

Article 1:
His Britannic Majesty acknowledges the said United States, viz., New Hampshire, Massachusetts Bay, Rhode Island and Providence Plantations, Connecticut, New York, New Jersey, Pennsylvania, Delaware, Maryland, Virginia, North Carolina, South Carolina and Georgia, to be free sovereign and independent states, that he treats with them as such, and for himself, his heirs, and successors, relinquishes all claims to the government, propriety, and territorial rights of the same and every part thereof.

Article 2:
And that all disputes which might arise in future on the subject of the boundaries of the said United States may be prevented, it is hereby agreed and declared, that the following are and shall be their boundaries, viz.; from the northwest angle of Nova Scotia, viz., that angle which is formed by a line drawn due north from the source of St. Croix River to the highlands; along the said highlands which divide those rivers that empty themselves into the river St. Lawrence, from those which fall into the Atlantic Ocean, to the northwestern most head of Connecticut River; thence down along the middle of that river to the forty-fifth degree of north latitude; from thence by a line due west on said latitude until it strikes the river Iroquois or Cataraquy; thence along the middle of said river into Lake Ontario; through the middle of said lake until it strikes the communication by water between that lake and Lake Erie; thence along the middle of said communication into Lake Erie, through the middle of said lake until it arrives at the water communication between that lake and Lake Huron; thence along the middle of said water communication into Lake Huron, thence through the middle of said lake to the water communication between that lake and Lake Superior; thence through Lake Superior northward of the Isles Royal and Phelipeaux to the Long Lake; thence through the middle of said Long Lake and the water communication between it and the Lake of the Woods, to the said Lake of the Woods; thence through the said lake to the most northwestern most point thereof, and from thence on a due west course to the river Mississippi; thence by a line to be drawn along the middle of the said river Mississippi until it shall intersect the northernmost part of the thirty-first degree of north latitude, South, by a line to be drawn due east from the determination of the line last mentioned in the latitude of thirty-one

degrees of the equator, to the middle of the river Apalachicola or Chattahoochee; thence along the middle thereof to its junction with the Flint River, thence straight to the head of Saint Mary's River; and thence down along the middle of Saint Mary's River to the Atlantic Ocean; east, by a line to be drawn along the middle of the river Saint Croix, from its mouth in the Bay of Fundy to its source, and from its source directly north to the aforesaid highlands which divide the rivers that fall into the Atlantic Ocean from those which fall into the river Saint Lawrence; comprehending all islands within twenty leagues of any part of the shores of the United States, and lying between lines to be drawn due east from the points where the aforesaid boundaries between Nova Scotia on the one part and East Florida on the other shall, respectively, touch the Bay of Fundy and the Atlantic Ocean, excepting such islands as now are or heretofore have been within the limits of the said province of Nova Scotia.

Article 3:
It is agreed that the people of the United States shall continue to enjoy unmolested the right to take fish of every kind on the Grand Bank and on all the other banks of Newfoundland, also in the Gulf of Saint Lawrence and at all other places in the sea, where the inhabitants of both countries used at any time heretofore to fish. And also that the inhabitants of the United States shall have liberty to take fish of every kind on such part of the coast of Newfoundland as British fishermen shall use, (but not to dry or cure the same on that island) and also on the coasts, bays and creeks of all other of his Britannic Majesty's dominions in America; and that the American fishermen shall have liberty to dry and cure fish in any of the unsettled bays, harbors, and creeks of Nova Scotia, Magdalen Islands, and Labrador, so long as the same shall remain unsettled, but so soon as the same or either of them shall be settled It shall not be lawful for the said fishermen to dry or cure fish at such settlement without a previous agreement for that purpose with the inhabitants, proprietors, or possessors of the ground

Article 4:
It is agreed that creditors on either side shall meet with no lawful impediment to the recovery of the full value in sterling money of all bona fide debts heretofore contracted.

Article 5:

It is agreed that Congress shall earnestly recommend it to the legislatures of the respective states to provide for the restitution of all estates, rights, and properties, which have been confiscated belonging to real British subjects; and also of the estates, rights, and properties of person's resident in districts in the possession on his Majesty's arms and who have not borne arms against the said United States. And that persons of any other description shall have free liberty to go to any part or parts of any of the thirteen United States and therein to remain twelve months unmolested in their endeavors to obtain the restitution of such of their estates, rights, and properties as may have been confiscated; and that Congress shall also earnestly recommend to the several states a reconsideration and revision of all acts or laws regarding the premises, so as to render the said laws or acts perfectly consistent not only with justice and equity but with that spirit of conciliation which on the return of the blessings of peace should universally prevail. And that Congress shall also earnestly recommend to the several states that the estates, rights, and properties, of such last-mentioned persons shall be restored to them, they refunding to any persons who may be now in possession the bona fide price (where any has been given) which such persons may have paid on purchasing any of the said lands, rights, or properties since the confiscation.

And it is agreed that all persons who have any interest in confiscated lands, either by debts, marriage settlements, or otherwise, shall meet with no lawful impediment in the prosecution of their just rights.

Article 6:
That there shall be no future confiscations made nor any prosecutions commenced against any person or persons for, or by reason of, the part which he or they may have taken in the present war, and that no person shall on that account suffer any future loss or damage, either in his person, liberty, or property; and that those who may be in confinement on such charges at the time of the ratification of the treaty in America shall be immediately set at liberty, and the prosecutions so commenced be discontinued.

Article 7:
There shall be a firm and perpetual peace between his Brittanic Majesty and the said states, and between the subjects of the one and the citizens of the other, wherefore all hostilities both by sea and land shall from henceforth cease.

All prisoners on both sides shall be set at liberty, and his Brittanic Majesty shall with all convenient speed, and without causing any destruction, or carrying away any Negroes or other property of the American inhabitants, withdraw all his armies, garrisons, and fleets from the said United States, and from every post, place, and harbor within the same; leaving in all fortifications, the American artillery that may be therein; and shall also order and cause all archives, records, deeds, and papers belonging to any of the said states, or their citizens, which in the course of the war may have fallen into the hands of his officers, to be forthwith restored and delivered to the proper states and persons to whom they belong.

Article 8:
The navigation of the river Mississippi, from its source to the ocean, shall forever remain free and open to the subjects of Great Britain and the citizens of the United States.

Article 9:
In case it should so happen that any place or territory belonging to Great Britain or to the United States should have been conquered by the arms of either from the other before the arrival of the said Provisional Articles in America, it is agreed that the same shall be restored without difficulty and without requiring any compensation

Article 10:
The solemn ratifications of the present treaty expedited in good and due form shall be exchanged between the contracting parties in the space of six months or sooner, if possible, to be computed from the day of the signatures of the present treaty. In witness, whereof we the undersigned, their ministers plenipotentiary, have in their name and in virtue of our full powers, signed with our hands the present definitive treaty and caused the seals of our arms to be affixed thereto.
Done at Paris, this third day of September in the year of our Lord, one thousand seven hundred and eighty-three.
D. HARTLEY (SEAL)
JOHN ADAMS (SEAL)
B. FRANKLIN (SEAL)
JOHN JAY (SEAL)

THERE IS NO ARTICLE 11 OR 12!!!!

APPENDIX X

CONSTITUTION OF THE UNITED STATES OF AMERICA

Preamble
We the people of the United States, to form a more perfect union, establish justice, insure domestic tranquility, provide for the common defense, promote the general welfare, and secure blessings of liberty to ourselves and our posterity, do ordain and establish this Constitution for the United States of America.

Article. I.
Section. 1.
All legislative powers herein granted shall be vested in a Congress of the United States, which shall consist of a Senate and House of Representatives.

Section. 2.
The House of Representatives shall be composed of members chosen every second year by the people of the several states, and the electors in each state shall have the qualifications requisite for electors of the most numerous branches of the state legislature.

No person shall be a Representative who shall not have attained to the age of twenty-five years and been seven years a citizen of the United States, and who shall not, when elected, be an inhabitant of that state in which he shall be chosen.

Representatives and | direct taxes | shall be apportioned among the several states which may be included within this union, according to their respective numbers, which shall be determined by adding to the whole number of free persons, including those bound to service for a term of years, and excluding Indians not taxed, three fifths of all other persons.

The actual enumeration shall be made within three years after the first meeting of the Congress of the United States, and within every subsequent term of ten years, in such manner as they shall by law direct.

The number of Representatives shall not exceed one for every thirty thousand, but each state shall have at least one Representative; and until such enumeration shall be made, the state of New Hampshire shall be entitled to chuse three, Massachusetts eight, Rhode-Island and

Providence Plantations one, Connecticut five, New-York six, New Jersey four, Pennsylvania eight, Delaware one, Maryland six, Virginia ten, North Carolina five, South Carolina five, and Georgia three.

When vacancies happen in the representation from any state, the executive authority thereof shall issue writs of election to fill such vacancies.
The House of Representatives shall chuse their speaker and other officers; and shall have the sole power of impeachment.

Section. 3.
The Senate of the United States shall be composed of two Senators from each state, chosen by the legislature thereof for six years; and each Senator shall have one vote.

Immediately after they shall be assembled in consequence of the first election, they shall be divided as equally as may be into three classes. The seats of the Senators of the first class shall be vacated at the expiration of the second year, of the second class at the expiration of the fourth year, and of the third class at the expiration of the sixth year, so that one third may be chosen every second year; and if vacancies happen by resignation, or otherwise, during the recess of the legislature of any state, the executive thereof may make temporary appointments until the next meeting of the legislature, which shall then fill such vacancies.

No person shall be a Senator who shall not have attained to the age of thirty years and been nine years a citizen of the United States, and who shall not, when elected, be an inhabitant of that state for which he shall be chosen.

The Vice President of the United States shall be President of the Senate, but shall have no vote, unless they be equally divided. The Senate shall chuse their other officers, and a President pro tempore, in the absence of the Vice President, or when he shall exercise the office of President of the United States.

The Senate shall have the sole power to try all impeachments. When sitting for that purpose, they shall be on oath or affirmation. When the President of the United States is tried, the Chief Justice shall preside: and no person shall be convicted without the concurrence of two thirds of the members present.

Judgment in cases of impeachment shall not extend further than to removal from office, and disqualification to hold and enjoy any office of honor, trust or profit under the United States: but the party convicted shall nevertheless be liable and subject to indictment, trial, judgment and punishment, according to law.

Section. 4.
The times, places and manner of holding elections for Senators and Representatives, shall be prescribed in each state by the legislature thereof; but the Congress may at any time by law make or alter such regulations, except as to the places of choosing Senators. The Congress shall assemble at least once in every year, and such meeting shall be on the first Monday in December, unless they shall by law appoint a different day.

Section.. 5.

Each House shall be the judge of the elections, returns and qualifications of its own members, and a majority of each shall constitute a quorum to do business; but a smaller number may adjourn from day to day, and may be authorized to compel the attendance of absent members, in such manner, and under such penalties as each House may provide.

Each House may determine the rules of its proceedings, punish its members for disorderly behavior, and, with the concurrence of two thirds, expel a member.

Each House shall keep a journal of its proceedings, and from time to time publish the same, excepting such parts as may in their judgment require secrecy; and the yeas and nays of the members of either House on any question shall, at the desire of one fifth of those present, be entered on the journal.
Neither House, during the session of Congress, shall, without the consent of the other, adjourn for more than three days, nor to any other place than that in which the two Houses shall be sitting.
Section. 6.
The Senators and Representatives shall receive a compensation for their services, to be ascertained by law, and paid out of the treasury of the United States. They shall in all cases, except treason, felony and breach of the peace, be privileged from arrest during their attendance at the session of their respective Houses, and in going to and returning from the

same; and for any speech or debate in either House, they shall not be questioned in any other place.

Senator or Representative shall, during the time for which he was elected, be appointed to any civil office under the authority of the United States, which shall have been created, or the emoluments whereof shall have been increased during such time; and no person holding any office under the United States, shall be a member of either House during his continuance in office

Section. 7.
All bills for raising revenue shall originate in the House of Representatives; but the Senate may propose or concur with amendments as on other bills.

Every bill which shall have passed the House of Representatives and the Senate, shall, before it become a law, be presented to the President of the United States: If he approve he shall sign it, but if not he shall return it, with his objections to that House in which it shall have originated, who shall enter the objections at large on their journal, and proceed to reconsider it. If after such reconsideration two thirds of that House shall agree to pass the bill, it shall be sent, together with the objections, to the other House, by which it shall likewise be reconsidered, and if approved by two thirds of that House, it shall become a law. But in all such cases the votes of both Houses shall be determined by yeas and nays, and the names of the persons voting for and against the bill shall be entered on the journal of each House respectively. If any bill shall not be returned by the President within ten days (Sundays excepted) after it shall have been presented to him, the same shall be a law, in like manner as if he had signed it, unless the Congress by their adjournment prevent its return, in which case it shall not be a law.

Every order, resolution, or vote to which the concurrence of the Senate and House of Representatives may be necessary (except on a question of adjournment) shall be presented to the President of the United States; and before the same shall take effect, shall be approved by him, or being disapproved by him, shall be repassed by two thirds of the Senate and House of Representatives, according to the rules and limitations prescribed in the case of a bill.

Section. 8.

The Congress shall have power to lay and collect taxes, duties, imposts and excises, to pay the debts and provide for the common defence and general welfare of the United States; but all duties, imposts and excises shall be uniform throughout the United States;

To borrow money on the credit of the United States;

To regulate commerce with foreign nations, and among the several states, and with the Indian tribes;

To establish a uniform rule of naturalization, and uniform laws about bankruptcies throughout the United States;

To coin money, regulate the value thereof, and of foreign coin, and fix the standard of weights and measures;

To provide for the punishment of counterfeiting the securities and current coin of the United States; To establish post offices and post roads;

To promote the progress of science and useful arts, by securing for limited times to authors and inventors the exclusive right to their respective writings and discoveries;

To constitute tribunals inferior to the Supreme Court;

To define and punish piracies and felonies committed on the high seas, and offences against the law of nations;

To declare war, grant letters of mark and reprisal, and make rules concerning captures on land and water;

To raise and support armies, but no appropriation of money to that use shall be for a longer term than two years;

To provide and maintain a navy;

To make rules for the government and regulation of the land and naval forces;

To provide for calling forth the militia to execute the laws of the union, suppress insurrections and repel invasions;

To provide for organizing, arming, and disciplining, the militia, and for governing such part of them as may be employed in the service of the United States, reserving to the states respectively, the appointment of the officers, and the authority of training the militia according to the discipline prescribed by Congress;

To exercise exclusive legislation in all cases whatsoever, over such district (not exceeding ten miles square) as may, by cession of particular states, and the acceptance of Congress, become the seat of the government of the United States, and to exercise like authority over all places purchased by the consent of the legislature of the state in which the same shall be, for the erection of forts, magazines, arsenals, dockyards, and other needful buildings; — And

To make all laws which shall be necessary and proper for carrying into execution the foregoing powers, and all other powers vested by this Constitution in the government of the United States, or in any department or officer thereof.

Section. 9.
The migration or importation of such persons as any of the states now existing shall think proper to admit, shall not be prohibited by the Congress prior to the year one thousand eight hundred and eight, but a tax or duty may be imposed on such importation, not exceeding ten dollars for each person.
The privilege of the writ of habeas corpus shall not be suspended, unless when in cases of rebellion or invasion the public safety may require it.
No bill of attainder or ex post facto law shall be passed.

No capitation, or other direct, tax shall be laid, unless in proportion to the census or enumeration herein before directed to be taken. No tax or duty shall be laid on articles exported from any state. No preference shall be given by any regulation of commerce or revenue to the ports of one state over those of another; nor shall vessels bound to, or from, one state, be obliged to enter, clear, or pay duties in another.

No money shall be drawn from the treasury, but in consequence of appropriations made by law; and a regular statement and account of the receipts and expenditures of all public money shall be published from time to time.

No title of nobility shall be granted by the United States: and no person holding any office of profit or trust under them, shall, without the consent of the Congress, accept of any present, emolument, office, or title, of any kind whatever, from any king, prince, or foreign state.

Section. 10.
No state shall enter into any treaty, alliance, or confederation; grant letters of marque and reprisal; coin money; emit bills of credit; make anything but gold and silver coin a tender in payment of debts; pass any bill of attainder, ex post facto law, or law impairing the obligation of contracts, or grant any title of nobility.
No state shall, without the consent of the Congress, lay any imposts or duties on imports or exports, except what may be absolutely necessary

for executing it's inspection laws: and the net produce of all duties and imposts, laid by any state on imports or exports, shall be for the use of the treasury of the United States; and all such laws shall be subject to the revision and control of the Congress. No state shall, without the consent of Congress, lay any duty of tonnage, keep troops, or ships of war in time of peace, enter into any agreement or compact with another state, or with a foreign power, or engage in war, unless invaded, or in such imminent danger as will not admit of delay.

Article. II.
Section. 1.
The executive power shall be vested in a President of the United States of America. He shall hold his office during the term of four years, and, together with the Vice President, chosen for the same term, be elected, as follows:

Each state may direct, a number of electors, equal to the whole number of Senators and Representatives to which the state may be entitled in the Congress: but no Senator or Representative, or person holding an office of trust or profit under the United States, shall be appointed an elector.

The electors shall meet in their respective states, and vote by ballot for two persons, of whom one at least shall not be an inhabitant of the same state with themselves. And they shall make a list of all the persons voted for, and of the number of votes for each; which list they shall sign and certify and transmit sealed to the seat of the government of the United States, directed to the President of the Senate.
The President of the Senate shall, in the presence of the Senate and House of Representatives, open all the certificates, and the votes shall then be counted.

The person having the greatest number of votes shall be the President, if such number be a majority of the whole number of electors appointed; and if there be more than one who have such majority, and have an equal number of votes, then the House of Representatives shall immediately chuse by ballot one of them for President; and if no person have a majority, then from the five highest on the list the said House shall in like manner chuse the President.
But in chusing the President, the votes shall be taken by states, the representation from each state having one vote; A quorum for this purpose shall consist of a member or members from two thirds of the states, and a majority of all the states shall be necessary to a choice. In

every case, after the choice of the President, the person having the greatest number of votes of the electors shall be the Vice President. But if there should remain two or more who have equal votes, the Senate shall choose from them by ballot the Vice President.

The Congress may determine the time of choosing the electors, and the day on which they shall give their votes; which day shall be the same throughout the United States.

No person except a natural born citizen, or a citizen of the United States, at the time of the adoption of this Constitution, shall be eligible to the office of President; neither shall any person be eligible to that office who shall not have attained to the age of thirty-five years, and been fourteen years a resident within the United States.

In case of the removal of the President from office, or of his death, resignation, or inability to discharge the powers and duties of the said office, the same shall devolve on the Vice President, and the Congress may by law provide for the case of removal, death, resignation, or inability, both of the President and Vice President, declaring what officer shall then act as President, and such officer shall act accordingly, until the disability be removed, or a President shall be elected.

The President shall, at stated times, receive for his services, a compensation, which shall neither be increased nor diminished during the period for which he shall have been elected, and he shall not receive within that period any other emolument from the United States, or any of them.

Before he enter on the execution of his office, he shall take the following oath or affirmation: — "I do solemnly swear (or affirm) that I will faithfully execute the office of President of the United States, and will to the best of my ability, preserve, protect and defend the Constitution of the United States."

Section. 2.
The President shall be commander in chief of the Army and Navy of the United States, and of the militia of the several states, when called into the actual service of the United States; he may require the opinion, in writing, of the principal officer in each of the executive departments, upon any subject relating to the duties of their respective offices, and he shall have

power to grant reprieves and pardons for offences against the United States, except in cases of impeachment.

He shall have power, by and with the advice and consent of the Senate, to make treaties, provided two thirds of the Senators present concur; and he shall nominate, and by and with the advice and consent of the Senate, shall appoint ambassadors, other public ministers and consuls, judges of the Supreme Court, and all other officers of the United States, whose appointments are not herein otherwise provided for, and which shall be established by law: but the Congress may by law vest the appointment of such inferior officers, as they think proper, in the President alone, in the courts of law, or in the heads of departments.

The President shall have power to fill up all vacancies that may happen during the recess of the Senate, by granting commissions which shall expire at the end of their next session.

Section. 3.
He shall from time to time give to the Congress information of the state of the union, and recommend to their consideration such measures as he shall judge necessary and expedient; he may, on extraordinary occasions, convene both Houses, or either of them, and in case of disagreement between them, with respect to the time of adjournment, he may adjourn them to such time as he shall think proper; he shall receive ambassadors and other public ministers; he shall take care that the laws be faithfully executed, and shall commission all the officers of the United States.

Section. 4. The President, Vice President and all civil officers of the United States, shall be removed from office on impeachment for, and conviction of, treason, bribery, or other high crimes and misdemeanors.

Article III.
Section. 1.
The judicial power of the United States shall be vested in one Supreme Court, and in such inferior courts as the Congress may from time to time ordain and establish.
The judges, both of the supreme and inferior courts, shall hold their offices during good behavior, and shall, at stated times, receive for their services a compensation, which shall not be diminished during their continuance in office.
Section. 2.

The judicial power shall extend to all cases, in law and equity, arising under this Constitution, the laws of the United States, and treaties made, or which shall be made, under their authority; — to all cases affecting ambassadors, other public ministers, and consuls; — to all cases of admiralty and maritime jurisdiction; — to controversies to which the United States shall be a party; —

to controversies between two or more states; — between a state and citizens of another state; — between citizens of different states; — between citizens of the same state claiming lands under grants of different states, and between a state, or the citizens thereof, and foreign states, citizens, or subjects.

In all cases affecting ambassadors, other public ministers, and consuls, and those in which a state shall be party, the Supreme Court shall have original jurisdiction. In all the other cases before mentioned, the Supreme Court shall have appellate jurisdiction, both as to law and fact, with such exceptions, and under such regulations as the congress shall make.

The trial of all crimes, except in cases of impeachment, shall be by jury; and such trial shall be held in the state where the said crimes shall have been committed; but when not committed within any state, the trial shall be at such place or places as the congress may by law have directed.

Section. 3.
Treason against the United States shall consist only in levying war against them, or in adhering to their enemies, giving them aid and comfort. No person shall be convicted of treason unless on the testimony of two witnesses to the same overt act, or on confession in open court. The Congress shall have power to declare the punishment of treason, but no attainder of treason shall work corruption of blood, or forfeiture except during the life of the person attainted.

Article. IV.

Section. 1.
Full faith and credit shall be given in each state to the public acts, records, and judicial proceedings of every other state. And the Congress may by general laws prescribe the manner in which such acts, records and proceedings shall be proved, and the effect thereof.
Section . 2.

The citizens of each state shall be entitled to all privileges and immunities of citizens in the several states.

A person charged in any state with treason, felony, or other crime, who shall flee from justice, and be found in another state, shall on demand of the executive authority of the state from which he fled, be delivered up, to be removed to the state having jurisdiction of the crime.

No person held to service or labor in one state, under the laws thereof, escaping into another, shall, in consequence of any law or regulation therein, be discharged from such service or labor, but shall be delivered up on claim of the party to whom such service or labor may be due.

Section. 3.

New states may be admitted by the Congress into this union; but no new state shall be formed or erected within the jurisdiction of any other state; nor any state be formed by the junction of two or more states, or parts of states, without the consent of the legislatures of the states concerned as well as of the congress.

The Congress shall have power to dispose of and make all needful rules and regulations respecting the territory or other property belonging to the United States; and nothing in this Constitution shall be so construed as to prejudice any claims of the United States, or of any state.

The United States shall guarantee to every state in this union a republican form of government, and shall protect each of them against invasion; and on application of the legislature, or of the executive (when the legislature cannot be convened), against domestic violence

Article. V.

The Congress, whenever two thirds of both houses shall deem it necessary, shall propose amendments to this Constitution, or, on the application of the legislatures of two thirds of the several states, shall call a convention for proposing amendments, which, in either case, shall be valid to all intents and purposes, as part of this the several states, or by conventions in three fourths thereof, as the one or the other mode of ratification may be proposed by the Congress; provided that no amendment which may be made prior to the year one thousand eight hundred and eight shall in any manner affect the first and fourth clauses in the ninth Section of the first Article; and that no state, without its consent, shall be deprived of its equal suffrage in the Senate.

Article. VI.

All debts contracted, and engagements entered, before the adoption of this Constitution, shall be as valid against the United States under this Constitution, as under the Confederation. This Constitution, and the laws of the United States which shall be made in pursuance thereof; and all treaties made, or which shall be made, under the authority of the United States, shall be the supreme law of the land; and the judges in every state shall be bound thereby, anything in the Constitution or laws of any State to the notwithstanding.

Fellow Citizens of the Senate and the House of Representatives.
Among the vicissitude's incident to life, no event could have filled me with greater anxieties than that of which the notification was transmitted by your order and received on the fourteenth day of the present month.

On the one hand, I was summoned by my Country, whose voice I can never hear but with veneration and love, from a retreat which I had chosen with the fondest predilection, and, in my flattering hopes, with an immutable decision, as the asylum of my declining years: a retreat which was rendered every day more necessary as well as more dear to me, by the addition of habit to inclination, and of frequent interruptions in my health to the gradual waste committed on it by time.

 On the other hand, the magnitude and difficulty of the trust to which the voice of my Country called me, being sufficient to awaken in the wisest and most experienced of her citizens, a distrustful scrutiny into his qualifications, could not but overwhelm with despondence, one, who, inheriting inferior endowments from nature and unpractised in the duties of civil administration, ought to be peculiarly conscious of his own deficiencies

. In this conflict of emotions, all I dare aver, is, that it has been my faithful study to collect my duty from a just appreciation of every circumstance, by which it might be affected.

All I dare hope, is, that, if in executing this task I have been too much swayed by a grateful remembrance of former instances, or by an affectionate sensibility to this transcendent proof, of the confidence of my fellow-citizens; and have thence too little consulted my incapacity as well as disinclination for the weighty and untried cares before me; my error will be palliated by the motives which misled me, and its consequences be judged by my Country, with some share of the partiality in which they originated.

Such being the impressions under which I have, in obedience to the public summons, repaired to the present station; it would be peculiarly improper to omit in this first official Act, my fervent supplications to that Almighty Being who rules over the Universe, who presides in the Councils of Nations, and whose providential aids can supply every human defect, that his benediction may consecrate to the liberties and happiness of the People of the United States, a Government instituted by themselves for these essential purposes: and may enable every instrument employed in its administration to execute with success, the functions allotted to his charge.

In tendering this homage to the Great Author of every public and private good I assure myself that it expresses your sentiments not less than my own; nor those of my fellow-citizens at large, less than either.

No People can be bound to acknowledge and adore the invisible hand, which conducts the Affairs of men more than the People of the United States.

Every step, by which they have advanced to the character of an independent nation, seems to have been distinguished by some token of providential agency.

And in the important revolution just accomplished in the system of their United Government, the tranquil deliberations and voluntary consent of so many distinct communities, from which the event has resulted, cannot be compared with how most Governments have been established, without some return of pious gratitude along with a humble anticipation of the future blessings which the past seem to presage.

These reflections, arising out of the present crisis, have forced themselves too strongly on my mind to be suppressed. You will join with me I trust in thinking, that there are none under the influence of which, the proceedings of a new and free Government can more auspiciously commence.

By the article establishing the Executive Department, it is made the duty of the President "to recommend to your consideration, such measures as he shall judge necessary and expedient. "The circumstances under which I now meet you, will acquit me from entering into that subject, farther than to refer to the Great Constitutional Charter under which you are assembled; and which, in defining your powers, designates the objects to which your attention is to be given.

It will be more consistent with those circumstances, and far more congenial with the feelings which actuate me, to substitute, in place of a recommendation of measures, the tribute that is due to the talents, trectitude and the patriotism which adorn the characters selected to devise and adopt them

In these honorable qualifications, I behold the surest pledges, that as on one side, no local prejudices, or attachments; no seperate views, nor party animosities, will misdirect the comprehensive and equal eye which ought to watch over this great assemblage of communities and interests: so, on another, that the foundations of our National policy will be laid in the pure and immutable principles of private morality; and the pre-eminence of a free Government, be exemplified by all the attributes which can win the affections of its Citizens, and command the respect of the world.

I dwell on this prospect with every satisfaction which an ardent love for my Country can inspire: since there is no truth more thoroughly established, than that there exists in the economy and course of nature, an indissoluble union between virtue and happiness, between duty and advantage, between the genuine maxims of an honest and magnanimous policy, and the solid rewards of public prosperity and felicity:

 Since we ought to be no less persuaded that the propitious smiles of Heaven, can never be expected on a nation that disregards the eternal rules of order and right, which Heaven itself has ordained:
And since the preservation of the sacred fire of liberty, and the destiny of the Republican model of Government, are justly considered as deeply, perhaps as finally staked, on the experiment entrusted to the hands of the American people.
Besides the ordinary objects submitted to your care, it will remain with your judgment to decide, how far an exercise of the occasional power delegated by the Fifth article of the Constitution is rendered expedient at the present juncture by the nature of objections which have been urged against the System, or by the degree of inquietude which has given birth to them.

Instead of undertaking recommendations on this subject, in which I could be guided by no lights derived from official opportunities, I shall again give way to my entire confidence in your discernment and pursuit of the public good:

For I assure myself that whilst you carefully avoid every alteration which might endanger the benefits of a United and effective Government, or which ought to await the future lessons of experience; a reverence for the characteristic rights of freemen, and a regard for the public harmony, will sufficiently influence your deliberations on the question how far the former can be more impregnably fortified, or the latter be safely and advantageously promoted. most properly addressed to the House of Representatives.

It concerns myself, and will therefore be as brief as possible.

When I was first honoured with a call into the Service of my Country, then on the eve of an arduous struggle for its liberties, the light in which I contemplated my duty required that I should renounce every pecuniary compensation.

From this resolution, I have in no instance departed.

And being still under the impressions which produced it, I must decline as inapplicable to myself, any share in the personal emoluments, which may be indispensably included in a permanent provision for the Executive Department; and must accordingly pray that the pecuniary estimates for the Station in which I am placed, may, during my continuance in it, be limited to such actual expenditures as the public good may be thought to require.awakened by the occasion which brings us together, I shall take my present leave; but not without resorting once more to the benign parent of the human race, in humble supplication that since he has been pleased to favour the American people, with opportunities for deliberating in perfect tranquility, and dispositions for deciding with unparellelled unanimity on a form of Government, for the security of their Union, and the advancement of their happiness; so his divine blessing may be equally conspicuous in the enlarged views, the temperate consultations, and the wise measures on which the success of this Government must depend.

APPENDIX XII

HENRY'S REMARKS ON CONSTITUTION

(The author has carefully researched Henry's numerous speeches during the Constitution ratification process. These are Henry's actual words and the author has collected them from the numerous times he spoke and given weight to his strongest fears and concerns They were not necessarily said in the order that the author has placed them.)

"THAT GOVERNMENT HAS ALWAYS BEEN A CHOICE BETWEEN TWO EVILS HAS BEEN A LONG-STANDING MAXIM. EVILS ADMITTED IN RDER TO BE REMOVED SUBSEQUENTLY, AND TRYANNY SUBMITTED TO IN ORDER TO BE EXCLUEED BY A SUBSQNENT ALTERATION, ARE THINGS TOTALLY NEW TO ME.

I ASK, DOES EXPERIENCE WARRANT SUCH A THING FROM THE BEGINNING OF THE WORLD TO THIS DAY? DO YOU ENTER INTO A COMPACT FIRST, AND AFTERWARDS SETTLE THE TERMS OF THE GOVERNMENT?

THIS CONFEDERATION MERITS THE HIGHEST VALUE
IT CARRIED US THROUGH A LONG AND DANGEROUS WAR;

IT HAS SECURED US A TERRITORY GREATER THAN ANY EUROPEAN MONARCH POSSESSES; AND SHALL A GOVERNMENT WHICH HAS BEEN STRONG AND VIGOROUS, BE ABANONED SO QUICKLY?

THIS SIR IS THE LANGUAGE OF DEMOCRACY-THAT A MAJORITY HAVE A RIGHT TO ALTER GOVERNMENT WHEN FOUND TO BE OPPRESSIVE.

BUT HOW DIFFERENT IS YOUR NEW CONSITIUTION FROM THIS!

THIS CONSITUTION IS SAID TO HAVE BEAUTIFUL FEATURES; BUT WHEN I COME TO EXAMINE THESE FEATURES SIR, THEY APPEAR TO ME HORRIBLY FRIGHTFUL.

IT SQUINTS TOWARDS MONARCY, AND DOES NOT THIS RAISE INDIGNATION IN THE BREAST OF EVERY TRUE AMERICAN?

YOUR PRESIDENT MAY EASILY BECOME KING. IF HE BE A MAN OF AMBITION, HOW EASY FOR HIM TO RENDER HIMSELF ABSOLUTE. THE ARMY IS IN HIS HANDS, AND HE MAY SEIZE THE FIRST AUSPICIOUS MOMENT TO ACCOMPLISH HIS DESIGN,

YOUR SENATE IS SO IMPERFECTLY STRUCTURED THAT YOUR DEAREST RIGHTS MAY BE SACRIFICED TO WHAT MAY BE A CONTINUE FOR EVER UNCHANGEABLY THIS GOVERNMENT, ALTHO HORRIDLY DEFECTIVE.

HOW DIFFERENT FROM THE SENTIMENTS OF FREEMEN THAT A CONTEMPTIBLE MINORITY CAN PREVENT THE GOOD OF THE MAJORITY.

THE SENATE, BY MAKING TREATIES, MAY DESTROY YOUR LIBERTY AND LAWS FOR WANT OF ANY RESPONSIBILITY. AND THAT THE PRESERVATION OF OUR LIBERTY DEPENDS ON THE SINGLE CHANCE OF MEN BEING VIRTIOUS ENOUGH TO MAKE LAWS TO PUNISH THEMSELVES???

SHOW ME THAT COUNTRY WHERE THE RIGHTS AND LIBERTIES OF THE PEOPLE WERE PLACED ON THE SOLE CHANCE OF THEIR RULERS BEING GOOD MEN WITHOUT A CONSEQUENT LOSS OF LIBERTY.

WHERE ARE YOUR CHECKS IN THS GOVERNMENT?

POWER IS THE GREAT EVIL WITH WHICH WE ARE CONTENDING.

WE CURRENTLY HAVE DIVIDED POWER BETWEEN THREE BRANCHES OF GOVERNMENT AND ERECTED CHECKS AND BALANCES TO PREVENT ABUSE OF POWER.

HOWEVER, WHERE IN THIS NEW DOCUMENT IS THE CHECK ON THE POWER OF THE JUDICARY?

IF WE FAIL TO CHECK THE POWER OF THE JUDICIARY, I PREDICT THAT WE WILL EVENTUALLY LIVE UNDER JUDICIAL TYRANNY.

THE RIGHTS OF TRIAL BY JURY, LIBERTY OF THE PRESS, ALL PRETENSIONS TO HUMAN RIGHTS AND PRIVILEDGES, ARE RENDERED INSECURE, IF NOT LOST.

HOW DOES YOUR TRIAL BY JURY STAND? IN CIVIL CASES GONENOT SUFFICENTLY SECURED IN CRIMINAL. WHEREFORE ARE YOUR RELIGIOUS RIGHTS?

IS IT NECESSARY FOR YOUR LIBERTY THAT YOU SHOULD ABANDON THOSE GREAT RIGHTS?

BUT WE ARE TOLD WE NEED NOT FEAR, BECAUSE THOSE IN POWER, BEING OUR REPRESENTATIVES, WILL NOT ABUSE THAT POWER WE PUT IN THEIR HANDS.

I AM NOT WELL VERSED IN HISTORY BUT HAS LIBERTY BEEN DESTROYED MORE BY THE PEOPLE OR BY THE TYRANNY OF RULERS?

YOU WILL FIND THE BALANCE ON THE SIDE OF TYRANNY.

HAPPY YOU WILL BE IF YOU MISS THE FATE OF THOSE NATIONS, WHO SUFFERED THEIR LIBERTY
TO BE WRESTED FROM THEM, WHO NOW GROAN UNDER INTOLERABLE DESPOTISM?

MOST OF THOSE NATIONS HAVE BEEN THE VICTIMS OF THEIR OWN FOLLY. WHILE THEY ACQUIRED THEIR VISIONARY BLESSINGS, THEY LOST THEIR FREEDOMS.

LIBERTY, THE GREATEST OF ALL EARTHLY BLESSINGS, GIVE US THAT JEWEL AND YOU MAY HAVE ALL THE REST. SUSPECT EVERYONE WHO APPROACHES THAT JEWEL. NOTHING WILL PRESERVE BUT DOWNRIGHT FORCE.

WHEN YOU GIVE UP THAT FORCE, YOU ARE INEVITABLY RUINED.

 MY GREATEST OBJECTION TO THIS GOVERNMENT IS THAT WE HAVE NO MEANS OF DEFENDING OUR RIGHTS.

HAVE WE THE MEANS OF RESISTING DISCIPLINED ARMIES, WHEN OUR ONLY DEFENSE, THE MILITIA, IS PUT INTO THE HANDS OF CONGRESS?

THIS ACQUISTION WILL TRAMPLE ON OUR FALLEN LIBERTY. WHERE HAS THE SPIRIT OF AMERICA GONE?

WHAT SERVICE WOULD THE MILITIA BE TO YOU, WHEN MOST PROBABLY, YOU WILL NOT HAVE A SINGLE MUSKET IN THE STATE? OUR ARMS ARE TO BE PROVIDED BY CONGRESS, THEY MAY, OR MAY NOT ARM YOU.

DID YOU EVER READ OF ANY REVOLUTION IN A NATION, BROUGHT ABOUT BY THE PUNISHMENT OF THOSE IN POWER, INFLICTED BY THOSE WHO HAD NO POWER?

CONGRESS, BY THE POWER OF TAXATION, BY THAT OF RAISING AN ARMY, AND BY THEIR CONTROL OVER THE MILITIA, HAVETHE POWEROF THE SWORD IN ONE HAND, AND THE PURSE IN THE OTHER

WHERE AND WHEN DID FREEDOM EXIST, WHEN THE SWORD AND PURSE WERE GIVEN UP FROM THE PEOPLE?

UNLESS A MIRACLE IN HUMAN AFFAIRS INTERPOSED, NO NATION EVER RETAINED ITS LIBERTY AFTER THE LOSS OF THE SWORD AND PURSE.
A STANDING ARMY WE SHALL HAVE, AND HOW ARE YOU TO PUNISH THEM? WHAT RESISTANCE COULD BE MADE? THE ATTEMPT WOULD BE MADNESS.

YOUR ARMS, WHEREWITH YOU COULD DEFEND YOURSELVES ARE GONE.

YOU READ OF A RIOT ACT IN A COUNTRY WHICH IS CALLED ONE OF THE FREEST IN THE WORLD, WHERE A FEW NEIGHBORS CANNOT ASSEMBLE WITHOUT THE RISK OF BEING SHOT BY A HIRED SOLDIERY.

WE MAY SEE SUCH AN ACT IN AMERICA.

IT IS SAID THAT EIGHT STATES HAVE ADOPTED THIS PLAN. I DECLARE THAT IF 12 AND ½ HAD ADOPTED IT, I WOULD, WITH MANLY FIRMNESS, REJECT IT.

I HAVE NOT SAID THE ONE HUNDRED THOUSAND PART OF WHAT I HAD ON MY MIND AND WISH TO IMPART.

BEFORE YOU ABANDON YOUR PRESENT SYSTEM, MAY YOU BE FULLY APPRIZED OF THE DANGERS OF THIS CONSTITUTION, NOT BY FATAL EXPERIENCE, BUT BY A MOREABLER ADVOCATE THAN I.

APPENDIX XIII
BILL OF RIGHTS

THE FIRST 10 AMENDMENTS TO THE CONSTITUTION AS RATIFIE BY THE STATES

Preamble

Congress OF THE United States *begun and held at the City of New York, on Wednesday the Fourth of March one thousand seven hundred and eighty-nine.*

THE Conventions of a number of the States having at the time of their adopting the Constitution, expressed a desire, in order to prevent **misconstruction** or **abuse** of its powers, that further **declaratory** and **restrictive** clauses should be added: And as extending the ground of **public confidence** in the Government, will best insure the **beneficent ends** of its institution.

RESOLVED by the Senate and House of Representatives of the United States of America, in Congress assembled, two thirds of both Houses concurring, that the following Articles be proposed to the Legislatures of the **several** States, as Amendments to the Constitution of the United States, all or any of which Articles, when ratified by three fourths of the said Legislatures, to be valid to all intents and purposes, as part of the said Constitution; viz.:

ARTICLES in addition to, and Amendment of the Constitution of the United States of America, proposed by Congress, and ratified by the Legislatures   of the **several** States, pursuant to the fifth Article of the original Constitution.

Amendment I
Congress shall make no law respecting an establishment of religion, or prohibiting the free exercise thereof; or abridging the freedom of speech, or of the press; or the right of the people peaceably to assemble, and to petition the government for a redress of grievances.

Amendment II
A well-regulated militia, being necessary to the security of a free state, the right of the people to keep and bear arms, shall not be infringed.

Amendment III

No soldier shall, in time of peace be quartered in any house, without the consent of the owner, nor in time of war, but in a manner to be prescribed by law.

Amendment IV

The right of the people to be secure in their persons, houses, papers, and effects, against unreasonable searches and seizures, shall not be violated, and no warrants shall issue, but upon probable cause, supported by oath   or affirmation, and particularly describing the place to be searched, and the persons or things to be seized.

Amendment V

No person shall be held to answer for a capital, or otherwise infamous crime, unless on a presentment or indictment of a grand jury, except in cases arising in the land or naval forces, or in the militia, when in actual service in time of war or public danger; nor shall any person be subject for the same offense to be twice put in jeopardy of life or limb; nor shall be compelled in any criminal case to be a witness against himself, nor be deprived of life, liberty, or property, without due process of law; nor shall private property be taken for public use, without just compensation.

Amendment VI

In all criminal prosecutions, the accused shall enjoy the right to a speedy and public trial, by an impartial jury of the state and district wherein the crime shall have been committed, which district shall have been previously ascertained by law, and to be informed of the nature and cause of the accusation; to be confronted with the witnesses against him; to have compulsory process for obtaining witnesses in his favor, and to have the assistance of counsel for his defense.

Amendment VII

In suits at common law, where the value in controversy shall exceed twenty dollars, the right of trial by jury shall be preserved, and no fact tried by a jury, shall be otherwise reexamined in any court of the United States, than according to the rules of the common law

Amendment VIII

Excessive bail shall not be required, nor excessive fines imposed, nor cruel and unusual punishments inflicted.

Amendment IX

he enumeration in the Constitution, of certain rights, shall not be construed to deny or disparage others retained by the people.

Amendment X

The powers not delegated to the United States by the Constitution, nor prohibited by it to the states, are reserved to the states respectively, or to the people.

APPENDIX XIV

GEORGE WASHINGTON'S FAREWELL ADDRESS

Friends and Citizens:
The period for a new election of a citizen to administer the executive government of the United States being not far distant, and the time actually arrived when your thoughts must be employed in designating the person who is to be clothed with that important trust, it appears to me proper, especially as it may conduce to a more distinct expression of the public voice, that I should now apprise you of the resolution I have formed, to decline being considered among the number of those out of whom a choice is to be made.

I beg you, at the same time, to do me the justice to be assured that this resolution has not been taken without a strict regard to all the considerations appertaining to the relation which binds a dutiful citizen to his country; and that in withdrawing the tender of service, which silence in my situation might imply,

I am influenced by no diminution of zeal for your future interest, no deficiency of grateful respect for your past kindness, but am supported by a full conviction that the step is compatible with both.

The acceptance of, and continuance hitherto in, the office to which your suffrages have twice called me have been a uniform sacrifice of inclination to the opinion of duty and to a deference for what appeared to be your desire.

I constantly hoped that it would have been much earlier in my power, consistently with motives which I was not at liberty to disregard, to return to that retirement from which I had been reluctantly drawn.

The strength of my inclination to do this, previous to the last election, had even led to the preparation of an address to declare it to you; but mature reflection on the then perplexed and critical posture of our affairs with foreign nations, and the unanimous advice of persons entitled to my confidence, impelled me to abandon the idea.

I rejoice that the state of your concerns, external as well as internal, no longer renders the pursuit of inclination incompatible with the sentiment of duty or propriety, and am persuaded, whatever partiality may be retained for my services, that, in the present circumstances of our country, you will not disapprove my determination to retire.

The impressions with which I first undertook the arduous trust were explained on the proper occasion. In the discharge of this trust, I will only say that I have, with good intentions, contributed towards the organization and administration of the government the best exertions of which a very fallible judgment was capable.

 Not unconscious in the outset of the inferiority of my qualifications, experience in my own eyes, perhaps still more in the eyes of others, has strengthened the motives to diffidence of myself; and every day the increasing weight of years admonishes me more and more that the shade of retirement is as necessary to me as it will be welcome.

Satisfied that if any circumstances have given peculiar value to my services, they were temporary,
 I have the consolation to believe that, while choice and prudence invite me to quit the political scene, patriotism does not forbid it.

 In looking forward to the moment which is intended to terminate the career of my public life, my feelings do not permit me to suspend the deep acknowledgment of that debt of gratitude which I owe to my beloved country for the many honors it has conferred upon me; still more for the steadfast confidence with which it has supported me; and for the opportunities

I have thence enjoyed of manifesting my inviolable attachment, by services faithful and persevering, though in usefulness unequal to my zeal.

 If benefits have resulted to our country from these services, let it always be remembered to your praise, and as an instructive example in our annals, that under circumstances in which the passions, agitated in every direction, were liable to mislead, amidst appearances sometimes dubious, vicissitudes of fortune often discouraging, in situations in which not infrequently want of success has countenanced the spirit of criticism, the constancy of your support was the essential prop of the efforts, and a guarantee of the plans by which they were effected.

Profoundly penetrated with this idea, I shall carry it with me to my grave, as a strong incitement to unceasing vows that heaven may continue to you the choicest tokens of its beneficence; that your union and brotherly affection may be perpetual; that the free Constitution, which is the work of your hands, may be sacredly maintained; that its administration in every department may be stamped with wisdom and virtue; that, in fine, the happiness of the people of these States, under the auspices of liberty, may be made complete by so careful a preservation and so prudent a use of this blessing as will acquire to them the glory of recommending it to the applause, the affection, and adoption of every nation which is yet a stranger to it.

Here, perhaps, I ought to stop.

But a solicitude for your welfare, which cannot end but with my life, and the apprehension of danger, natural to that solicitude, urge me, on an occasion like the present, to offer to your solemn contemplation, and to recommend to your frequent review, some sentiments which are the result of much reflection, of no inconsiderable observation, and which appear to me all-important to the permanency of your felicity as a people.

These will be offered to you with the more freedom, as you can only see in them the disinterested warnings of a parting friend, who can possibly have no personal motive to bias his counsel.

Nor can I forget, as an encouragement to it, your indulgent reception of my sentiments on a former and not dissimilar occasion.

Interwoven as is the love of liberty with every ligament of your hearts, no recommendation of mine is necessary to fortify or confirm the attachment.

The unity of government which constitutes you one people is also now dear to you.

It is justly so, for it is a main pillar in the edifice of your real independence, the support of your tranquility at home, your peace abroad; of your safety; of your prosperity; of that very liberty which you so highly prize.

But as it is easy to foresee that, from different causes and from different quarters, much pains will be taken, many artifices employed to weaken in your minds the conviction of this truth; as this is the point in your political fortress against which the batteries of internal and external enemies will be most constantly and actively (though often covertly and insidiously) directed, it is of infinite moment that you should properly estimate the immense value of your national union to your collective and individual happiness; that you should cherish a cordial, habitual, and immovable attachment to it; accustoming yourselves to think and speak of it as of the palladium of your political safety and prosperity; watching for its preservation with jealous anxiety; discountenancing whatever may suggest even a suspicion that it can in any event be abandoned; and indignantly frowning upon the first dawning of every attempt to alienate any portion of our country from the rest, or to enfeeble the sacred ties which now link together the various parts.

For this you have every inducement of sympathy and interest. Citizens, by birth or choice, of a common country, that country has a right to concentrate your affections. The name of American, which belongs to you in your national capacity, must always exalt the just pride of patriotism more than any appellation derived from local discriminations.

With slight shades of difference, you have the same religion, manners, habits, and political principles. You have in a common cause fought and triumphed together; the independence and liberty you possess are the work of joint counsels, and joint efforts of common dangers, sufferings, and successes.

But these considerations, however powerfully they address themselves to your sensibility, are greatly outweighed by those which apply more immediately to your interest. Here every portion of our country finds the most commanding motives for carefully guarding and preserving the union of the whole.

The North, in an unrestrained intercourse with the South, protected by the equal laws of a common government, finds in the productions of the latter great additional resources of maritime and commercial enterprise and precious materials of manufacturing industry. The South, in the same intercourse, benefiting by the agency of the North, sees its agriculture grow and its commerce expand.

Turning partly into its own channels the seamen of the North, it finds its particular navigation invigorated; and, while it contributes, in different ways, to nourish and increase the general mass of the national navigation, it looks forward to the protection of a maritime strength, to which itself is unequally adapted.

The East, in a like intercourse with the West, already finds, and in the progressive improvement of interior communications by land and water, will more and more find a valuable vent for the commodities which it brings from abroad, or manufactures at home.

The West derives from the East supplies requisite to its growth and comfort, and, what is perhaps of still greater consequence, it must of necessity owe the secure enjoyment of indispensable outlets for its own productions to the weight, influence, and the future maritime strength of the Atlantic side of the Union, directed by an indissoluble community of interest as one nation.

Any other tenure by which the West can hold this essential advantage, whether derived from its own separate strength, or from an apostate and unnatural connection with any foreign power, must be intrinsically precarious.

While then particular interest in union, all the parts combined cannot fail to find in the united mass of means and efforts greater strength, greater resource, proportionally greater security from external danger, a less frequent interruption of their peace by foreign nations; and, what is of inestimable value, they must derive from union an exemption from those broils and wars between themselves, which so frequently afflict neighboring countries not tied together by the same governments, which their own rival ships alone would be sufficient to produce, but which opposite foreign alliances, attachments, and intrigues would stimulate and embitter.

Hence, likewise, they will avoid the necessity of those overgrown military establishments which, under any form of government, are inauspicious to liberty, and which are to be regarded as particularly hostile to republican liberty. In this sense, it is that your union ought to be considered as a main prop of your liberty, and that the love of the one ought to endear to you the preservation of the other.

These considerations speak a persuasive language to every reflecting and virtuous mind, and exhibit the continuance of the Union as a primary object of patriotic desire. Is there a doubt whether a common government can embrace so large a sphere? Let experience solve it.

To listen to mere speculation in such a case were criminal. We are authorized to hope that a proper organization of the whole with the auxiliary agency of governments for the respective subdivisions, will afford a happy issue to the experiment. It is well worth a fair and full experiment.

With such powerful and obvious motives to union, affecting all parts of our country, while experience shall not have demonstrated its impracticability, there will always be reason to distrust the patriotism of those who in any quarter may endeavor to weaken its bands.

In contemplating the causes which may disturb our Union, it occurs as matter of serious concern that any ground should have been furnished for characterizing parties by geographical discriminations, Northern and Southern, Atlantic and Western; whence designing men may endeavor to excite a belief that there is a real difference of local interests and views.

One of the expedients of party to acquire influence within particular districts is to misrepresent the opinions and aims of other districts. You cannot shield yourselves too much against the jealousies and heart burnings which spring from these misrepresentations; they tend to render alien to each other those who ought to be bound together by fraternal affection.

The inhabitants of our Western country have lately had a useful lesson on this head; they have seen, in the negotiation by the Executive, and in the unanimous ratification by the Senate, of the treaty with Spain, and in the universal satisfaction at that event, throughout the United States, a decisive proof how unfounded were the suspicions propagated among them of a policy in the General Government and in the Atlantic States unfriendly to their interests in regard to the Mississippi; they have been witnesses to the formation of two treaties, that with Great Britain, and that with Spain, which secure to them everything they could desire, in respect to our foreign relations, towards confirming their prosperity.

Will it not be their wisdom to rely for the preservation of these advantages on the Union by which they were procured? Will they not henceforth be deaf to those advisers, if such there are, who would sever them from their brethren and connect them with aliens?

To the efficacy and permanency of your Union, a government for the whole is indispensable. No alliance, however strict, between the parts can be an adequate substitute; they must inevitably experience the infractions and interruptions which all alliances in all times have experienced.

Sensible of this momentous truth, you have improved upon your first essay, by the adoption of a constitution of government better calculated than your former for an intimate union, and for the efficacious management of your common concerns.

This government, the offspring of our own choice, uninfluenced and unawed, adopted upon full investigation and mature deliberation, completely free in its principles, in the distribution of its powers, uniting security with energy, and containing within itself a provision for its own amendment, has a just claim to your confidence and your support.

Respect for its authority, compliance with its laws, acquiescence in its measures, are duties enjoined by the fundamental maxims of true liberty. The basis of our political systems is the right of the people to make and to alter their constitutions of government.

But the Constitution which at any time exists, till changed by an explicit and authentic act of the whole people, is sacredly obligatory upon all. The very idea of the power and the right of the people to establish government presupposes the duty of every individual to obey the established government.

All obstructions to the execution of the laws, all combinations and associations, under whatever plausible character, with the real design to direct, control, counteract, or awe the regular deliberation and action of the constituted authorities, are destructive of this fundamental principle, and of fatal tendency. to put, in the place of the delegated will of the nation the will of a party, often a small but artful and enterprising minority of the community; and, according to the alternate triumphs of different parties, to make the public administration the mirror of the ill-concerted and incongruous projects of faction, rather than the organ of consistent and wholesome plans digested by common counsels and modified by mutual interests.

However combinations or associations of the above description may now and then answer popular ends, they are likely, in the course of time and things, to become potent engines, by which cunning, ambitious, and unprincipled men will be enabled to subvert the power of the people and to usurp for themselves the reins of government, destroying afterwards the very engines which have lifted them to unjust dominion.

Towards the preservation of your government, and the permanency of your present happy state, it is requisite, not only that you steadily discountenance irregular oppositions to its acknowledged authority, but also that you resist with care the spirit of innovation upon its principles, however specious the pretexts. One method of assault may be to effect, in the forms of the Constitution, alterations which will impair the energy of the system, and thus to undermine what cannot be directly overthrown.

In all the changes to which you may be invited, remember that time and habit are at least as necessary to fix the true character of governments as of other human institutions; that experience is the surest standard by which to test the real tendency of the existing constitution of a country; that facility in changes, upon the credit of mere hypothesis and opinion, exposes to perpetual change, from the endless variety of hypothesis and opinion; and remember, especially, that for the efficient management of your common interests, in a country so extensive as ours, a government of as much vigor as is consistent with the perfect security of liberty is indispensable.

Liberty itself distributed and adjusted, its surest guardian. It is, indeed, little else than a name, where the government is too feeble to withstand the enterprises of faction, to confine each member of the society within the limits prescribed by the laws, and to maintain all in the secure and tranquil enjoyment of the rights of person and property.

I have already intimated to you the danger of parties in the State, with particular reference to the founding of them on geographical discriminations. Let me now take a more comprehensive view, and warn you in the most solemn manner against the baneful effects of the spirit of party generally.

This spirit, unfortunately, is inseparable from our nature, having its root in the strongest passions of the human mind. It exists under different shapes in all governments, more or less stifled, controlled, or repressed; but, in those of the popular form, it is seen in its greatest rankness, and is truly their worst enemy.

The alternate domination of one faction over another, sharpened by the spirit of revenge, natural to party dissension, which in different ages and countries has perpetrated the most horrid enormities, is itself a frightful despotism. But this leads at length to a more formal and permanent despotism.

The disorders and miseries which result gradually incline the minds of men to seek security and repose in the absolute power of an individual; and sooner or later the chief of some prevailing faction, more able or more fortunate than his competitors, turns this disposition to the purposes of his own elevation, on the ruins of public liberty.

Without looking forward to an extremity of this kind (which nevertheless ought not to be entirely out of sight), the common and continual mischief of the spirit of party are sufficient to make it the interest and duty of a wise people to discourage and restrain it.

It serves always to distract the public councils and enfeeble the public administration. It agitates the community with ill-founded jealousies and false alarms, kindles the animosity of one part against another, foments occasionally riot and insurrection. It opens the door to foreign influence and corruption, which finds a facilitated access to the government itself through the channels of party passions. Thus the policy and the will of one country are subjected to the policy and will of another.

There is an opinion that parties in free countries are useful checks upon the administration of the government and serve to keep alive the spirit of liberty. This within certain limits is probably true; and in governments of a monarchical cast, patriotism may look with indulgence, if not with favor, upon the spirit of party.

But in those of the popular character, in governments purely elective, it is a spirit not to be encouraged.

From their natural tendency, it is certain there will always be enough of that spirit for every salutary purpose. And there being constant danger of excess, the effort ought to be by force of public opinion, to mitigate and assuage it.

A fire not to be quenched, it demands a uniform vigilance to prevent its bursting into a flame, lest, instead of warming, it should consume.

It is important, likewise, that the habits of thinking in a free country should inspire caution in those entrusted with its administration, to confine themselves within their respective constitutional spheres, avoiding in the exercise of the powers of one department to encroach upon another.

The spirit of encroachment tends to consolidate the powers of all the departments in one, and thus to create, whatever the form of government, a real despotism.

A just estimate of that love of power, and proneness to abuse it, which predominates in the human heart, is sufficient to satisfy us of the truth of this position.

The necessity of reciprocal checks in the exercise of political power, by dividing and distributing it into different depositaries, and constituting each the guardian of the public weal against invasions by the others, has been evinced by experiments ancient and modern; some of them in our country and under our own eyes.

To preserve them must be as necessary as to institute them. If, in the opinion of the people, the distribution or modification of the constitutional powers be in any particular wrong, let it be corrected by an amendment in the way which the Constitution designates.

But let there be no change by usurpation; for though this, in one instance, may be the instrument of good, it is the customary weapon by which free governments are destroyed. The precedent must always greatly overbalance in permanent evil any partial or transient benefit, which the use can at any time yield. prosperity, religion and morality are indispensable supports.

In vain would that man claim the tribute of patriotism, who should labor to subvert these great pillars of human happiness, these firmest props of the duties of men and citizens.

The mere politician, equally with the pious man, ought to respect and to cherish them. A volume could not trace all their connections with private and public felicity.

Where is the security for property, for reputation, for life, if the sense of religious obligation desert the oaths which are the instruments of investigation in courts of justice?

And let us with caution indulge the supposition that morality can be maintained without religion.

Whatever may be conceded to the influence of refined education on minds of peculiar structure, reason and experience both forbid us to expect that national morality can prevail in exclusion of religious principle.

It is substantially true that virtue or morality is a necessary spring of popular government. The rule, indeed, extends with more or less force to every species of free government.

Who that is a sincere friend to it can look with indifference upon attempts to shake the foundation of the fabric?

Promote then, as an object of primary importance, institutions for the general diffusion of knowledge. In proportion as the structure of a government gives force to public opinion, it is essential that public opinion should be enlightened.

As a very important source of strength and security, cherish public credit. One method of preserving it is to use it as sparingly as possible, avoiding occasions of expense by cultivating peace, but remembering also that timely disbursements to prepare for danger frequently prevent much greater disbursements to repel it, avoiding likewise the accumulation of debt, not only by shunning occasions of expense, but by vigorous exertion in time of peace to discharge the debts which unavoidable wars may have occasioned, not ungenerously throwing upon posterity the burden which we ourselves ought to bear.

The execution of these maxims belongs to your representatives, but it is necessary that public opinion should co-operate. To facilitate to them the performance of their duty, it is essential that you should practically bear in mind that towards the payment of debts there must be revenue; that to have revenue there must be taxes; that no taxes can be devised which are not more or less inconvenient and unpleasant; that the intrinsic embarrassment, inseparable from the selection of the proper objects (which is always a choice of difficulties), ought to be a decisive motive for a candid construction of the conduct of the government in making it, and for a spirit of acquiescence in the measures for obtaining revenue, which the public exigencies may at any time dictate.

Observe good faith and justice towards all nations; cultivate peace and harmony with all. Religion and morality enjoin this conduct; and can it be, that good policy does not equally enjoin it - It will be worthy of a free, enlightened, and at no distant period, a great nation, to give to mankind the magnanimous and too novel example of a people always guided by an exalted justice and benevolence.

Who can doubt that, in the course of time and things, the fruits of such a plan would richly repay any temporary advantages which might be lost by a steady adherence to it?

Can it be that Providence has not connected the permanent felicity of a nation with its virtue? The experiment, at least, is recommended by every sentiment which ennobles human nature.

Alas! is it rendered impossible by its vices?

In the execution of such a plan, nothing is more essential than that permanent, inveterate antipathies against particular nations, and passionate attachments for others, should be excluded; and that, in place of them, just and amicable feelings towards all should be cultivated.

The nation which indulges towards another a habitual hatred or a habitual fondness is in some degree a slave. It is a slave to its animosity or to its affection, either of which is sufficient to lead it astray from its duty and its interest.

Antipathy in one nation against another disposes each more readily to offer insult and injury, to lay hold of slight causes of umbrage, and to be haughty and intractable, when accidental or trifling occasions of dispute occur.
Hence, frequent collisions, obstinate, envenomed, and bloody contests.

The nation, prompted by ill-will and resentment, sometimes impels to war the government, contrary to the best calculations of policy.

The government sometimes participates in the national propensity, and adopts through passion what reason would reject; at other times it makes the animosity of the nation subservient to projects of hostility instigated by pride, ambition, and other sinister and pernicious motives.

The peace often, sometimes perhaps the liberty, of nations, has been the victim. So likewise, a passionate attachment of one nation for another produces a variety of evils.
imaginary common interest in cases where no real common interest exists, and infusing into one the enmities of the other, betrays the former into a participation in the quarrels and wars of the latter without adequate inducement or justification.

It leads also to concessions to the favorite nation of privileges denied to others which is apt doubly to injure the nation making the concessions; by unnecessarily parting with what ought to have been retained, and by exciting jealousy, ill-will, and a disposition to retaliate, in the parties from whom equal privileges are withheld.

devote themselves to the favorite nation), facility to betray or sacrifice the interests of their own country, without odium, sometimes even with popularity; gilding, with the appearances of a virtuous sense of obligation, a commendable deference for public opinion, or a laudable zeal for public good, the base or foolish compliances of ambition, corruption, or infatuation.

As avenues to foreign influence in innumerable ways, such attachments are particularly alarming to the truly enlightened and independent patriot.

How many opportunities do they afford to tamper with domestic factions, to practice the arts of seduction, to mislead public opinion, to influence or awe the public councils. powerful nation dooms the former to be the satellite of the latter.

Against the insidious wiles of foreign influence (I conjure you to believe me, fellow-citizens) the jealousy of a free people ought to be constantly awake, since history and experience prove that foreign influence is one of the most baneful foes of republican government. But that jealousy to be useful must be impartial; else it becomes the instrument of the very influence to be avoided, instead of a defense against it.

 Excessive partiality for one foreign nation and excessive dislike of another cause those whom they actuate to see danger only on one side, and serve to veil and even second the arts of influence on the other.

 Real patriots who may resist the intrigues of the favorite are liable to become suspected and odious, while its tools and dupes usurp the applause and confidence of the people, to surrender their interests.

The great rule of conduct for us in regard to foreign nations is in extending our commercial relations, to have with them as little political connection as possible.

 So far as we have already formed engagements, let them be fulfilled with perfect good faith. Here let us stop. Europe has a set of primary interests which to us have none; or a very remote relation.

Hence, she must be engaged in frequent controversies, the causes of which are essentially foreign to our concerns. Hence, therefore, it must be unwise in us to implicate ourselves by artificial ties in the ordinary vicissitudes of her politics, or the ordinary combinations and collisions of her friendships or enmities.

Our detached and distant situation invites and enables us to pursue a different course. off when we may defy material injury from external annoyance; when wemay take such an attitude as will cause the neutrality we may at any time resolve upon to be scrupulously respected; when belligerent nations, under the impossibility of making acquisitions upon us, will not lightly hazard the giving us provocation; when we may choose peace or war, as our interest, guided by justice, shall counsel.

Why forego the advantages of so peculiar a situation? Why quit our own to stand upon foreign ground?

Why, by interweaving our destiny with that of any part of Europe, entangle our peace and prosperity in the toils of European ambition, rivalship, interest, humor, or caprice?

It is our true policy to steer clear of permanent alliances with any portion of the foreign world; so far, I mean, as we are now at liberty to do it; for let me not be understood as capable of patronizing infidelity to existing engagements.

I hold the maxim no less applicable to public than to private affairs, that honesty is always the best policy.

I repeat it, therefore, let those engagements be observed in their genuine sense. But, in my opinion, it is unnecessary and would be unwise to extend them.

Taking care always to keep ourselves by suitable establishments on a respectable defensive posture, we may safely trust to temporary alliances for extraordinary emergencies.

Harmony, liberal intercourse with all nations, are recommended by policy, humanity, and interest. But even our commercial policy should hold an equal and impartial hand; neither seeking nor granting exclusive favors or preferences; consulting the natural course of things; diffusing and diversifying by gentle means the streams of commerce, but forcing nothing; establishing (with powers so disposed, in order to give trade a stable course, to define the rights of our merchants, and to enable the government to support them) conventional rules of intercourse, the best that present circumstances and mutual opinion will permit, but temporary, and liable to be from time to time abandoned or varied, as experience and circumstances shall dictate; constantly keeping in view that it is folly in one nation to look for disinterested favors from another; that it must pay with a portion of its independence for whatever it may accept under that character; that, by such acceptance, it may place itself in the condition of having given equivalents for nominal favors, and yet of being reproached with ingratitude for not giving more.

"There can be no greater error than to expect or calculate upon real favors from nation to nation. It is an illusion, which experience must cure, which a just pride ought to discard. Affectionate friend, I dare not hope they will make the strong and lasting impression I could wish; that they will control the usual current of the passions, or prevent our nation from running the course which has hitherto marked the destiny of nations.

But, if I may even flatter myself that they may be productive of some partial benefit, some occasional good; that they may now and then recur to moderate the fury of party spirit, to warn against the mischiefs of foreign intrigue, to guard against the impostures of pretended patriotism; this hope will be a full recompense for the solicitude for your welfare, by which they have been dictated.

How far in the discharge of my official duties I have been guided by the principles which have been delineated, the public records and other evidences of my conduct must witness to you and to the world.

To myself, the assurance of my own conscience is, that I have at least believed myself to be guided by them. the twenty-second of April, 1793, is Sanctioned by your approving voice, and by that of your representatives in both houses of Congress, the spirit of that measure has continually governed me, uninfluenced by any attempts to deter or divert me from it.

After deliberate examination, with the aid of the best lights I could obtain, I was well satisfied that our country, under all the circumstances of the case, had a right to take, and was bound in duty and interest to take, a neutral position.

 Having taken it, I determined, as far as should depend upon me, to maintain it, with moderation, perseverance, and firmness
.
The considerations which respect the right to hold this conduct, it is not necessary on this occasion to detail. I will only observe that, according to my understanding of the matter, that right, so far from being denied by any of the belligerent powers, has been virtually admitted by all.

The duty of holding a neutral conduct may be inferred, without anything more, from the obligation which justice and humanity impose on every nation, in cases in which it is free to act, to maintain inviolate the relations of peace and amity towards other nations.

The inducements of interest for observing that conduct will best be referred to your own reflections and experience.

With me a predominant motive has been to endeavor to gain time to our country to settle and mature its yet recent institutions, and to progress without interruption to that degree of strength and consistency which is necessary to give it, humanly speaking, the command of its own fortunes. Though, in reviewing the incidents of my administration, I am unconscious of intentional error, I am nevertheless too sensible of my defects not to think it probable that I may have committed many errors. Whatever they may be, I fervently beseech the Almighty to avert or mitigate the evils to which they may tend.

I shall also carry with me the hope that my country will never cease to view them with indulgence; and that, after forty-five years of my life dedicated to its service with an upright zeal, the faults of incompetent abilities will be consigned to oblivion, as myself must soon be to the mansions of rest.

Relying on its kindness in this as in other things, and actuated by that fervent love towards it, which is so natural to a man who views in it the native soil of himself and his progenitors for several generations, I anticipate with pleasing expectation that retreat in which I promise myself to realize, without alloy, the sweet enjoyment of partaking, in the midst of my fellow-citizens, the benign influence of good laws under a free government, the ever favorite object of my heart, and the happy reward, as I trust, of our mutual cares, labors, and dangers.

NOTE: WASHINGTON NEVER GAVE THIS ADDRESS IN PERSON. HE RELEASED IT TO ALL THE MAJOR NEWSPAPERS FOR PUBLISHMENT.

APPENDIX XV
21 GOALS OF THE ILLUMINATI AND THE COMMITTEE
OF 300

Dr. John Coleman (ca. 1993)
From: Conspirators' Hierarchy: The Story of The Committee of 300

1. To establish a One World Government/New World Order with a **unified church and monetary system** under their direction. The One World Government began to set up its church in the 1920: s and 30: s, for they realized the need for a religious belief inherent in mankind must have an outlet and, therefore, set up a "church" body to channel that belief in the direction they desired.

2. To bring about the utter **destruction of all national identity and national pride**, which was a primary consideration if the concept of a One World Government was to work.

3. To engineer and bring about the **destruction of religion**, and more **especially, the Christian Religion**, with the one exception, their own creation, as mentioned above.

4. To establish the ability to control of each and every person through means of mind control and what Zbignew Brzezinski called techonotronics, which would create human-like robots and a system of terror which would make Felix Dzerzinhski's Red Terror look like children at play.

5. To bring about the **end to all industrialization** and to end the production of nuclear generated electric power in what they call "the post-industrial zero-growth society". Excepted are the computer- and service industries. US industries that remain will be exported to countries such as Mexico where abundant slave labor is available. As we saw in 1993, this has become a fact through the passage of the **North American Free Trade Agreement**, known as **NAFTA**. Unemployables in the US, in the wake of industrial destruction, will either become opium-heroin and/or

cocaine addicts, or become statistics in the elimination of the "excess population" process we know of today as **Global 2000**.

6. To encourage, and eventually **legalize the use of drugs** and **make pornography an "art-form"**, which will be widely accepted and, eventually, become quite commonplace.

7. To bring about **depopulation of large cities** according to the trial run carried out by the Pol Pot regime in Cambodia. It is interesting to note that Pol Pot's genocidal plans were drawn up in the US by one of the Club of Rome's research foundations, and overseen by **Thomas Enders**, a high-ranking State Department official. It is also interesting that the committee is currently seeking to reinstate the Pol Pot butchers in Cambodia.

8. To **suppress all scientific development** except for those deemed beneficial by the Illuminati. Especially targeted is nuclear energy for peaceful purposes. Particularly hated are the fusion experiments currently being scorned and ridiculed by the Illuminati and its jackals of the press. Development of the **fusion torch** would blow the Illuminati's conception of "limited natural resources" right out of the window. A fusion torch, properly used, could create unlimited and as yet untapped natural resources, even from the most ordinary substances. Fusion torch uses are legion, and would benefit mankind in a manner which, as yet, is not even remotely comprehended by the public.

9. To cause. by means of A) **limited wars** in the advanced countries, B) by means of **starvation** and **diseases** in the **Third World** countries, **the death of three billion people by the year 2050**, people they call "useless eaters". The Committee of 300 (Illuminati) commissioned **Cyrus Vance** to write a paper on this subject of how to bring about such genocide. The paper was produced under the title "**Global 2000 Report**" and was accepted and approved for action by former President James Earl Carter, and Edwin Muskie, then Secretary of States, for and on behalf of the US Government. **Under the terms of the Global 2000 Report, the population of the US is to be reduced by 100 million by the year of 2050**.

10. To **weaken the moral fiber of the nation** and to **demoralize workers** in the labor class **by creating mass unemployment**. As jobs dwindle due to the postindustrial zero growth policies introduced by the Club of Rome, the report envisages demoralized and discouraged

workers resorting to alcohol and drugs. The youth of the land will be encouraged by means of rock music and drugs to rebel against the status quo, thus undermining and eventually destroying the family unit. In this regard, the Committee commissioned Tavistock Institute to prepare a blueprint as to how this could be achieved. Tavistock directed **Stanford Research** to undertake the work under the direction of **Professor Willis Harmon**. This work later became known as the "**Aquarian Conspiracy**".

11. To **keep people everywhere from deciding their own destinies by means of one created crisis after another and then "managing" such crises**. This will confuse and demoralize the population to the extent where faced with too many choices, apathy on a massive scale will result. In the case of the US, an agency for Crisis Management is already in place. It is called the **Federal Emergency Management Agency (FEMA)**, whose existence I first enclosed in 1980.

12. To introduce new cults and continue to boost those already functioning which include rock music gangsters such as **the Rolling Stones** (a gangster group much favored by European Black Nobility), and all of the Tavistock-created rock groups which began with the Beatles.

13. To continue to **build up the cult of Christian Fundamentalism** begun by the British East India Company's servant Darby, which will be misused to strengthen the Zionist State of Israel by identifying with the Jews through the myth of "God's chosen people", and by donating very substantial amounts of money to what they mistakenly believe is a religious cause in the furtherance of Christianity.

14. To press for the spread of religious cults such as **the Moslem Brotherhood**, **Moslem Fundamentalism**, the Sikhs, and to carry out mind control experiments of the Jim Jones and "Son of Sam" type. It is worth noting that the late **Khomeini was a creation of British Military Intelligence Div. 6, MI6**. This detailed work spelled out the step-by-step process which <u>the US Government implemented to put Khomeini in power</u>.

15. To **export "religious liberation" ideas** around the world so as **to undermine all existing religions, but more especially the Christian religion**. This began with the "Jesuit Liberation Theology", that brought an end to the Somoza Family rule in Nicaragua, and which today is destroying El Salvador, now 25 years into a "civil war". Costa Rica and

Honduras are also embroiled in revolutionary activities, instigated by the Jesuits. One very active entity engaged in the so-called liberation theology, is the Communist-oriented Mary Knoll Mission.

This accounts for the extensive media attention to the murder of four of Mary Knoll's so-called nuns in El Salvador a few years ago. The four nuns were Communist subversive agents and their activities were widely documented by the Government of El Salvador. The US press and the new media refused to give any space or coverage to the mass of documentation possessed by the Salvadorian Government, which proved what the Mary Knoll Mission nuns were doing in the country. Mary Knoll is in service in many countries and placed a leading role in bringing Communism to Rhodesia, Mozambique, Angola and South Africa.

16. To **cause a total collapse of the world's economies** and engender total political chaos.

17. To take control of all foreign and domestic policies of the US

18. To give the fullest support to supranational institutions such as the **United Nations**, the **International Monetary Fund (IMF)**, the Bank of International Settlements, the **World Court** and, as far as possible, **make local institutions less effective**, by gradually phasing them out **or bringing them under the mantle of the UN.**

19. To **penetrate** and **subvert** all governments, and work from within them to **destroy the sovereign integrity of the nations** represented by them.

20. Qaeda, ISIS, ISIL, etc.] and to negotiate with terrorists whenever terrorist activities take place. It will be recalled that it was Bettino Crax, who persuaded the Italian and US Governments to negotiate with the **Red Brigades** kidnapers of Prime Minister Moro and General Dozier. As an aside, Dozier was placed under strict orders not to talk what happened to him. Should he ever break that silence, he will no doubt be made "a horrible example of", in the manner in which Henry Kissinger dealt with Aldo Moro, Ali Bhutto and General Zia ul Haq.

21. To **take control of education in America** with the intent and purpose **of utterly and completely destroying it.**

APPENDIX XVI

SPANGLED BANNER
FRANCIS SCOTT KEY

O say can you see, by the dawn's early light,
What so proudly we hailed at the twilight's last gleaming,
Whose broad stripes and bright stars through the perilous fight,
O'er the ramparts we watched, were so gallantly streaming?
And the rockets' red glare, the bombs bursting in air,
Gave proof through the night that our flag was still there;
O say does that star-spangled banner yet wave
O'er the land of the free and the home of the brave?

On the shore dimly seen through the mists of the deep,
Where the foe's haughty host in dread silence reposes,
What is that which the breeze, o'er the towering steep,
As it fitfully blows, half conceals, half discloses?
Now it catches the gleam of the morning's first beam,
In full glory reflected now shines in the stream:
'Tis the star-spangled banner, O long may it wave
O'er the land of the free and the home of the brave.

And where is that band who so vauntingly swore
That the havoc of war and the battle's confusion,
A home and a country, should leave us no more?
Their blood has washed out their foul footsteps' pollution.
No refuge could save the hireling and slave
From the terror of flight, or the gloom of the grave:
And the star-spangled banner in triumph doth wave,
O'er the land of the free and the home of the brave.

O thus be it ever, when freemen shall stand
Between their loved homes and the war's desolation.
Blest with vict'ry and peace, may the Heav'n rescued land
Praise the Power that hath made and preserved us a nation!
Then conquer we must, when our cause it is just,
And this be our motto: 'In God is our trust.'
And the star-spangled banner in triumph shall wave
O'er the land of the free and the home of the brave

GENERAL GAGE'S MARTIAL LAW ORDER BY HIS

EXCELLENCY

The Hon. Thomas Gage, Esq; Governor, and Commander in Chief in and over his Majesty's Province of Massachusetts-Bay, a Vice Admiral of the same.

A PROCLAMATION.

WHEREAS the infatuated multitudes, who have long suffered themselves to be conducted by certain well known Incendiaries and Traitors, in a fatal progression of crimes, against the constitutional authority of the state, have at length proceeded to avowed rebellion; and the good effects which were expected arise from the patience and lenity of the King's government, have been often frustrated, and are now rendered hopeless, by the influence of the same evil counsels; it only remains for those who are entrusted with supreme rule, as well for the punishment of the guilty, as the protection of the well-affected, to prove they do not bear the sword in vain.

The infringements which have been committed upon the most sacred rights of the crown and people of Great-Britain, are too many to enumerate on one side, and are all too atrocious to be palliated on the other.

All unprejudiced people who have been witnesses of the late transactions, in this and the neighboring provinces, will find upon a transient review, marks of premeditation and conspiracy that would justify the fulness of chastisement:

And even those who are least acquainted with facts, cannot fail to receive a just impression of their enormity, in proportion as they discover the arts and assiduity by which they have been falsified or concealed. authors of the present unnatural revolt never daring to trust their cause or their actions to the judgment of an impartial public, or even to the dispassionate reflection of their followers, have uniformly placed their chief confidence in the suppression of truth: And while indefatigable and shameless pains have been taken to obstruct every appeal to the real interest of the people of America; the grossest forgeries, calumnies and absurdities that ever insulted human understanding, have been imposed upon their credulity.

The press, that distinguished appendage of public liberty, and when fairly and impartially employed its best support, has been invariably prostituted to the most contrary purposes; The animated language of ancient and virtuous times calculated to vindicate and promote the just rights and interest of mankind, have been applied to countenance the most abandoned violation of those sacred blessings; and not only from the flagitious prints, but from the popular harangues of the times, men have been taught to depend upon activity in treason, for the security of their persons and properties; 'till to compleat the horrid profanation of terms, and of ideas, the name of God has been introduced in the pulpits to excite and justify devastation and massacre.

The minds of men have been thus gradually prepared for the worst extremities; a number of armed persons, to the amount of many thousands assembled on the 19th of April last, and from behind walls, and lurking holes, attacked a detachment of the King's troops, who not expecting so consummate an act of phrenzy, unprepared for vengeance, and willing to decline it, made use of their arms only in their own defence

Since that period, the rebels, deriving confidence from impunity, have added insult to outrage; have repeatedly fired upon the King's ships and subjects, with cannon and small arms, have possessed the roads, and other communications by which the town of Boston was supplied with provisions, and with a preposterous parade of military arrangement, they affect to hold the army besieged, while part of their body make daily and indiscriminate invasions upon private property, and with a wantonness of cruelty ever incident to lawless tumult, carry depredation and distress wherever they turn their steps.

The actions of the 19th of April are of such notoriety, as must baffle all attempts to contradict them, and the flames of buildings and other property from the islands, and adjacent country, for some weeks past, spread a melancholy confirmation or the subsequent assertions.

in this exigency of complicated calamities, I avail myself of the last effort within the bounds of my duty, to spare the effusion of blood; to offer, and I do hereby in his Majesty's name, offer and promise, his most gracious pardon in all who shall forthwith lay down their arms, and return to the duties of peaceable subjects, excepting only from the benefit of such pardon, Samuel Adams and John

Hancock, whose offences are of too flagitious a nature to admit of any other consideration about that of {Omitted text, 1w} punishments.

And to the end that no person within the limits of this proffered mercy, may plead ignorance of the consequences of refusing it, I by these presents proclaim not only the persons above-named and excepted, but also all their adherents, associates and abettors, meaning to comprehend in those terms, all and every person, and persons of what class, denomination or description so ever, who have appeared in arms against the King's government, and shall not lay down the same as afore-mentioned, and likewise all such as shall so take arms after the date hereof, or who shall in any-wise protects or conceal such offenders, or assist them with money, provision, cattle, arms, ammunition, carriages, or any other necessary for subsistence or offence; or shall hold secret correspondence with them by letter, message, signal, or otherwise, to be rebels and traitors, and as such as to be treated.

And whereas, during the continuance of the present unnatural rebellion, justice cannot be administered by the common law of the land, the course whereof has, for a longtime past, been violently impeded, and wholly interrupted; from whence results a necessity for using and exercising the law martial; I have therefore thought fit, by the authority vested in me, by the Royal Charter to this province, to publish, and I do hereby publish, proclaim and order the use and exercise of the law martial, within and throughout this province, for so long time as the present unhappy occasion shall necessarily require; whereof all persons are hereby required to take notice, and govern themselves, as well to maintain order and regularity among the peaceable inhabitants of the province, as to resist, encounter, and subdue the Rebels and Traitors above-described by such as shall be called upon those purposes.

To these inevitable, but I trust salutary measures, it is a far more pleasing part of my duty, to add the assurances of protection and support, to all who in so trying a Crisis, shall manifest their allegiance to the King, and affection to the parent state.

So that such persons as may have been intimidated to quit their habitations in the course of this alarm, may return to their respective callings and professions; and stand distinct and separate from the parricides of the constitution, till God in his Mercy shall restore to his creatures, in this distracted land, that system of happiness from which they have be seduced, the religion of peace, and liberty founded upon law.

GIVEN at BOSTON, this Twelfth Day of June, in the Fifteenth Year of the Reign of his Majesty GEORGE the Third, by the Grace of GOD, of Great Britain, France and Ireland, KING, Defender of the Faith, & Annoque Domini, 1775.

By His Excellency's Command,
Tho's Flucker, Secr'y.

APPENDIX XVIII   CULPEPPER COUNTY "HENRY'S" FLAG

The Culpeper Minutemen were formed by an act of the Third Virginia Convention in July 1775 in response to the growing British threat. The group was made up of men from Orange, Fauquier and Culpeper counties.

Patrick Henry was their senior colonel, to whom the lower ranked officers reported. Words from Henry's famous **"Give me Liberty or give me death!"** speech to the Virginia House of Burgesses were included on the Culpeper Flag.

The Culpeper Minutemen were first called into duty when John Murray, Lord Dunmore, Royal Governor of Virginia, confiscated the colonist's gunpowder at the Virginia capital, Williamsburg.

 The colonists were alarmed, and Patrick Henry immediately sent word to Culpeper County. The Culpeper Minutemen met at the Culpeper Courthouse carrying their Culpeper Flag and marched for Williamsburg.

According to sixteen-year old Philip Slaughter who fought with the Culpeper Minutemen wrote the following:

"The whole regiment appeared according to orders in hunting shirts made of strong brown linen, dyed the color of the leaves of the trees, and on the breast was worked in large white letters the words, "Liberty or Death"! and all that could procure for love or money buck's tails, wore them in their hats. Each man had a leather belt around his shoulders, with a tomahawk and scalping knife."

Slaughter also reported the flag that the Culpeper Minutemen were carrying, the Culpeper Flag:

"The flag had in the center a rattlesnake coiled in the act to strike. Below it were the words, 'Don't tread on me!' At the sides, 'Liberty or Death!' and at the top, 'The Culpeper Minute Men.'" **

This is the definitive proof that the Culpeper Flag was indeed carried by the Culpeper Minutemen.

This makes the Culpeper Flag somewhat unique because many of the flags that many people consider to be "historic American flags" cannot definitively be tied directly to the American Revolution.

The Culpeper Minutemen were dissolved in February 1776, most of them then joined the Continental Army, many joining Colonel Daniel Morgan's 11th Virginia Continental Regiment. John Marshall, who would later become the 4th Chief Justice of the United States Supreme Court, was one of the original Culpeper Minutemen.

** Excerpts from the book: "Culpeper: A Virginia County's History Through 1920,: written by the Culpeper Historical Society Inc. and Eugene M. Scheel, © 1920published by Green Publishers, Inc.: Orange

APPENDIX X1X

VIRGINIA'S CONSTITUTIONPROPOSED AMENDMENTS
VIRGINIA RATIFICATION OF CONSTITUTITON

Ratification of the Constitution by the State of Virginia, June 26, 1788. Virginia ratified the Constitution in two steps. The first was the declaration of ratification. The second was a recommendation that a bill of rights be added to the Constitution, and that a list of amendments also be added in accordance with Article 5. The following text is taken from the Library of Congress's Continental Congress Broadside Collection.

WE the Delegates of the people of Virginia, duly elected in pursuance of a recommendation from the General Assembly, and now met in Convention, having fully and freely investigated and discussed the proceedings of the Federal Convention, and being prepared as well as the most mature deliberation hath enabled us, to decide thereon, **DO** in the name and in behalf of the people of Virginia, declare and make known that the powers granted under the Constitution, being derived from the people of the United States may be resumed by them whensoever the same shall be perverted to their injury or oppression, and that every power not granted thereby remains with them and at their will: that therefore no right of any denomination, can be cancelled, abridged, restrained or modified, by the Congress, by the Senate or House of Representatives acting in any capacity, by the President or any department or officer of the United States, except in those instances in which power is given by the Constitution for those purposes: and that among other essential rights, the liberty of conscience and of the press cannot be cancelled, abridged, restrained or modified by any authority of the United States.

With these impressions, with a solemn appeal to the searcher of hearts for the purity of our intentions, and under the conviction, that, whatsoever imperfections may exist in the Constitution, ought rather to be examined in the mode prescribed therein, than to bring the Union into danger by a delay, with a hope of obtaining amendments previous to the ratification:

We the said Delegates, in the name and in behalf of the people of Virginia, do by these presents assent to, and ratify the Constitution recommended on the seventeenth day of September, one thousand seven hundred and eighty seven, by the Foederal Convention for the Government of the United States; hereby announcing to all those whom it may concern, that the said Constitution is binding upon the said People, according to an authentic copy hereto annexed, in the words following:

A copy of the Constitution was included in the ratification document.

On motion, Ordered, That the Secretary of this Convention cause to be engrossed, forthwith, two fair copies of the form of ratification, and of the proposed Constitution of Government, as recommended by the Foederal Convention on the seventeenth day of September, one thousand seven hundred and eighty seven.

MR. Wythe reported, from the Committee appointed, such amendments to the proposed Constitution of Government for the United States, as were by them deemed necessary to be recommended to the consideration of the Congress which shall first assemble under the said Constitution, to be acted upon according to the mode prescribed in the fifth article thereof; and he read the same in his place, and afterwards delivered them in at the clerk's table, where the same were again read, and are as followeth:

That there be a Declaration or Bill of Rights asserting and securing from encroachment the essential and unalienable rights of the people in some such manner as the following:

1st. That there are certain natural rights of which men when they form a social compact cannot deprive or divest their posterity, among which are the enjoyment of life, and liberty, with the means of acquiring, possessing and protecting property, and pursuing and obtaining happiness and safety.

2d. That all power is naturally vested in, and consequently derived from, the people; that magistrates therefore are their trustees, and agents, and at all times amenable to them.

3d. That the Government ought to be instituted for the common benefit, protection and security of the people; and that the doctrine of non-resistance against arbitrary power and oppression, is absurd, slavish, and destructive to the good and happiness of mankind.

4th. That no man or set of men are entitled to exclusive or separate public emoluments or privileges from the community, but in consideration of public services; which not being descendible, neither ought the offices of magistrate, legislator or judge, or any other public office to be hereditary.

5th. That the legislative, executive and judiciary powers of government should be separate and distinct, and that the members of the two first may be restrained from oppression by feeling and participating the public burthens, they should at fixed periods be reduced to a private station, return into the mass of the people; and the vacancies be supplied by certain and regular elections, in which all or any part of the former members to be eligible or ineligible, as the rules of the Constitution of Government, and the laws shall direct.

6th. That elections of Representatives in the legislature ought to be free and frequent, and all men having sufficient evidence of permanent common interest with, and attachment to the community, ought to have the right of suffrage: and no aid, charge, tax or fee can be set, rated, or levied upon the people without their own consent, or that of their representatives, so elected, nor can they be bound by any law, to which they have not in like manner assented for the public good.

7th. That all power of suspending laws, or the execution of laws by any authority without the consent of the representatives, of the people in the legislature, is injurious to their rights, and ought not to be exercised.

8th. That in all capital and criminal prosecutions, a man hath a right to demand the cause and nature of his accusation, to be confronted with the accusers and witnesses, to call for evidence and be allowed counsel in his favor, and to a fair and speedy trial by an impartial jury of his vicinage, without whose unanimous consent he cannot be found guilty (except in the government of the land and naval forces) nor can he be compelled to give evidence against himself.

9th. That no freeman ought to be taken, imprisoned, or disseized of his freehold, liberties, privileges or franchises, or outlawed or exiled, or in any manner destroyed or deprived of his life, liberty, or property but by the law of the land.

10th. That every freeman restrained of his liberty is entitled to a remedy to enquire into the lawfulness thereof, and to remove the same, if unlawful, and that such remedy ought not to be denied nor delayed.

11th. That in controversies respecting property, and in suits between man and man, the ancient trial by jury is one of the greatest securities to the rights of the people, and ought to remain sacred and inviolable.

12th. That every freeman ought to find a certain remedy by recourse to the laws for all injuries and wrongs he may receive in his person, property, or character. He ought to obtain right and justice freely without sale, completely and without denial, promptly and without delay, and that all establishments, or regulations contravening these rights, are oppressive and unjust.

13th. That excessive bail ought not to be required, nor excessive fines imposed, nor cruel and unusual punishments inflicted.

14th. That every freeman has a right to be secure from all unreasonable searches, and seizures of his person, his papers, and property; all warrants therefore to search suspected places, or seize any freeman, his papers or property, without information upon oath (or affirmation of a person religiously scrupulous of taking an oath) of legal and sufficient cause, are grievous and oppressive, and all general warrants to search suspected places, or to apprehend any suspected person without specially naming or describing the place or person, are dangerous and ought not to be granted.

15th. That the people have a right peaceably to assemble together to consult for the common good, or to instruct their representatives; and that every freeman has a right to petition or apply to the Legislature for redress of grievances.

16th. That the people have a right to freedom of speech, and of writing and publishing their sentiments; that the freedom of the press is one of the greatest bulwarks of liberty, and ought not to be violated.

17th. That the people have a right to keep and bear arms; that a well regulated militia composed of the body of the people trained to arms, is the proper, natural and safe defence of a free state. That standing armies in time of peace are dangerous to liberty, and therefore ought to be avoided, as far as the circumstances and protection of the community will admit; and that in all cases, the military should be under strict subordination to and governed by the civil power.

18th. That no soldier in time of peace ought to be quartered in any house without the consent of the owner, and in time of war in such manner only as the laws direct.

19th. That any person religiously scrupulous of bearing arms ought to be exempted upon payment of an equivalent to employ another to bear arms in his stead.

20th. That religion, or the duty which we owe to our Creator, and the manner of discharging it, can be directed only by reason and conviction, not by force or violence, and therefore all men have an equal, natural and unalienable right to the exercise of religion according to the dictates of conscience, and that no particular sect or society ought to be favored or established by law in preference to others.

AMENDMENTS TO THE CONSTITUTION.

1st. That each state in the union shall respectively retain every power, jurisdiction and right, which is not by this constitution delegated to the Congress of the United States, or to the departments of the Foederal Government.

2d. That there shall be one representative for every thirty thousand, according to the enumeration or census mentioned in the Constitution, until the whole number of representatives amounts to two hundred; after which that number shall be continued or increased as Congress shall direct, upon the principles fixed in the Constitution, by apportioning the representatives of each state to some greater number of people from time to time as population increases.

3d. When Congress shall lay direct taxes or excises, they shall immediately inform the executive power of each state, of the quota of such state according to the census herein directed, which is proposed to be thereby raised; and if the legislature of any state shall pass a law which shall be effectual for raising such quota at the time required by Congress, the taxes and excises laid by Congress, shall not be collected in such state.

4th. That the members of the Senate and House of Representatives shall be ineligible to, and incapable of holding any civil office under the authority of the United States, during the time for which they shall respectively be elected.

5th. That the journals of the proceedings of the Senate and House of Representatives shall be published at least once in every year, except such parts thereof relating to treaties, alliances, or military operations, as in their judgment require secrecy.

6th. That a regular statement and account of the receipts and expenditures of all public money, shall be published at least once in every year.

7· concurrence of two thirds of the whole number of the members of the Senate; and no treaty, ceding, contracting, or restraining or suspending the territorial rights or claims of the United States, or any of them, or their, or any of their rights or claims to fishing in the American seas, or navigating the American rivers, shall be made, but in cases of the most urgent and extreme necessity, nor shall any such treaty be ratified without the concurrence of three fourths of the whole number of the members of both houses respectively.

8th. That no navigation law or law regulating commerce shall be passed without the consent of two thirds of the members present, in both houses.

9th. That no standing army or regular troops shall be raised, or kept up in time of peace, without the consent of two thirds of the members present, in both houses.

10th. That no soldier shall be inlisted for any longer term than four years, except in time of war, and then for no longer term than the continuance of the war.

11th. That each state respectively shall have the power to provide for organizing, arming and disciplining its own militia, whensoever Congress shall omit or neglect to provide for the same. That the militia shall not be subject to martial law, except when in actual service in time of war, invasion or rebellion, and when not in the actual service of the United States, shall be subject only to such fines, penalties and punishments as shall be directed or inflicted by the laws of its own state.

12th. That the exclusive power of legislation given to Congress over the Foederal Town and its adjacent district, and other places purchased or to be purchased by Congress of any of the states, shall extend only to such regulations as respect the police and good government thereof.

13th. That no person shall be capable of being President of the United States for more than eight years in any term of sixteen years.

14th. That the judicial power of the United States shall be vested in one Supreme Court, and in such Courts of Admiralty as Congress may from time to time ordain and establish in any of the different states: The judicial power shall extend to all cases in law and equity arising under treaties made, or which shall be made under the authority of the United States; to all cases affecting ambassadors, other foreign ministers and consuls; to all cases of admiralty and maritime jurisdiction; to controversies to which the United States shall be a party; to controversies between two or more States, and between parties claiming lands under the grants of different States. In all cases affecting ambassadors, other foreign ministers and consuls, and those in which a state shall be a party, the Supreme Court shall have original jurisdiction; in all other cases before mentioned, the Supreme Court shall have appellate jurisdiction, as to matters of law only: except in cases of equity, and of admiralty and maritime jurisdiction, in which the Supreme Court shall have a appellate jurisdiction both as to law and fact, with such exceptions and under such regulations as the Congress shall make: But the judicial power of the United States shall extend to no case where the cause of action shall have originated before the ratification of this Constitution; except in disputes between States about their territory; disputes between persons claiming lands under the grants of different States, and suits for debts due to the United States.

15th. That in criminal prosecutions, no man shall be restrained in the exercise of the usual and accustomed right of challenging or excepting to the jury.

16th. That Congress shall not alter, modify, or interfere in the times, places, or manner of holding elections for Senators and Representatives, or either of them, except when the Legislature of any state shall neglect, refuse, or be disabled by invasion or rebellion to prescribe the same

17th. That those clauses which declare that Congress shall not exercise certain powers, be not interpreted in any manner whatsoever, to extend the powers of Congress; but that they be construed either as making exceptions to the specified powers where this shall be the case, or otherwise, as inserted merely for greater caution.

18th. That the laws ascertaining the compensation of Senators and representatives for their services, be postponed in their operation, until after the election of representatives immediately succeeding the passing thereof; that excepted, which shall first be passed on the subject.

19th. That some tribunal other than the Senate be provided for trying impeachments of Senators.

20th. That the salary of a judge shall not be increased or diminished during his continuance in office otherwise than by general regulations of salary, which may take place on a revision of the subject at stated periods of not less than seven years, to commence from the same such salaries shall be first ascertained by Congress.

AND the Convention do, in the name and behalf of the people of this Commonwealth, enjoin it upon their representatives in Congress to exert all their influence and use all reasonable and legal methods to obtain a **RATIFICATION** of the foregoing alterations and provisions in the manner provided by the fifth article of the said Constitution; and in all Congressional laws to be passed in the meantime, to conform to the spirit of these amendments as far as the said Constitution will admit.

APPENDIX XX RED SKELTON'S PATRIOTIC TRIBUTE

The following words were spoken by the late Red Skelton on his television program, January 14, 1969, as he related the story of his teacher, Mr. Laswell, who felt his students had come to think of the Pledge of Allegiance as merely something to recite in class each day.

Now, more than ever, listen to the meaning of his words.

"I've been listening to you boys and girls recite the Pledge of Allegiance all semester and it seems as though it is becoming monotonous to you. If I may, may I recite it and try to explain to you the meaning of each word?"

I -- Me; an individual; a committee of one.

Pledge -- Dedicate all of my worldly good to give without self-pity.

Allegiance -- My love and my devotion.

To the Flag -- Our standard. "Old Glory"; a symbol of courage. And wherever she waves, there is respect, because your loyalty has given her a dignity that shouts "Freedom is everybody's job."

of the United -- That means we have all come together.

States -- Individual communities that have united into 48 great states; 48 individual communities with pride and dignity and purpose; all divided by imaginary boundaries, yet united to a common cause, and that's love of country --

Of America.

And to the Republic -- A Republic: a sovereign state in which power is invested into the representatives chosen by the people to govern; and the government is the people; and it's from the people to the leaders, not from the leaders to the people.

For which it stands

One Nation -- Meaning "so blessed by God."

[Under God][1]

Indivisible -- Incapable of being divided.

With Liberty -- Which is freedom; the right of power for one to live his own life without fears, threats, or any sort of retaliation.

And Justice -- The principle and qualities of dealing fairly with others.

For All -- For All. That means, boys and girls, it's as much your country as it is mine.

Now let me hear you recite the Pledge of Allegiance: *I pledge allegiance to the Flag of the United States of America ,and to the Republic, for which it stands ;one nation, indivisible, with liberty and justice for all.*

Since I was a small boy, two states have been added to our country, and two words have been added to the Pledge of Allegiance: <u>Under God</u>.

Wouldn't it be a pity if someone said, "That is a prayer" -- and that be eliminated from our schools, too?

Google: Red Skelton and the Pledge of Allegiance on you tube.

(The many faces of Red Skelton. He was truly one of the great ones.)

FOOTNOTES

1.Delmo C. West and August King, (Translation and commentary),1991, The Libra de las Prophecies' of Christopher Columbus

2.Professor Bryan F LA Beau (1999) Omaha, Nebraska, USA Center for the Study of Religion and Society(online) Vol 4, No 1.

3. Mayflower Compact, 1620,William Bradford, "Of Plymouth Plantation", 1647, (1901 Edition, Wright & Potter Printing,
 Moss state Printers

4.William Bradford, "Of Plymouth Plantation: 1620

5. James M. Wells, The Christian Philosophy of Patrick Henry

6.Elias Boudinot, The Life, Public Series, addresses, and
 Letters of Elias Boudinot, J.J. Boudinot, editor (Boston: Houghton, Mifflin & C o. 1896), Vol. I, PP. 19, 21.

7. Gary Delmar, "God and Country", Vol. 2(1984), p.108

8.John Adams letters to his wife

9."Declaration of Colonial Rights"

10.Patrick Henry speech to House of Burgesses, March 23, 1775

11."Necessity and Causes for taking up Arms"

12.Preamble, Declaration of Independence, July 4, 1776

13.George Bancroft, "History of the United States', Vol VI,(Boston,1878) ,p.32

14.bid, p.33 15

15.Samuel Adams, An Oration Delivered at the State-House, in Philadelphia, to a Very Numerous Audience; on Thursday, the 1st of August 1776

16.Abraham Clark, New Jersey delegate, to Elias Dayton, July 4, 1776

17. David Barton, "The Myth of Separation of Church and State ", Aledo, Texas, Wall builders Press, (1991), p. 91

18. Recollections and Private Memoirs of Washington, by George Washington Parke Custis, Edited by Benson J. Lossing, Vol. 1, page 248

19. George Washington address to the troops, July 2, 1776

20. Thomas Paine, December 23, 1776, The American Crisis
 "Common Sense" Thomas Paine (Reston, VA: Intercessors   for America   July/Aug 1993

21Barton, Ibid.

22.Verna M. Hall and Rosalie J. Slater, 'The Bible and the Constitution of the United States of America: (San Francisco, 1983) p. 248

23 F. Morris, "The Christian Life and Character of the
 Civil Institutions of the United States" (Philadelphia:
 George W. Childs, 1864) pp. 320-321, 323

24.Eleanor Custis Lewis letter written to Jared Spark, 1833

25. Ibid

26.. "George Washington, The Christian ", William J Johnston, p. 104

27.. 'The Light and the Glory" by Peter Marshall and David Manuel
 pp. 323-324.

28. William J Johnston, 'George Washington the Christian ', reprinted by Mott Media, 1976, p. 104

29. Ferrand, 1966, III, pp. 471-472

30. Ibid

31. 'The Federalists Papers ", p. 236
John Fiske, "The Critical Period of American History ",1783-1789 (New York, 1894) p. 231

32. W. Cleon Skousen, "The Making of America," (Washington D.C. 1985) p.5.

33. F. Morris," Christian Life and Character of the Civil Institutions of the United States' (Philadelphia, 1864), pp. 328.

34.Ford, Paul Leicester, ed. 'Essays on the Constitution of the United States Published during Its Discussion by the
 People" 1787--1788. Brooklyn: Historical Printing Club, 1892.

35 'Federalist Papers ', # 37, 233-39.

36 Correspondence to the Officers of the First Brigade of the
 Third Division of the Militia of Massachusetts 11 October 1798

37. Excerpt from George Washington's Farewell Address

38. James Madison, "Notes of Debates in the Federal Convention" 1787 (New York, 1787), p.32138. Ibid

39. Ibid

40.. Christine F Hart, 'One Nation Under God' (American
 Tract Society, reprinted by Gospel G Tract Society, Inc),p.2

41.Alexander Hamilton, the farmer Refuted: Or, a More "Impartial and Comprehensive view of the dispute Between Great Britain and the colonies "(New York: James Livingston, 1775), p.6

42 Blackstone's Commentaries with Notes and References St. George 'Tucker, editor (Philadelphia: William Young Birch, and Abraham Small, 1803), Vol. I, p. 300

43. Zephaniah Swift, 'A System of the Laws of the State of
 Connecticut" (Wyndham: John Byre, 1796) Vol. II, p 302)

44.Henry St. George tucker, 'A Few Lectures on Natural
 Law" (Charlottesville: James Alexander, 1844); pp. 10-11

45.William Rawle, "A View of the Constitution of the United
 States of America", second edition (Philadelphia: Philip
 H. Nicklin, 1829) pp. 125-126

46. James Wilson, "The Works of the Honorable James Wilson ", Bird Wilson, editor (Philadelphia: Bronson and Chauncey, 1804), Vol II, p. 466, form "Lectures on Law Delivered in the College of Philadelphia: Introductory Lecture: Of the Study of the Law in the United States."

47. Noah Webster, 'The Holy Bible…with Amendments of the Language" (New Haven: Durrie & Peck, 1833) p. iii.

48 James Madison, "Selections from the Private Correspondence of James Madison" from1813-1836.) J. C. McGuire, editor (Washington, 1853),

49. Thomas Jefferson, "Memoir, Correspondence, and Miscellanies ', Thomas Jefferson Randolph, editor Boston: Gray and Bowen, 1830) Vol. IV, p. 373 to Judge William Johnson on June 12, 1823

50.Debates and Other Proceedings of the Convention of Virginia, David Robertson, editor (Richmond: Ritchie & Wormsley and Augustine Davis, 1`805), p 275

51. Excerpts from Henry's speeches to the Virginia Provincial Council, February 6, 1788

52. Hamilton, Ibid., p. 6

53. Debates and Proceedings in the Convention of the Commonwealth of Massachusetts, Held in the Year 1788 (Boston: William White, 1856), pp. 86,

54.. Thomas Jefferson, Memoir, Correspondence, and Miscellanies Vol. II, p. 268 to Colonel Smith on November 13, 1787.

55. Richard Henry Lee, An additional Number of Letters from the federal Farmer to The Republican (New York: 1788), p. 170., Letter XVIII, January 215, 1788.

56. Alexander Hamilton, John Jay, and James Madison, "The Federalist on the New Constitution" (Philadelphia: Benjamin Warner, 1818), p. 259, Federalist No. 46 by James Madison

57.George Washington, "The Writings of George Washington ", Jared Sparks, editor (Boston: Ferdinand Andrews, 1838), Vol. XII, p. 8, from his First Annual Address to Congress on January 8, 1790

58. Noah Webster, "an Examination into the Principles of the Federal Constitution Proposed by the Late Convention Held at Philadelphia" (Prichard & Hall, 1787], p .32. 58. 57 vol. 9 (New York: Current Literature Publishing Company, 1913), pp. 202-224]

59. George Mason speech at Virginia Ratifying Convention 1788

60. Debate on a Standing Army, 1798-1800 [Excerpted from Great Debates in American History, Marion Mills Miller, ed, vol. 9 (New York: Current Literature Publishing Company, 1913), pp. 202-224]

61Jefferson, Notes on Virginia, 1803 Thomas Jefferson, 'The Writings of Jefferson ", p. 385

62; Alexander Hamilton, letter to James Bayard, 1803
Alexander Hamilton, "Famous American Statesman "p. 126

63.Treatise of the Religion of the Quakers, p. 355.

64. Bernard c Steiner, "One Hundred and Ten Years of Bible Maryland bible Society,1921) p. 21

65.Thomas Paine, 'Common Sense" Society Work in Maryland ', 810-1920 (Baltimore The

66. Sherman, "The Life of Roger Sherman ", pp 272-273

67.. Source: Bernard C. Steiner, 'The Life and Correspondence of James McHenry" (Cleveland: The Burrows Brothers, 1907), p. 475. In a letter from Charles Carroll to James McHenry of November 4, 1800.)

68.John Adams, Letter to Thomas Jefferson June 28, 1813

69.John Dickinson, "The Political Writings of John Dickinson"

70. John Hancock, 2nd Continental Congress, April 15, 1775

71.Benjamin Franklin, 'Works of Benjamin Franklin ', John Bigelow, editor (New York: Putnam's Sons, 1904), p. 185, to Ezra Stiles, March 9, 1790.

72.Elbridge Gerry, 'Proclamation for Day of Fasting and Prayer " Mar 6, 1812.

73. William Jay, "The Life of John Jay" (New York: J HEPWE 1833), Vol. II, p. 376, to John Murray Jr. on October 12, 1822.

74. James Madison, "The Papers of James Madison ", William T. Hutchinson, editor (Illinois: University of Chicago Press,1962), Vol. I, p. 96 to William Bradford on September 25, 1773

75. Notes of Debates in the Federal Convention of 1787", James Madison, (New York: W.W. Norton and Company), p. 504,

76. Benjamin Rush, "The Autobiography of Benjamin Rush ", George W. Corner, editor (Princeton: Princeton University Press, 1948), pp. 165-166.

77. Lewis Henry Boutella, "The Life of Roger Sherman" (Chicago: McClurg and Company, 1896), pp. 271-273.

78. John Witherspoon, The Works of the Reverend John Witherspoon (Philadelphia: William W. Woodward 1802), Vol. III, p. 42

79. As Governor of Massachusetts, A Proclamation for a day of Public Fasting, March 20, 1797

80. March 9, 1774, from a proclamation in our possession, Evans .Jonathan Trumbull, Proclamation for a Day of Fasting and Prayer,

13210.
81.   Haven: Durrie & Peck, 1832), p. 339, "Advice to the Young"
82. Joseph Story, "Life and Letters of Joseph Story ", William   W. Story, editor (Boston: Charles C. Little and James Brown, 1851), Vol. I, p.92, March 24, 1801.
83.Robert Treat Paine, "The Papers of Robert G. Treat Paine ", Stephen T. Riley and Edward W. Hanson, editors (Boston: Massachusetts Historical Society, 1992), Vol. I I, p. 4
84.Preamble, Treaty of Paris, 1783
85. Adams Diary entry, June 2, 1778
86/Marshall, Ibid., p. 370
87.William Wirt, "The Life and Character of Patrick Henry ", Philadelphia: James Webster, 1818), p.402
88. Many credit Abraham Lincoln, but never been substantiated
89.Rosalie Slater, from an essay in the preface to a Facsimile Edition of Noah Webster's 1828 Edition of "An American Dictionary of the English Language" (San Francisco, 1980), p.12.
90."America's Universities" from an unpublished paper by Mark Belies
91.Ibid
92.Ibid
93. Stephen K. McDowell and Mark A. Beliles, America's   Providential History (Charlottesville, VA: Providence Press 1988), p. 92.
94.David Barton, The Myth of Separation (Aledo, TX: Wall Builder Press, 1991), p. 91.
 95.Speech to Philadelphia State House 8/1/1776
96.Palladium Magazine, 9/20/1993 Ben Franklin, 1755, to the Pennsylvania State Legislature
97.Runkel v Winemiller, Harris&NcHenry 276 MD 1779
98. Charleston v. Benjamin, 2 Strob 508 SC1846
99. Church of the Holy Trinity v. United States. 143   U.S.457,458 (1892)
100.People v. Ruggles, 8 Johns R. 290 N.Y. 1811
101.Updegraph v. Commissioner, 11 Serg&Rawle 394   PA 1824
102.Vidal v. Girard's Executors, 432 U.S.126,132 (1844)
103.Everson v. Board of Education, 330 U.S. 1 1947
104.Zorach v Clausen, 343 U.S. 306 1952
105Jefferson letter to Danbury Baptist Convention 1802
106.1708 Kentucky Resolution
107. Jefferson second Inaugural address
 108. (Letters to the Methodist Episcopal Church at New London, Connecticut, Feb. 4, 1809)
109.Jefferson letter to Sam Miller Jan 23, 1808
110.Jefferson letter to Peter Carr, August 10, 1787

111.Engle v Vitale, 370 U.S. 421 1962

112. Judge Potters comments after the above decision

113.School District of Abbington v. Schempp 374 U.S. 203 1963

114.Wallace v Jaffries 472 US 38, 105 Sc.D. 2479, (1985)

115.Benjamin Rush, "A Plan for Schools, 1787

116.Constitutions, (1785), pp. 99-100, Delaware 1776,
    Article 22

117.William Jay, 'The Life of John Jay' (New York: J & J   Harper, 1833)
vol. II, p. 266

118. 'Biblical Principles' (NH. Plymouth Foundation 1981) p.31

119.Charles G. Finney, "Lectures on Revivals of Religion" (New York:
Fleming H. Revell Company,) 1868,

120.Benjamin Rush, "Letters of Benjamin Rush ", L. H. Butterfield, editor
(Princeton, NJ: Princeton University Press, 1951), Vol. I

121.Wert, Ibid, p. 89

122.Adams, Ibid, p.254 Letter from John Adams to Benjamin Rush, from
Quincy, Massachusetts, dated December 21, 1809,

123. Alex de Tocqueville," Democracy in America ", Vol 1 1835

124.'National Federation of Decency Journal ", Sept. 1988, p9.
"The New Freedom ", Garden city 1933

125.Page 405 of Rockefeller's autobiography, "Memoirs",

126. Ibid

127.Woodrow Wilson, Memoirs, Vol I 1913 "The New Freedom A Call For
 the Emancipation of the Generous Energies of a People" Speech to
World Affairs Press Conference, 4/19/1994

128.   Speech to the United Nations General Assembly 1992

129. Speech to Congress, Sept 11, 1991

130 Arthur Schlesinger, Foreign Affairs (July/August 1995

131. Jefferson, Ibid 132. Samuel Adams, "The Writings of Samuel
Adams", Harry Alonzo Cushing, editor (New York: G. P. Putnam's Sons,
908), Vol. III, p. 286, April 30, 1776

132. . April , 1799, in Jedidiah Morse's Election Sermon given at
Charleston 25, Mass., taken from an original in the Evans collection
compiled by the American Antiquarian Society, also States of America.

133.Samuel Adams, to John Scollay, April 30, 1776

134."Notes of Debates in the Federal Convention of 1787", James
Madison, (New York: W.W. Norton and Company), p. 504, said to the
delegates at the   Constitutional Convention)

135.Galatians 2: 4

136.John Adams, June 28, 1813 in a letter to Thomas Jefferson
 Richard K. Arno, "Adams to Jefferson/Jefferson to Adams", a dialogue from their correspondence (San Francisco Jericho Express) 1975, pp. 330-331
137. Inspirational Writings of Robert Schuller, Mass Marketing Paper Back, 1986
138. Edmund Burke, "Thoughts on the Causes of the Present Discontent", 23 April 1770
139.An Historical Review of the Constitution and Government of Pennsylvania." (1759);
140. Thomas Jefferson to William Stephens Smith, 13 Nov. 1787
141. James Bentley, Martin Niemoller 1892=1984 (NY Macmillan Free Press, 1984)
142. The Gathering Storm ", Houghton Mifflin Co. 1948, p.312

Made in the USA
Columbia, SC
08 October 2020